I0795912

IMAGES
of America

MARION

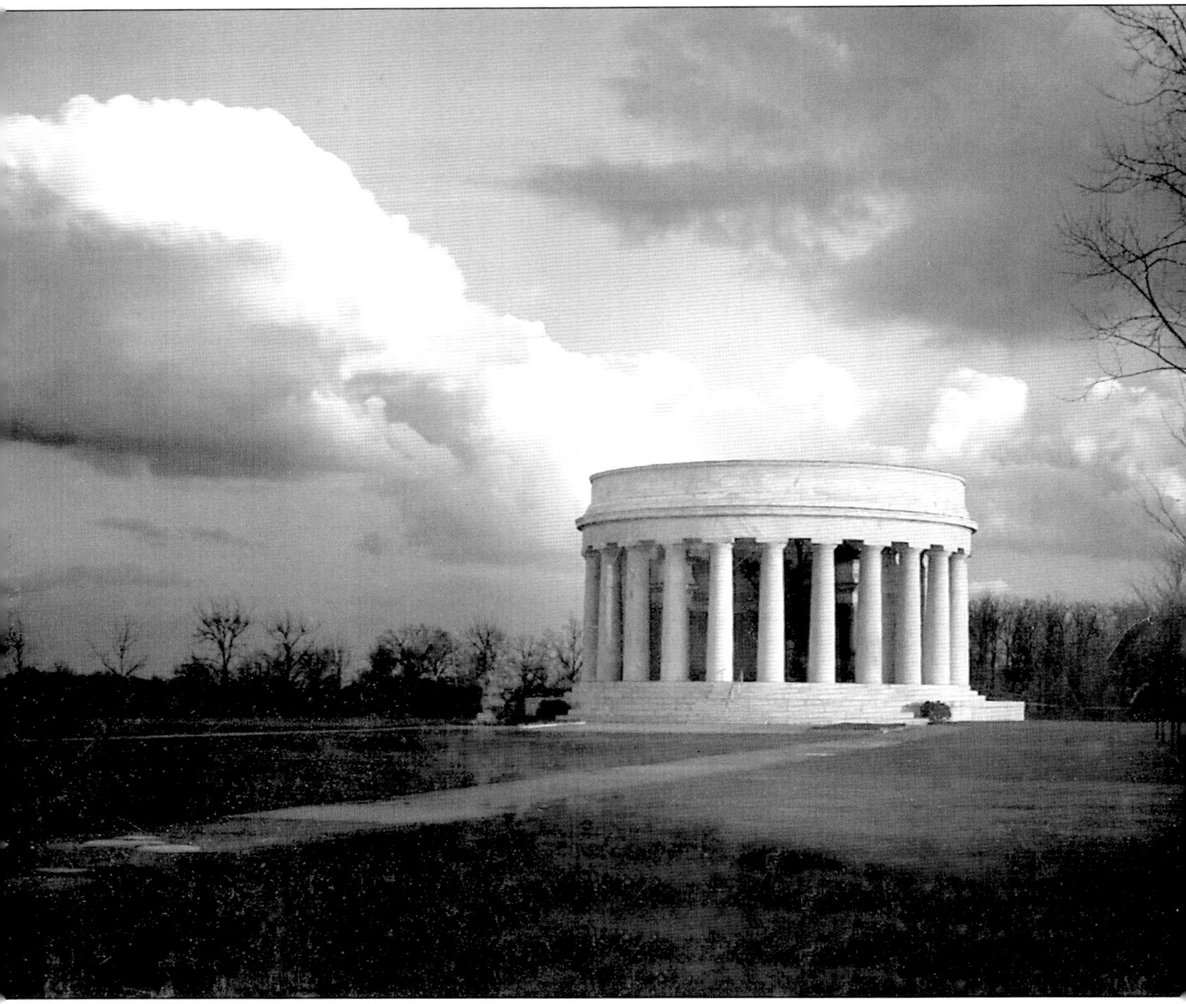

THE HARDING MEMORIAL, DELAWARE AVENUE AND VERNON HEIGHTS BOULEVARD. Completed in 1927, the Harding Memorial is perhaps the most beautiful structure ever constructed for a deceased president of the United States. The bodies of the late President Warren G. Harding and his wife, Florence Kling Harding, were removed to the memorial in December 1927; the memorial was dedicated by President Herbert Hoover in 1931. (Photograph courtesy of the Marion County Historical Society.)

IMAGES
of America

MARION

Stuart J. Koblentz

ARCADIA
PUBLISHING

ISBN 978-0-7385-3324-7

Published by Arcadia Publishing
Charleston, South Carolina

Printed in the United States of America

Library of Congress Catalog Card Number: 2004107705

For all general information contact Arcadia Publishing at:
Telephone 843-853-2070
Fax 843-853-0044
E-mail sales@arcadiapublishing.com
For customer service and orders:
Toll-Free 1-888-313-2665

Visit us on the Internet at www.arcadiapublishing.com

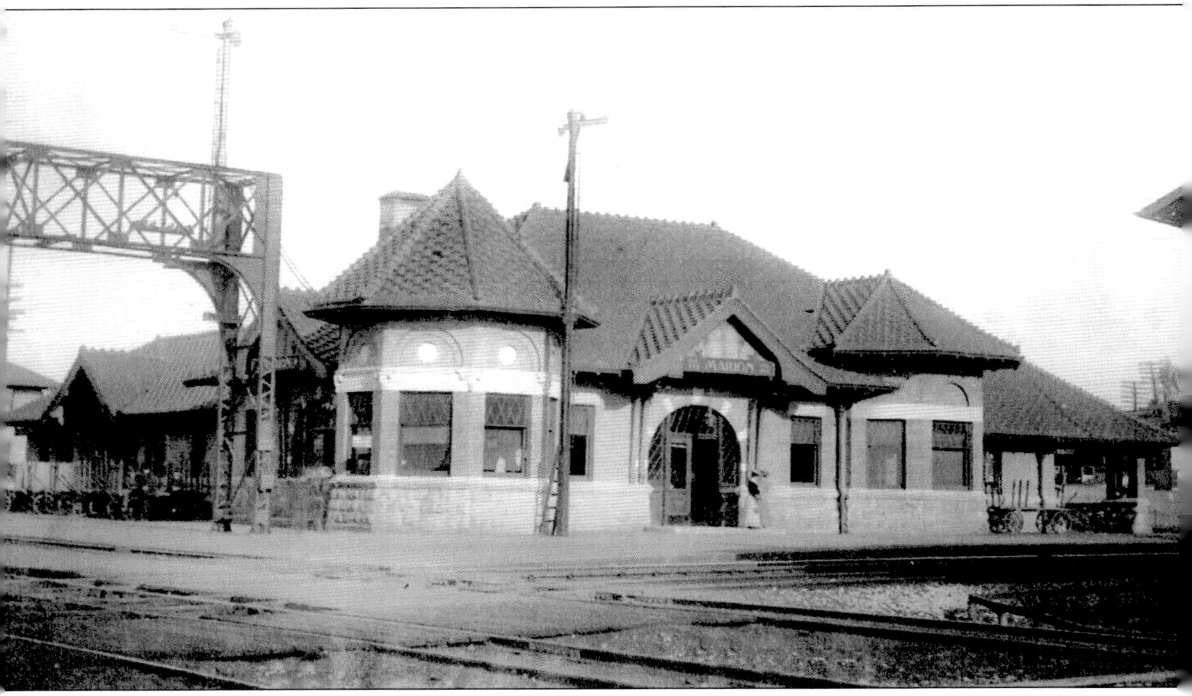

UNION STATION, MARION, OHIO, EARLY 1900S. Marion County owed a great deal of its growth as a community and manufacturing center to the railroads that served the city. In the late 1800s, city fathers recognized that the railroad stations serving Marion at that time did not bespeak Marion's prosperity. To remedy this, Union Station was built at the "crossroads" of Marion's rail lines on the city's west side. Saved from demolition, Union Station is now overseen by the Marion Union Station Association. (Photograph courtesy of the Marion County Historical Society.)

Contents

ACKNOWLEDGMENTS

Books such as these are not possible without the contributions and help provided by many people and organizations. I would like to thank my editor, Melissa Basilone, who was there when I needed help—I could not have brought this project to fruition without her encouragement and support. Trella Romine, Marion's First Lady of History, provided unending support, energy, inspiration, and enthusiasm. The Marion County Historical Society made their collection available to me for the purposes of writing this book; everyone in the society has been wonderfully supportive, and I am grateful for all that they do and all that they have done. Lynda Williams helped me navigate MCHS's vast photograph archive. Sharing their collections were Robert Turner, Gary Barnhart, Mike and Linda Perry, Shelby Needham, Carol Robinson, and Virginia Murphy. Brian Butko, Mary Ellen Withrow, and Rebecca Withrow Gooding also provided images. John Rall and Marsha Robinson of Hughes Photography helped immensely with their archive of industrial photographs. Carroll Niedhart and Scott Crider provided assistance and clarifications when necessary, as did Sam Norris at the Marion County Library. Eula Rhoads and Margaret Gracely helped by unlocking the doors of Heritage Hall's archives. Mary Jean Bowen, my mother, deserves recognition for unselfishly sharing her life stories about growing up in Marion; she has helped me to see this community with the benefit of more years of experience than I ever could have in my lifetime. Finally, I would like to acknowledge Mrs. Sonia Golden—though not directly involved in the work; any child who has had a teacher like her, and a friend such as she has been to me during my life, can do nothing short of the exceptional. And last but not least, this book is dedicated to E Haley and Bertie for their support and everything that I cannot put into words.

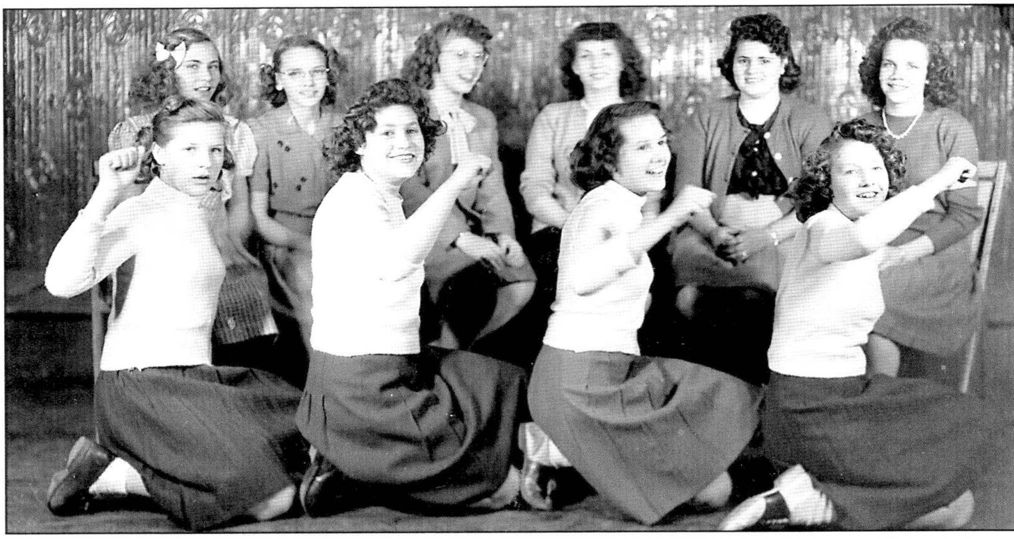

KIRKPATRICK SCHOOL CHEERLEADER'S, SCOTT TOWNSHIP, MARION COUNTY, OHIO, 1947. Students living in Scott Township attended Kirkpatrick School on State Route 98 until the advent of the county consolidated system in the 1950s. Given the size of the classes in the smaller township systems like Scott Township, those on the cheering squad represented the entire school quite well. Harriett Ann Monnette and Doris Boyd are third and forth from left, kneeling. (Photograph courtesy of the author.)

FOREWORD, AND FOREWARNED

Those who look through this work expecting to see familiar images may be surprised by what they find, and what they don't find. Previously published pictorial books on Marion have mostly documented Marion's history until World War II. It was my decision to cover topics not covered before, such as 1960s street scenes, the Sawyer Sanatoriums, Crystal Lake Amusement Park, the Isaly Dairy Company, and the Hardings before the "Front Porch Campaign" of 1920. Many topics, such as the Scioto Ordnance Plant and the Marion Engineer Depot during World War II, were reluctantly set aside due to lack of space.

For starters, Marion County, Ohio, is located in north central Ohio about 45 miles north of the state capital city of Columbus. It is one of 17 counties northwest of the Greenville Treaty Line that was not opened for settlement until after the defeat of the British and their Native American allies in the War of 1812. The first sign of civilization in the area came when a group of road surveyors for General William Henry Harrison's army had camped on the hill south of what is now downtown Marion. It included Jacob Foos, who, being thirsty, dug about until he discovered a fresh water spring. The spring became known as "Jacob's Well." Foos' digging was a telling event—for close to a century, Marion was the capital of steam shovel, drag lines, power shovels and other types of heavy, earth moving equipment. Marion shovels dug the Panama Canal, and products from the Marion Power Shovel Company moved NASA rockets into position for launch. To say that Marion citizens have moved heaven and earth is an honest observation.

The first land surveys in 1819 were followed by land sales in Delaware County in the summer of 1820. Eber Baker and his family arrived in 1821, and in 1822 he, along with Alexander Holmes, filed the plat for the Village of Marion. It was named after the county, which the state legislature had named for General Francis Marion of the Revolutionary War. In 1824, Marion County was separated from Delaware County and became a county with full powers to elect officials and conduct business.

Marion is proud of the contributions its residents and companies have made to the world. Warren G. Harding was publisher of the *Marion Star*, became a United States senator, and in 1920 was elected the 29th president of the United States. Only 40 or so communities in the United States are a part of this elite group of towns, which were called home by a United States president. Marion does have a rich history aside from Harding's impact. Norman Matoon Thomas, born and raised in Marion, was the Socialist Party presidential candidate six times and was cofounder of the America Civil Liberties Union. With the coming of the railroads in the 1850s, and Edward Huber in 1865, Marion entered the Industrial Age. Huber's nearly 100 inventions were the basis for the products of the Huber Manufacturing Company that rolled off assembly lines in Marion—steam engines, tractors, harvesting machines, the first gasoline powered tractors, and road machinery. Huber was also cofounder of the Marion Steam Shovel and other Marion industries. In 1955, Whirlpool Corporation opened and is now one of the largest facilities manufacturing consumer dryers in the world. The volume of high quality products coming off their assembly lines daily would seem, to the untrained eye, enough for the world for a lifetime. Mary Ellen Withrow was the 40th treasurer of the United States during the Clinton administration—the only person in the nation's history to hold the office of Treasurer on the local, state, and Federal levels of government.

Compiling a book such as this, I realized how quickly the familiar places and people we know slip from memory and into history. It is easy to take the here-and-now for granted; however, it is very hard to recreate these familiar scenes once they pass. For example, images of the interiors of the Crystal Lake Dance Pavilion, the Marion Theatre, or Isaly's Cafeteria on South Main Street could not be found. While working on the book, I also found myself having to explain to some people what "Green Stamps" were and how they were redeemed, or trying to convince younger residents that there really was an Isaly's Dairy on East Center Street.

In selecting the pictures for this book, I was privileged to use the collections of not only the Marion County Historical Society, but also those of many collectors of Marion memorabilia. If only I could share with you that rich treasure of local history and lore that passed before my eyes, you too would have a new appreciation for Marion's heritage.

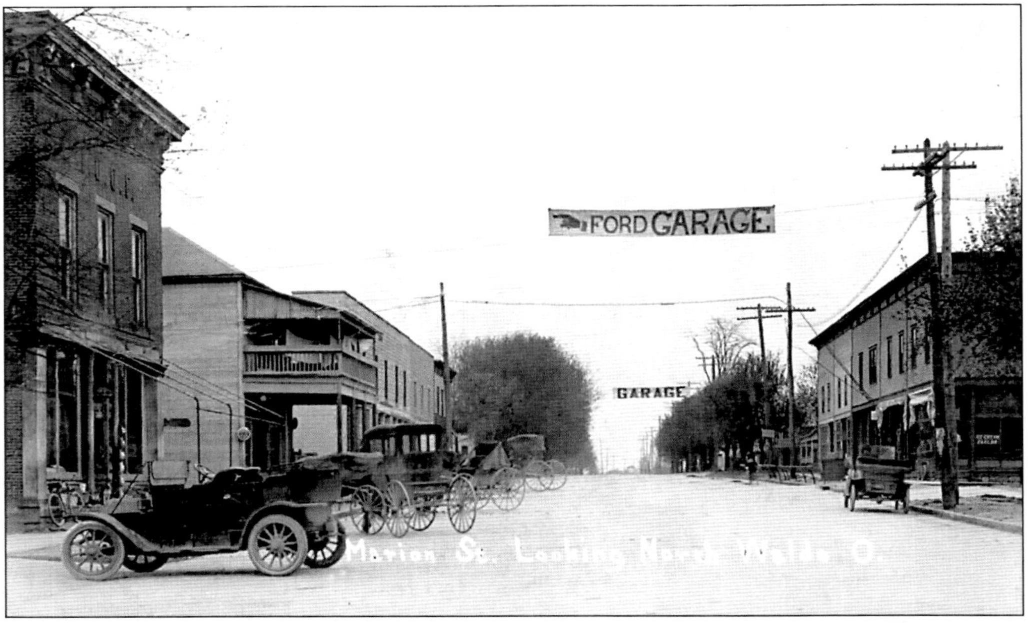

THE VILLAGE OF WALDO, WALDO TOWNSHIP, MARION COUNTY, EARLY 1900S. The question "Where's Waldo?" was often heard in central Ohio long before the advent of the popular children's books. Located in southern Marion County, the Village of Waldo was a bustling agricultural community when this photograph was taken in the early 1900s. Today, Waldo is regionally known as the home of Groll's Furniture and for the fried bologna sandwiches at the G&R Grill. (Photograph courtesy of the author.)

One

Around and About Marion

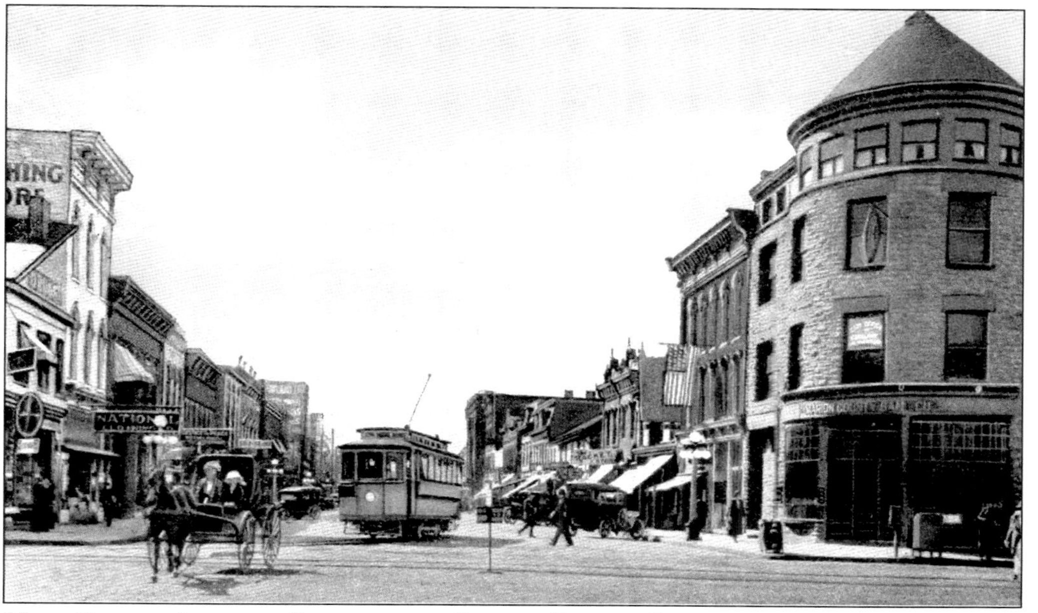

Main Street, Looking South from Center Street. Downtown Marion at the turn of the 20th century was the center of Marion County's economy. Horses and buggies shared the crowded streets with early automobiles, street cars, and interurban cars, making crossing the main streets a perilous undertaking in an age before modern traffic control. (Photograph courtesy of the author.)

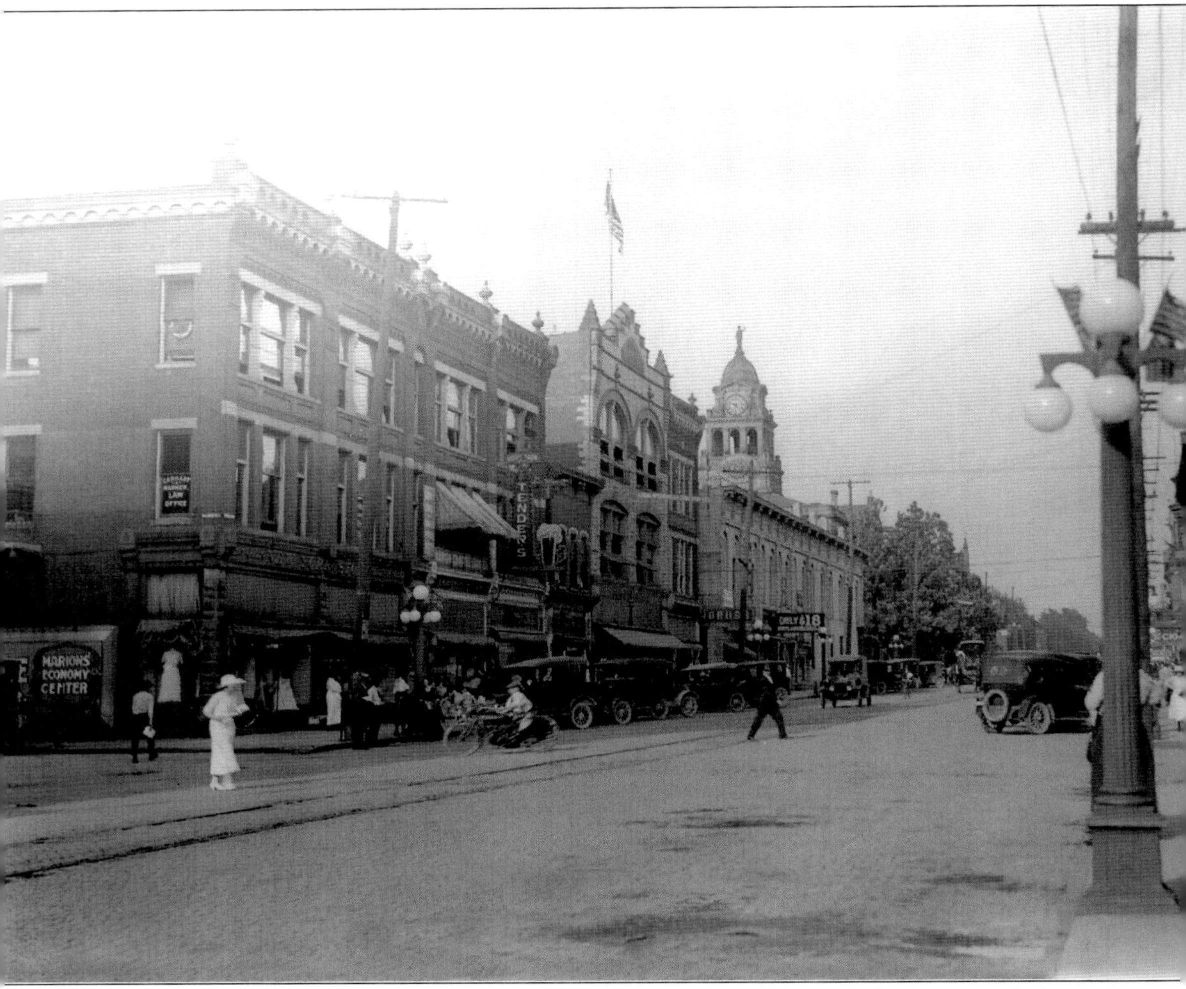

West Center Street, July 1920. Once Senator Warren G. Harding received the 1920 Republican Party nomination for presidency, news services began circulating photographs of Harding's hometown. This view shows West Center Street, looking eastwards towards the courthouse from the Frank Brothers' store at the corner of South Prospect Street. Businesses operating at the time included The New York Shop, Tender's Candies, Warner & Edwards Company, Hugh's Menswear (advertising men's suits from $18), and the National City Bank & Trust Corporation.

Interestingly, both of the major party presidential nominees in 1920 were newspaper publishers from the same state. Senator Harding owned and published the *Marion Star*, and Ohio Governor James Cox (the Democratic nominee), of Dayton, was the publisher and founder of Cox Newspapers. (Photograph courtesy of the author.)

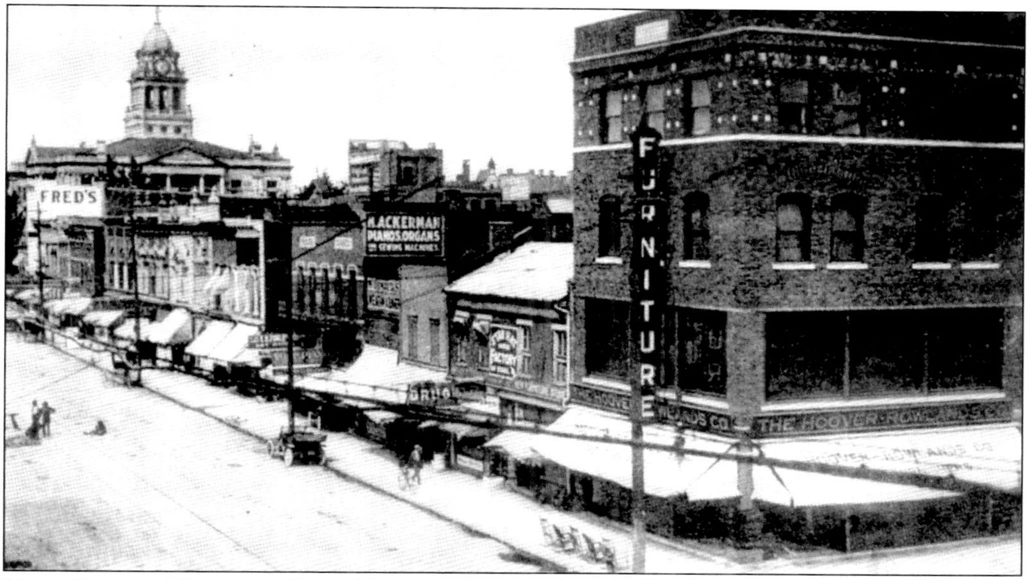

MAIN STREET, NORTH OF EAST CHURCH STREET. One's eye is drawn to the large brick Diebold building in the forefront that later housed the Schaffner Furniture and Mortuary Company—cabinetry and coffins had a great deal to do with one another in those days. However, the small two-story building to its immediate left shouldn't be overlooked: it was the birthplace of First Lady Florence Kling Harding. Mrs. Harding's birthplace was torn down in the 1910s and replaced by a small, two-story brick business block. (Photograph courtesy of Gary Barnhart.)

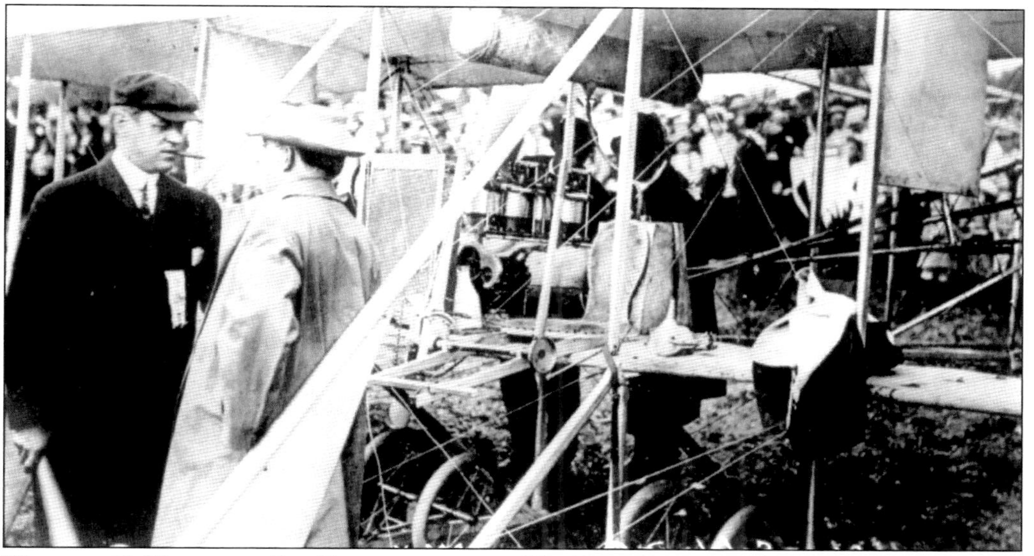

WARREN G. HARDING, CAL ROGERS, AND THE *VIN FIZZ*. On September 30, 1911, Cal Rogers (grandson of Oliver Hazard Perry) paid a visit to Marion while in a contest sponsored by the Hearst Newspaper Chain to fly coast to coast in 30 days. His flight aboard the *Vin Fizz* won the contest, even though it took 82 hours of airtime spread over 49 days, as he was the only one to make it to California. This was the first time that a plane flew over and landed in Marion County. Upon landing in Marion, Rogers was interviewed by Warren G. Harding for the *Marion Star*. (Photograph courtesy of Gary Barnhart.)

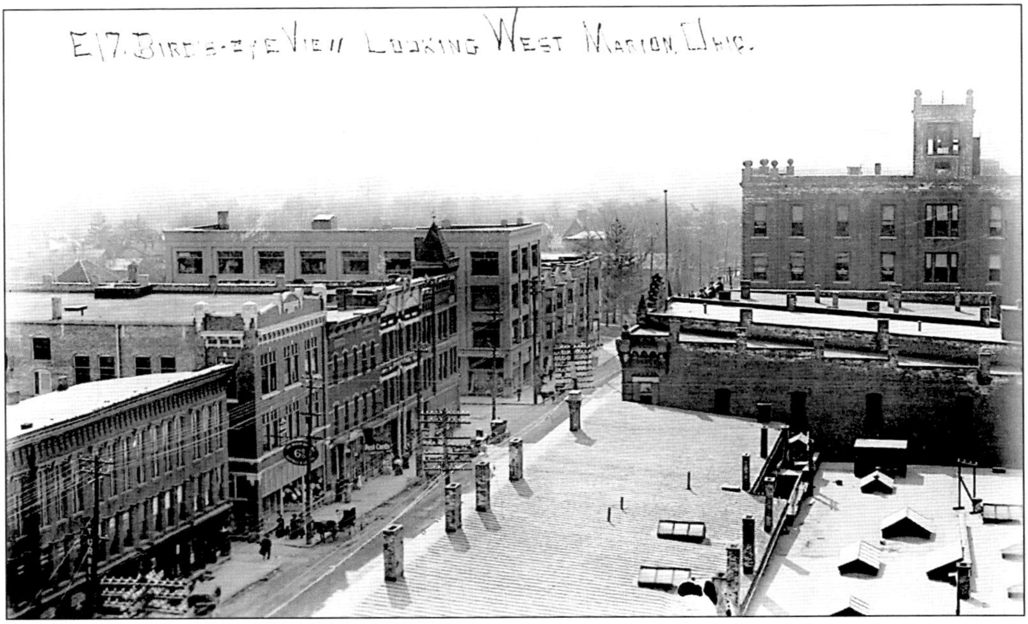

MARION, WEST FROM THE COURTHOUSE IN 1912. Looking west from the bell tower of the courthouse in the winter of 1912, Marion looks as if it was in for a very cold day. Draymen wait with their wagons along West Center Street, and D.A. Frank's new department store sits opposite of the Huber block. Beyond is West Center Street, still a residential neighborhood. (Photograph courtesy of the author.)

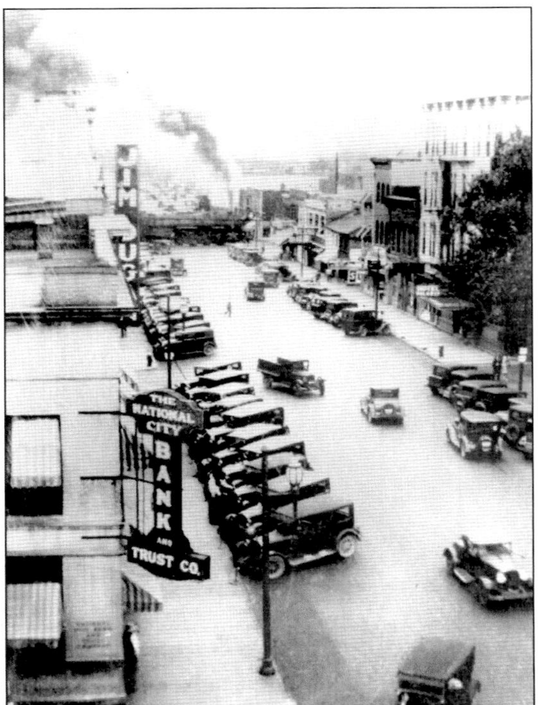

NORTH MAIN STREET. This image of North Main Street in the 1920s was taken from the Bennett Block. Cars, people, and trains all converged in the area near Jim Dugan's, the Courthouse, and the Pilgrim Inn. In the days before the current overpass system was instituted in the 1960s, the only clear passage connecting north Marion to points south was the Leader Street underpass. (Photograph courtesy of the Marion County Historical Society.)

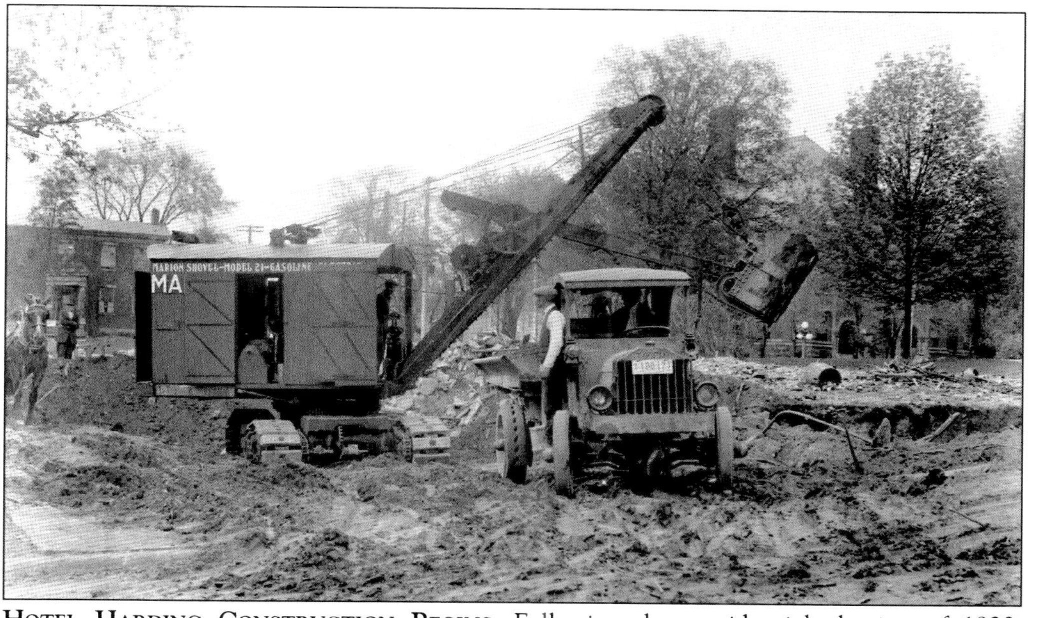

HOTEL HARDING CONSTRUCTION BEGINS. Following the presidential election of 1920, community leaders saw a need to construct a modern hotel of sufficient size and grandeur to suit the hometown of Warren G. Harding. A public campaign urged citizens to invest in "the Hotel Building" in order to help raise the first half of the capital needed to finance the structure. Work began on the site of the new hotel at West Center and Orchard Streets across from the Henderson-Campbell home, which itself would be replaced by the Palace Theatre by 1928. (Photograph courtesy of the Marion County Historical Society.)

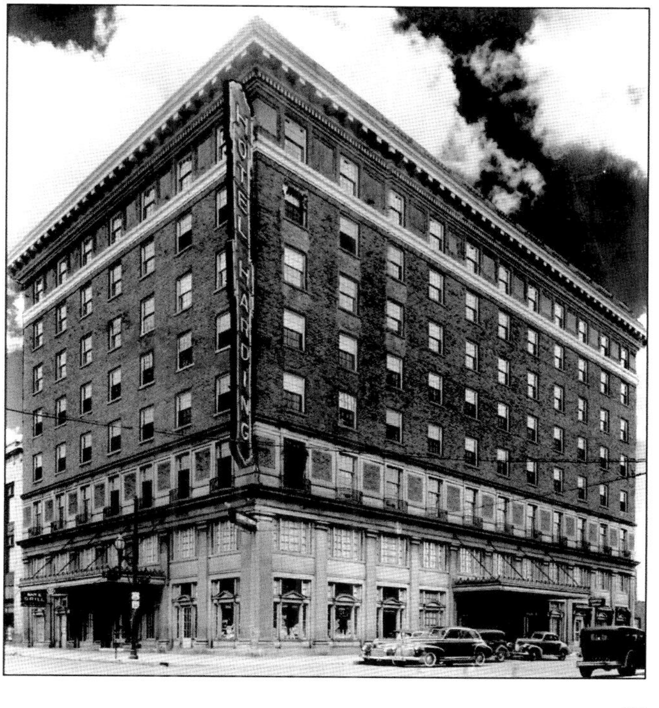

THE HOTEL HARDING. Following Warren G. Harding's presidential victory in 1920, city leaders felt that Marion should have a modern, first class hotel to house the VIPs that would be visiting the hometown of the president. Still under construction at the time of the president's death, the Hotel Harding nevertheless opened the following year in the fashion for which it was designed. Closed in March 1975, the eight-story hotel remained vacant until undergoing a full renovation and modernization in the 1990s. Now known as the Harding Center, the building provides apartment living for senior citizens. (Photograph courtesy of the Marion County Historical Society.)

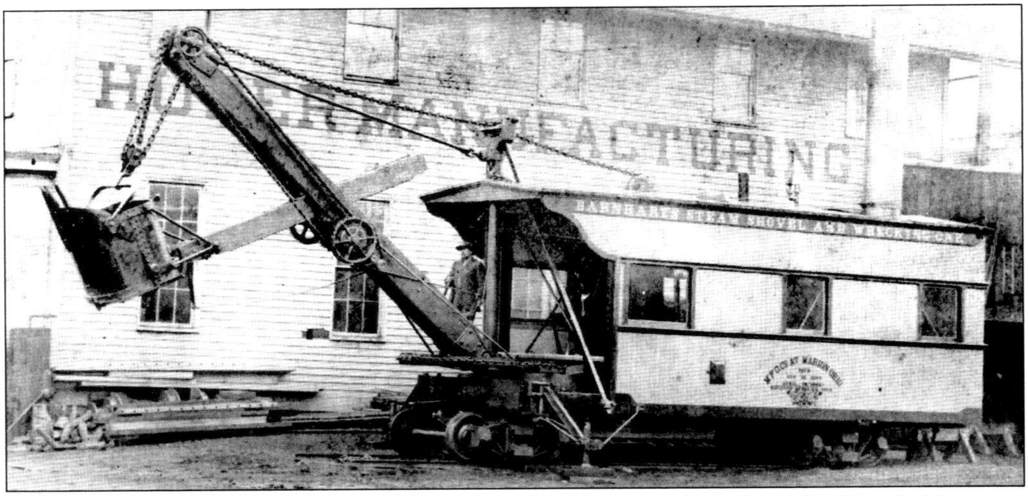

Barnhart's Steam Shovel and Wrecking Car. Frustrated by the lack of a reliable steam shovel, Henry Barnhart of Marion designed and built a better one. He patented it in 1884 with the help of Edward Huber, the same year the Marion Steam Shovel Company was incorporated, with Huber as president. By 1910, 80 percent of the steam shovels sold in the United States were manufactured in Marion. Twenty-seven "Marion shovels" were used in constructing the Panama Canal.

In 1948, the company was renamed the Marion Power Shovel Company, producing mammoth shovels for strip mining. They also manufactured creepers for NASA that still move space rockets to the launching pad. The facility was closed in 1997 by the Dresser Company, the last of a long line of out-of-town owners. (Photograph courtesy of Hughes Photography, John Rall, president.)

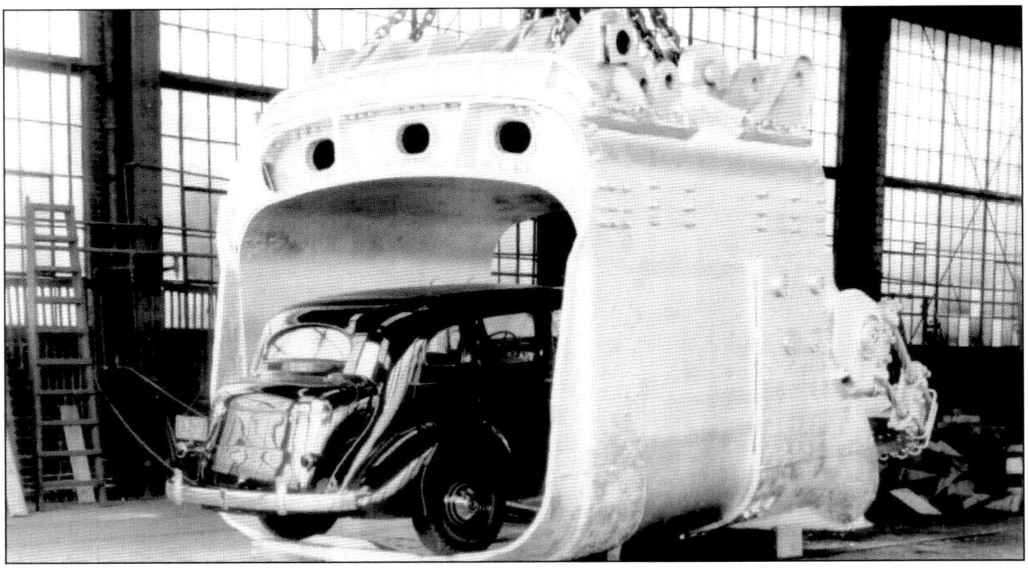

Marion Steam Shovel, 1935. As industrial requirements progressed, so did the need for larger and more powerful steam and power shovels. This 1935 image from the Marion County Historical Society's collection of Marion Power Shovel's industrial photographs shows how a standard car of the day could fit into one the shovel buckets produced in Marion. (Photograph courtesy of the Marion County Historical Society.)

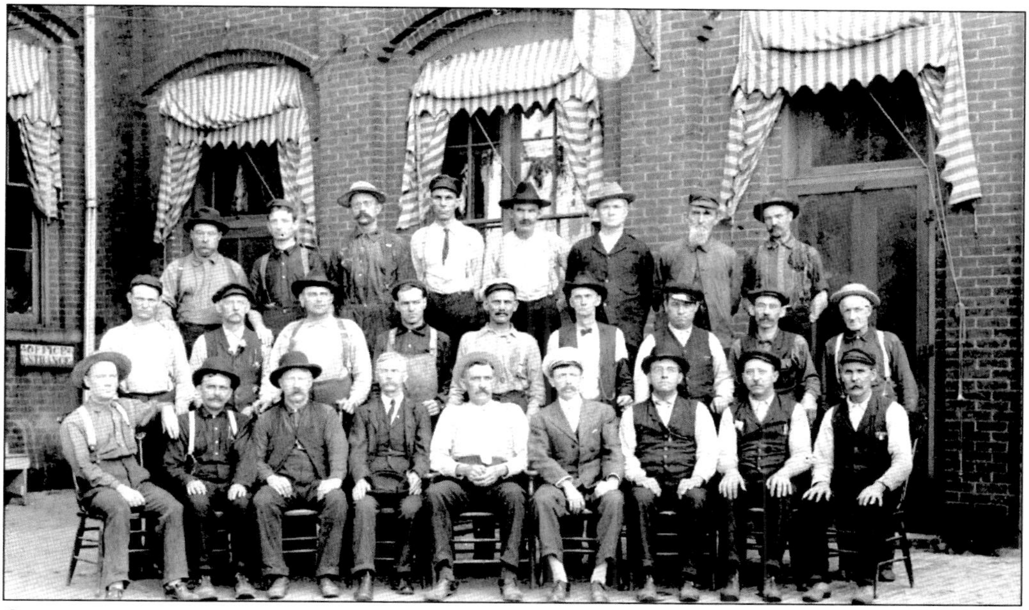

CARPENTRY DEPARTMENT, HUBER MANUFACTURING COMPANY, EARLY 1900S. Edward Huber revolutionized farming with the invention of the revolving hay rake in the mid 1850s. By the turn of the century, Huber had expanded his product line to include tractors, harvesting equipment, and steam rollers. Some of Huber's equipment in the early 1900s required wood parts, and thus the carpentry department was a vital part of Huber's manufacturing concern. Ellsworth Kennedy is fourth from the right in the back row. (Photograph courtesy of the Marion County Historical Society.)

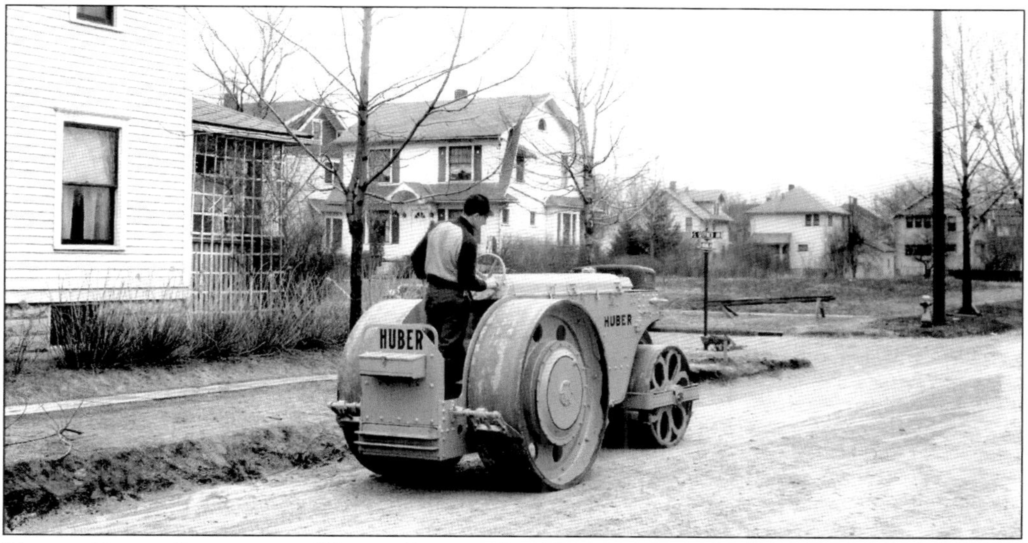

HUBER ROAD ROLLER AT WORK. During World War II, Huber Manufacturing Company converted to constructing road machinery, rather than farm machinery, and continued after the war until they closed in 1975. Modern road equipment, such as this road roller preparing Indiana Avenue's roadbed at South Seffner Avenue, helped communities around the world change the face of the earth. (Photograph courtesy of the Marion County Historical Society.)

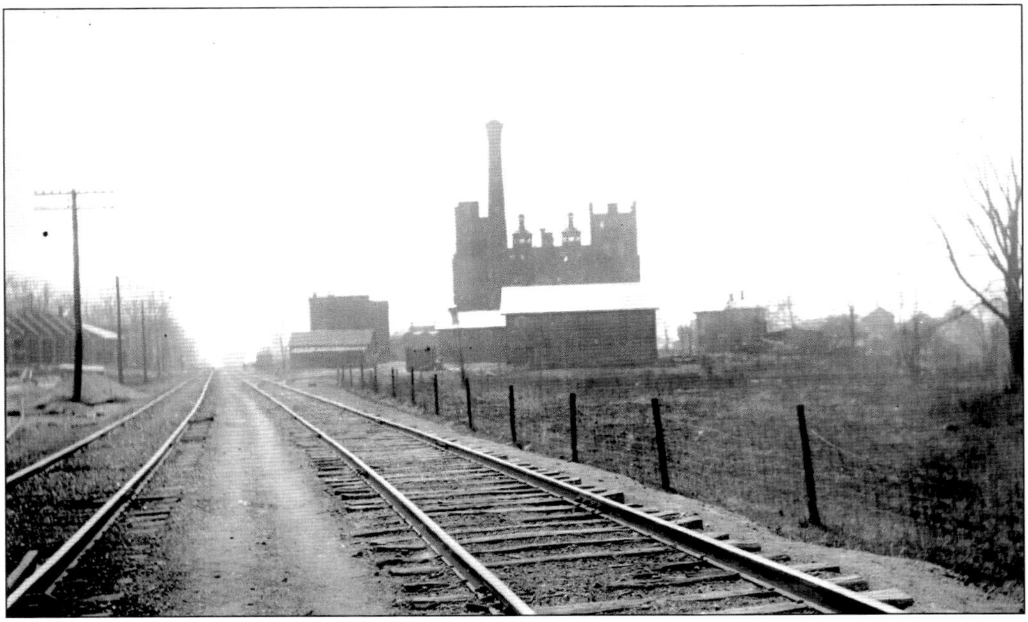

LOOKING SOUTH TOWARD MARION BREWERY, 1920S. The Marion Brewery on Bellefontaine Avenue prospered until the advent of Prohibition in the 1920s. This image was taken north of the idle building, looking south toward Pollack Steel. (Photograph courtesy of Hughes Photography, John Rall, president.)

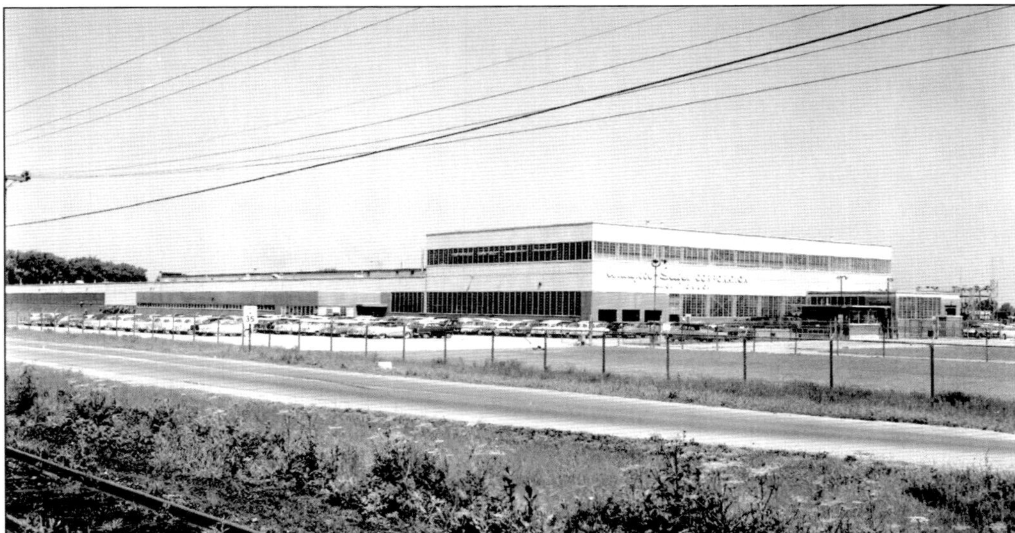

WHIRLPOOL-SEEGER DRYER PLANT, 1956. In 1955, the Whirlpool-Seeger Corporation purchased the Motor Products plant just west of Marion and began production of consumer dryers. Becoming RCA Whirlpool in 1959, and now known as the Whirlpool Corporation, the Marion facility has been enlarged and improved throughout its history. In addition to becoming one of the areas leading employers, Whirlpool has also generously supported numerous community projects, such as the restoration of the Palace Theatre, throughout its 50 years in Marion. (Photograph courtesy of the Marion County Historical Society.)

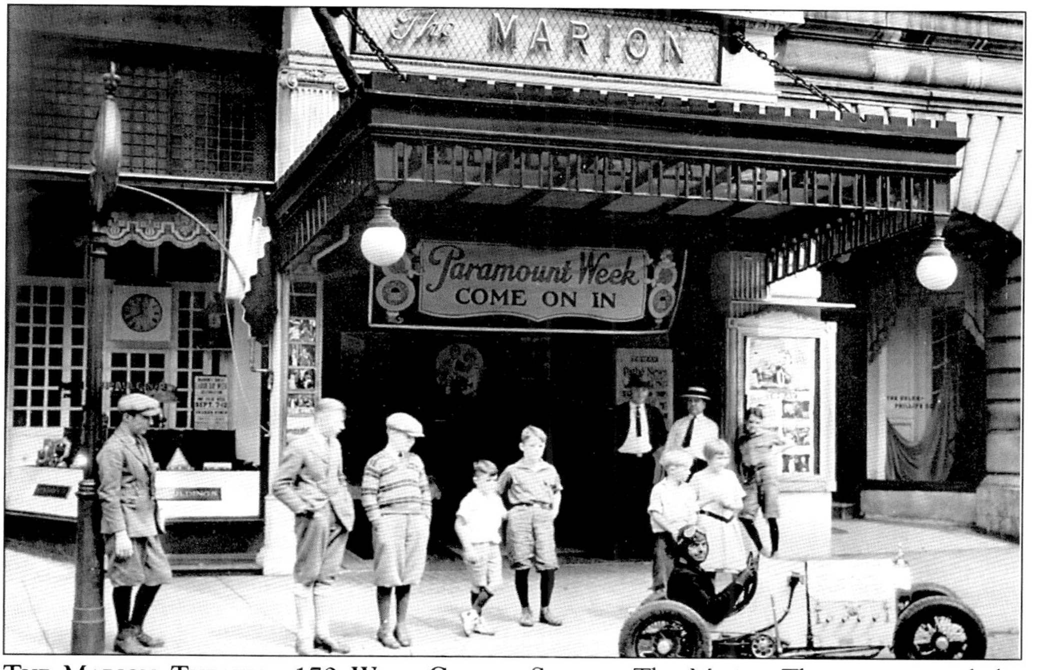

THE MARION THEATER, 170 WEST CENTER STREET. The Marion Theater occupied the building immediately west of the Uhler-Phillips department store at the northwest corner of Prospect Street. Opened in 1915 as a vaudeville house, it hosted Paramount films in the 1920s. It served the community well until 1953 along with the Ohio, Orpheum, and Oakland theaters. Along with the Palace, they were the backbone of entertainment in Marion during Hollywood's golden era. (Photograph courtesy of Gary Barnhart.)

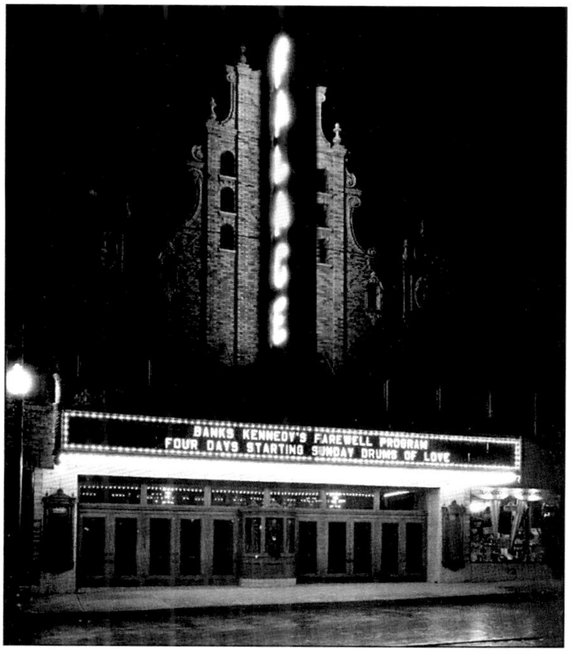

PALACE THEATRE AT NIGHT. Designed in the dramatic Spanish mission/Rococo style by John Ebberson, the Palace Theatre opened in 1928. Theater goers found themselves inside a courtyard of a Spanish village with the facades of buildings lining the walls. Clouds drifted overhead, projected by a small light and a metal disk. The crowning touch to this nighttime fantasy were lights that twinkled overhead. (Photograph courtesy Marion County Historical Society.)

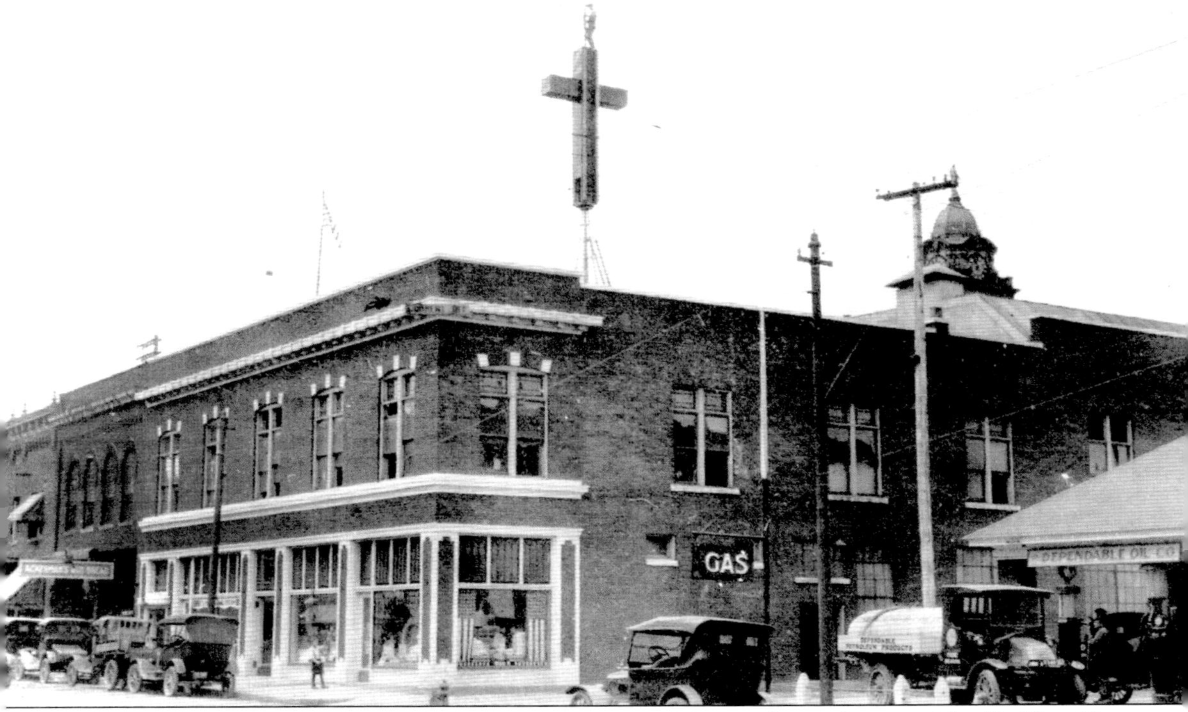

THE KU KLUX KLAN MARKET BUILDING, 139–143 NORTH STATE STREET. The Ku Klux Klan maintained an office in Marion in the Market Building during part of the 1920s. Marion was chosen in part because of the notoriety that the Harding presidency brought to the town. One must remember that in the Midwest in the 1920s, the Klan attracted large numbers of followers to its rallies, most of whom later regretted their involvement until their deaths. Exploiting the poor farm economy following World War I, the Klan in the upper Midwest focused on religious intolerance by targeting Jews and Catholics; racial hatred was not forgotten, but it did not enjoy the so called "popularity" that it did in the south. The building contained store fronts along North State Street and Klan offices on the second floor; a large auditorium was also located on the second floor of the building. In a twist of irony, the Knights of Columbus, a Catholic fraternal organization, held the mortgage on the Klan Market building for several years. Fearful of the Klan's possible bankruptcy, the Knights of Columbus foreclosed on the note in November 1924. The building was once crowned by a large, lighted, revolving cross. Vacant from 1925 to 1927, the building became the home of the *Marion Star* when the newspaper moved their office from East Center Street. The Market Building was remodeled in the 1960s and again after the newspaper was purchased by the Gannett Publishing Company, which still has its editorial and business offices there. (Photograph courtesy of Gary Barnhart.)

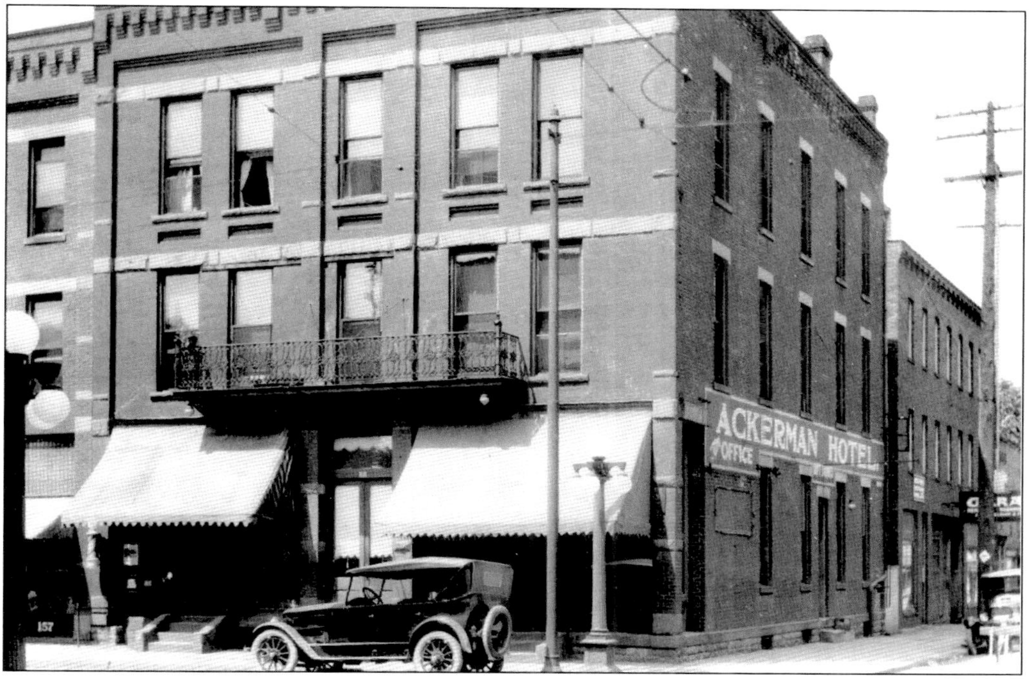

THE HOTEL ACKERMAN. Originally known as the Titus Hotel, the Ackerman Hotel was located on North State Street. It provided lodgings at a reasonable prize and had one modern convenience that the Pilgrim Inn on North Main Street lacked—an elevator. (Photograph courtesy of Hughes Photography Studio.)

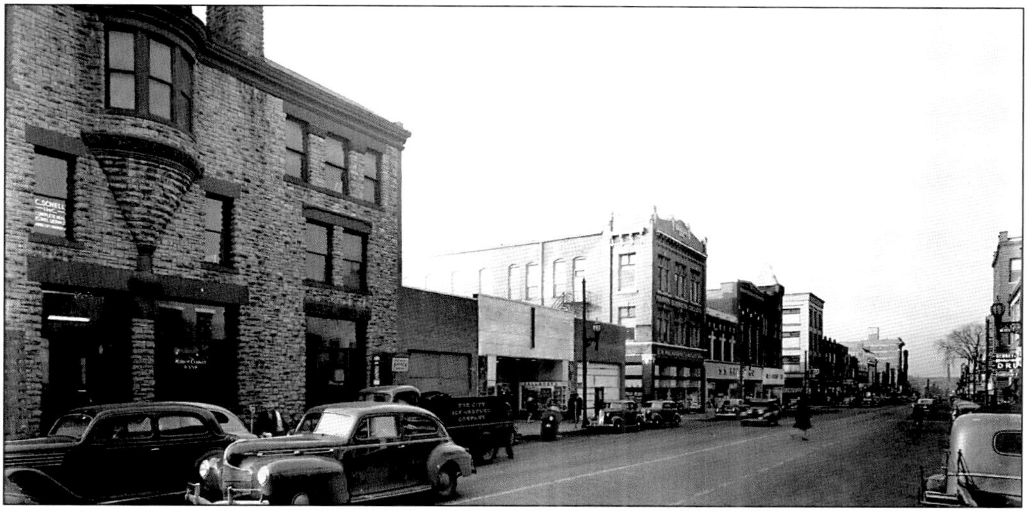

WEST CENTER STREET, c. 1941. This view of Center Street looking southwest from the North Main Street corner shows how downtown Marion looked before World War II. Immediately east of the limestone Bennett Block (which then housed the Marion County Bank) were a series of one-floor storefronts that would house Gallagher's Pharmacy and the Holly Shop. Marion's dime-store row was next, which included F.W. Woolworth, S.S. Kresge, and W.T. Grant & Company (housed in the Busby Block). (Photograph courtesy of the Marion County Historical Society.)

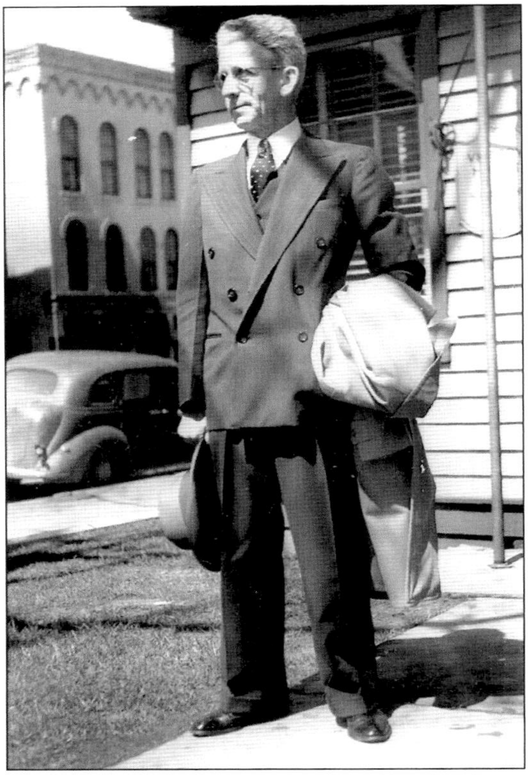

MORGAN BURKE, CHAIRMAN, UHLER-PHILLIPS COMPANY. Throughout his life, Morgan E. Burke represented style and civic involvement in Marion County, Ohio. Born in LaRue, Ohio, in 1885, Burke married Dorothy E. Bush, daughter of Eli and Margaret Bush, with whom he had one son, Morgan E. Burke Jr. Mr. Burke, who was always perfectly attired, served as president of the Marion Cemetery Association; he also served on the boards of the McDaniel Motor Company and the Home Federal Savings & Loan Association. (Photograph courtesy of Robin Burke Leffler.)

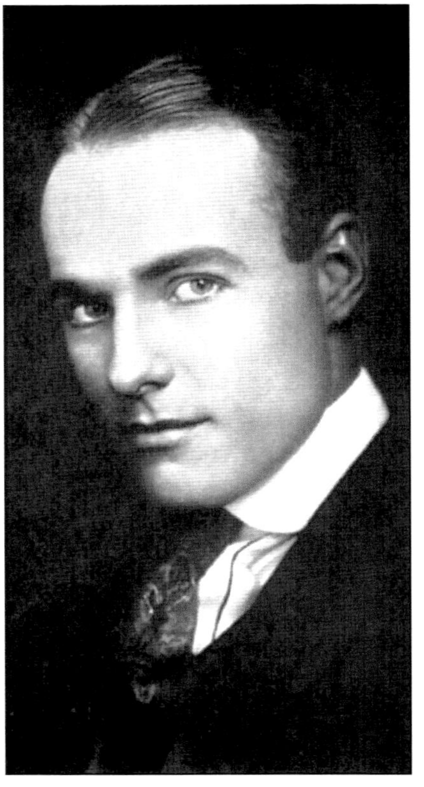

SAXON KLING, 1891–1940. Following his heart to Broadway, Marionite George M. Kling, son of Arthur and Gertrude (Wright) Kling, adopted the stage name Saxon Kling in New York, and joined the experimental Washington Square Players theater troupe, along with Samuel Jaffe. After making several silent films in California, Kling returned to New York, and his first love, the theater. In 1920, he played opposite Helen Hays in *Bab*. The 1928 comedy, *Crashing Through*, was his biggest success as a Broadway playwright. Kling's death in 1940 was front-page news in the *Marion Star*. At the time of his death, he was finalizing revisions with co-writer Ester Forbes (author of *Johnny Tremaine*) for their comedy, *What Every Woman Wants*, before its scheduled pre-Broadway run. He is buried in Marion Cemetery. (Photograph courtesy of the author.)

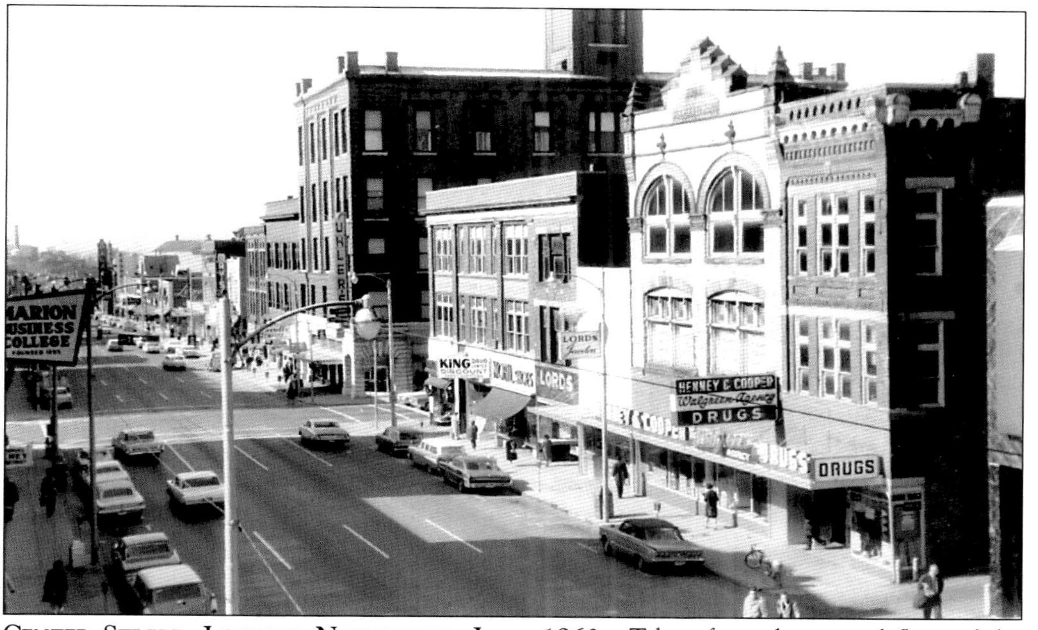

CENTER STREET, LOOKING NORTHWEST, LATE 1960S. Taken from the second floor of the Bennett Block, this view of West Center Street looks northwest toward the Huber Block, which was the longtime home of the Uhler-Phillips Company, "Marion's Friendly Department Store." In the foreground is the Warner & Edwards block, which housed Henney & Cooper Drug Store, now Rite Aid Pharmacy. (Photograph courtesy of the Marion County Historical Society.)

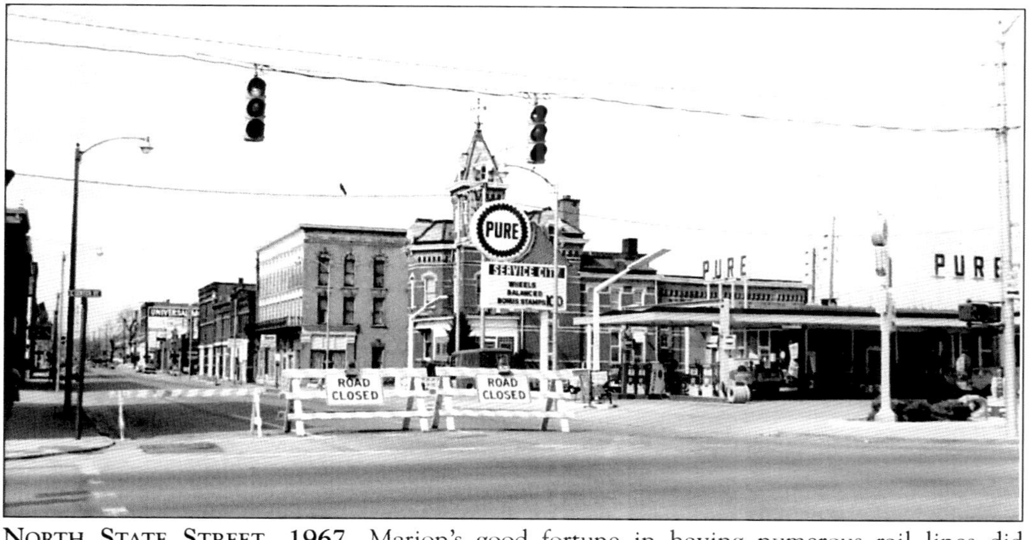

NORTH STATE STREET, 1967. Marion's good fortune in having numerous rail lines did contribute to significant traffic problems when trains passed through the heart of the city. As early as the 1920s, plans had been made for a system of overpasses to replace the grade crossings downtown and near the Marion Power Shovel Plant. At the State of Ohio's insistence, work on the first overpass at State Street was begun in 1967. Young's Pure Oil Station, the Marion County Sheriff's Residence and Jail, and the Snyder Hotel have all since been torn down. (Photograph courtesy of the Marion County Historical Society.)

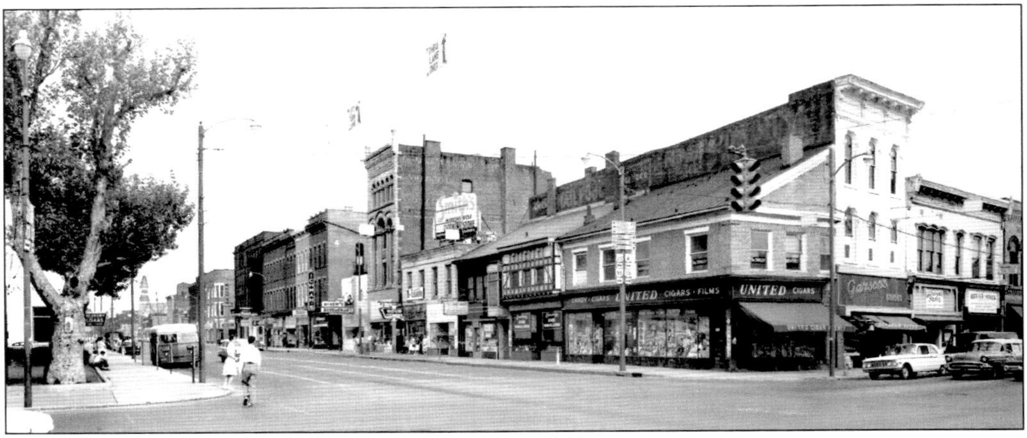

INTERSECTION OF CENTER AND MAIN STREETS, EARLY 1960S. The intersection pictured formed the commercial and governmental hub of Marion for over 150 years. While many of the structures in this photograph still exist and house businesses, many others have been leveled. The United Cigar Store still reigns supreme at this corner; but Tom McNew's Restaurant, once resplendent with its 1930s art-deco green Carrara glass façade and neon sign, was torn down in the 1980s. One of the greatest architectural losses in downtown Marion since 1975 was the destruction of the Marion National Bank building, to the immediate left of the "Smith's" billboard. (Photograph courtesy of Marion County Historical Society.)

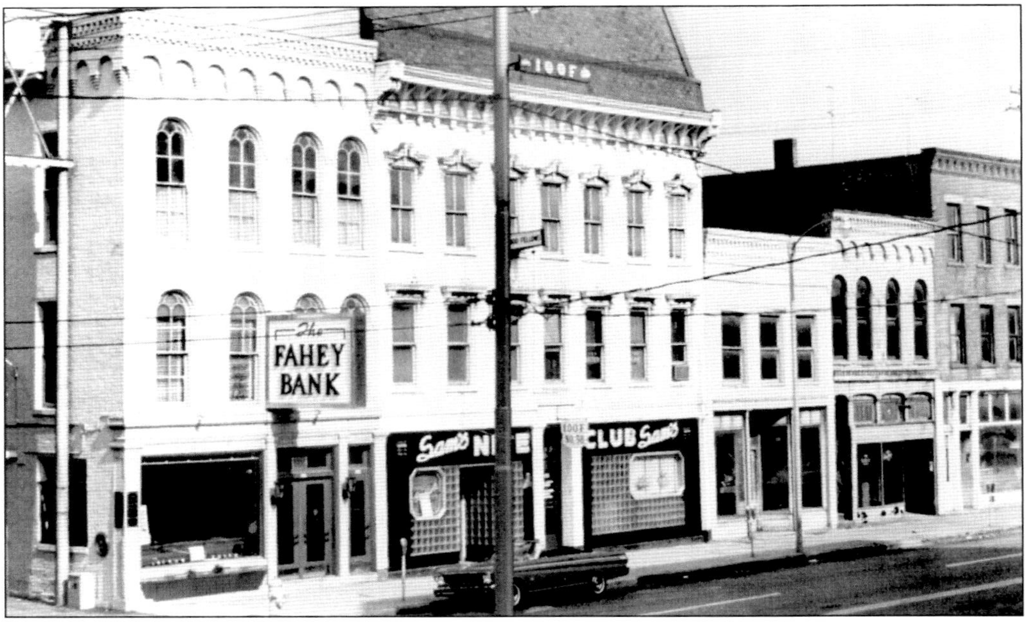

WEST SIDE OF NORTH MAIN STREET, 1965. In December 1965, The Fahey Bank announced that it would construct a new main office on the west side of North Main Street opposite the Courthouse. In order to do so, the bank had to purchase the remaining 887 years of a 1000-year lease held by the Lodge 58 of the International Order of Odd Fellows for the use of the upper floors of the Railroad Building. Fahey Bank's facility was constructed roughly the same as the previous bank building, with the remaining land used as a parking lot. (Photograph courtesy of Hughes Photography, John Rall, president.)

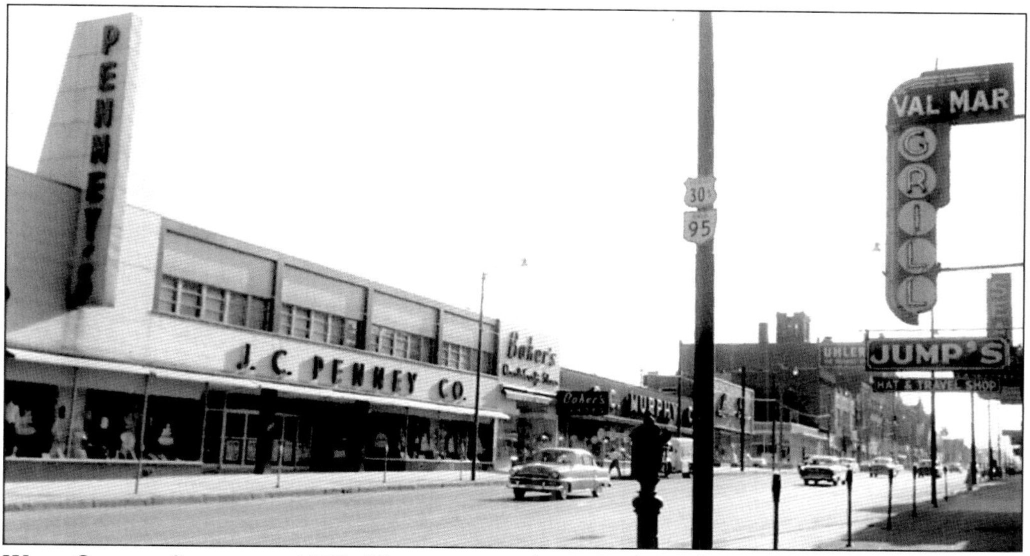

West Center Street, c. 1960. The commercial strip built on the site of Marion's old Central Junior High School on West Center Street was Marion's first shopping center. The J.C. Penney Co. moved into the largest store front allowing it to quadruple its floor space. Baker Shoes, G.C. Murphy Co., and Lerner Shops rounded out the selection. After years of sitting empty, this entire site was dramatically remodeled and now houses the new Marion County Administrative Offices. (Photograph courtesy of the Marion County Historical Society.)

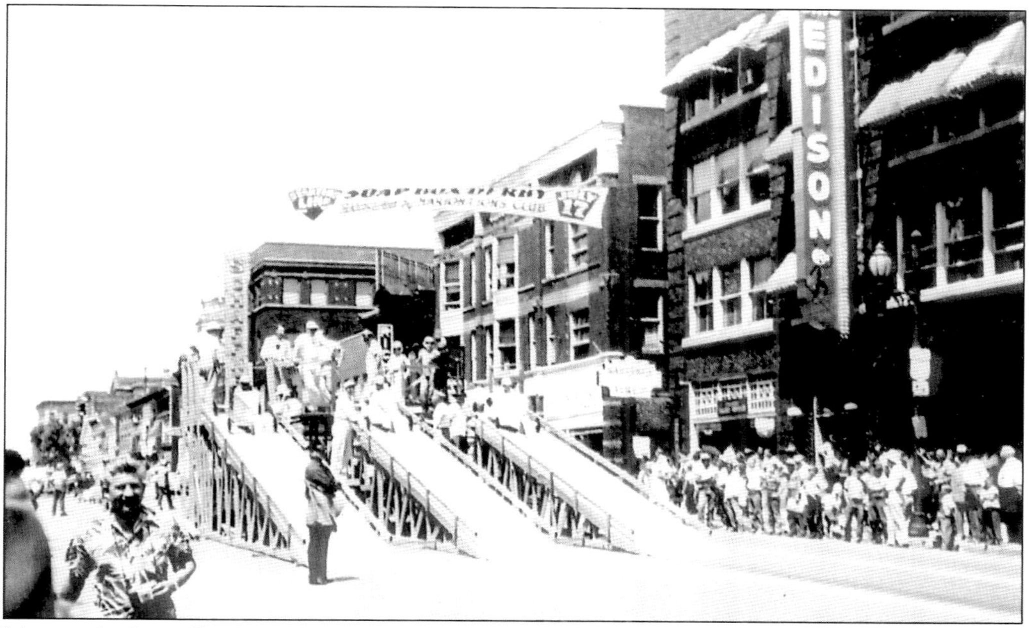

Marion's Soap Box Derby Races. In the 1950s and early 1960s, Marion hosted the local Soap Box Derby Races on the Main Street hill, just south of Church Street. Winners of this race advanced to the appropriate age-group qualifying races, which would hopefully take a local youngster to Akron for the National Soap Box Derby Races. (Photograph courtesy of Gary Barnhart.)

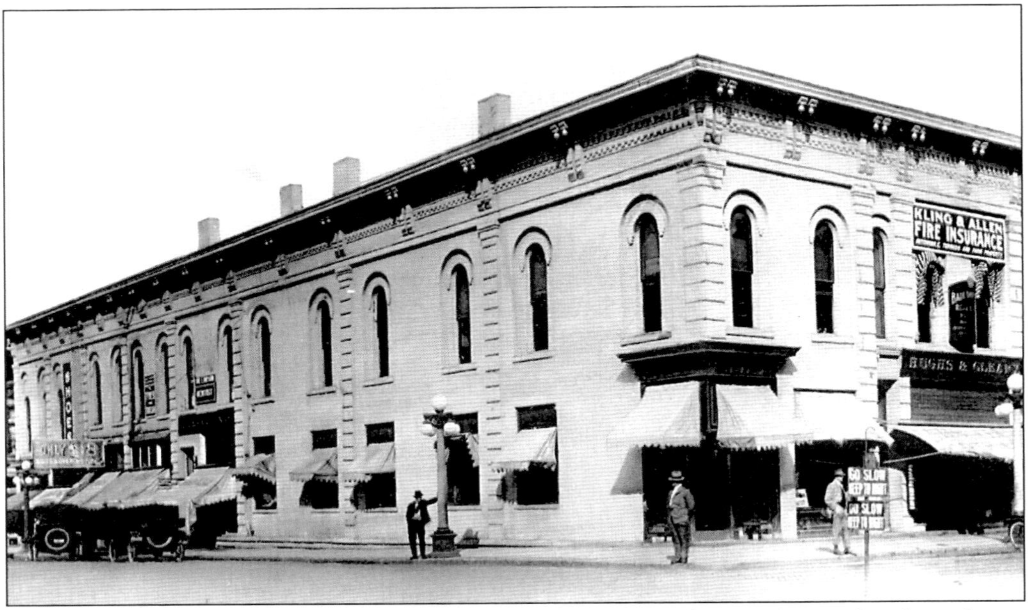

CITY NATIONAL BANK. The northwest corner of Center and Main Streets has been home to financial institutions since the 1880s. This cream-colored brick was the home of the City National Bank in 1911, with D.R. Crissinger as vice president. (Photograph courtesy of the Marion County Historical Society.)

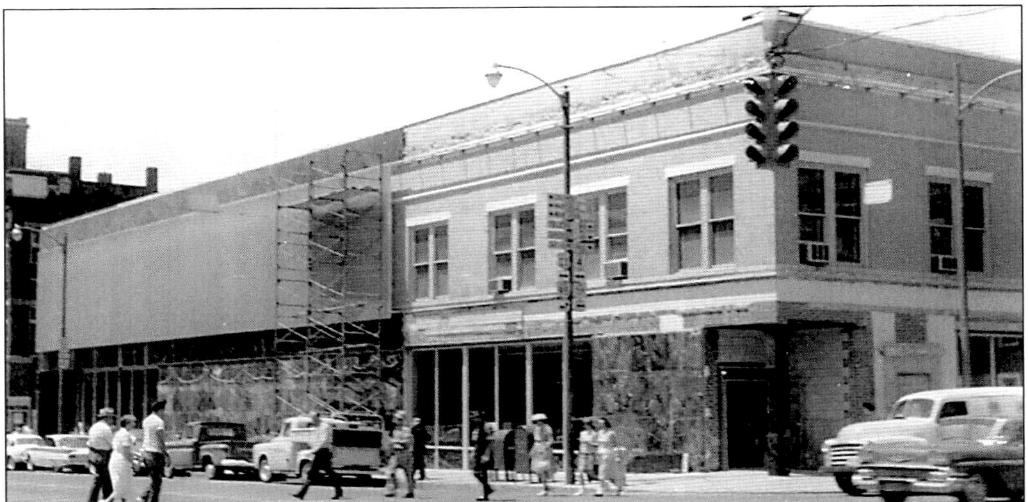

NATIONAL CITY BANK BUILDING REMODELING, 1960. In the summer of 1960, the National City Bank on the northwest corner of West Center and North Main Streets began the process of modernizing their downtown office. Using a black and green marble veneer on the first floor and along the cornice, the design also called for a curtain of aluminum screen to mask the second floor windows and brick. The effect was dramatic; however, the late judge and historian Charlton Myers was less than enthusiastic, writing in January 1961, "each little hole is a birdhouse…and it collects snow! Just how long will this last?" (Photograph courtesy of the Marion County Historical Society.)

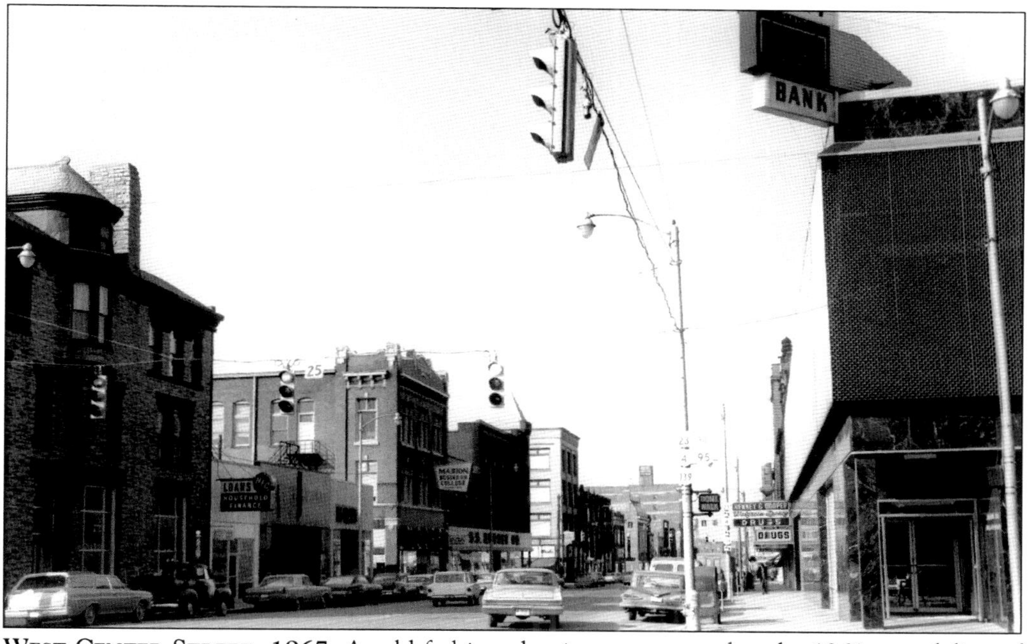

West Center Street, 1967. As old-fashioned as it may seem today, the 1961 remodeling of the National City Bank Building brought downtown Marion its first digital electric clock and thermometer and its first drive-through banking. (Photograph courtesy of the Marion County Historical Society.)

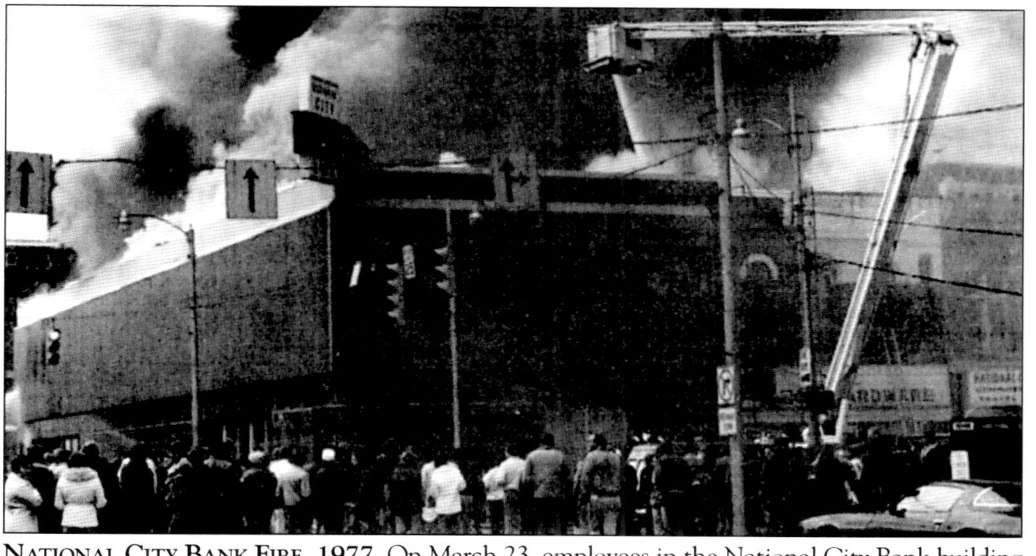

National City Bank Fire, 1977. On March 23, employees in the National City Bank building in downtown Marion smelled smoke. Around the same time, Harry Crawbaugh, of Crawbaugh Hardware, went to investigate a loud crash that seemed to come from the upper floors of his store. The fire destroyed the bank and the hardware store as well as the House of Brides store; and it heavily damaged Jim Dugan's. Fire Chief Ken Wakley told the *Marion Star* that he had "never seen a fire as tough as this." A new building was erected and occupied by the BancOhio National Bank, and later sold to National City Bank of Cleveland. (Photograph courtesy of Robert Turner.)

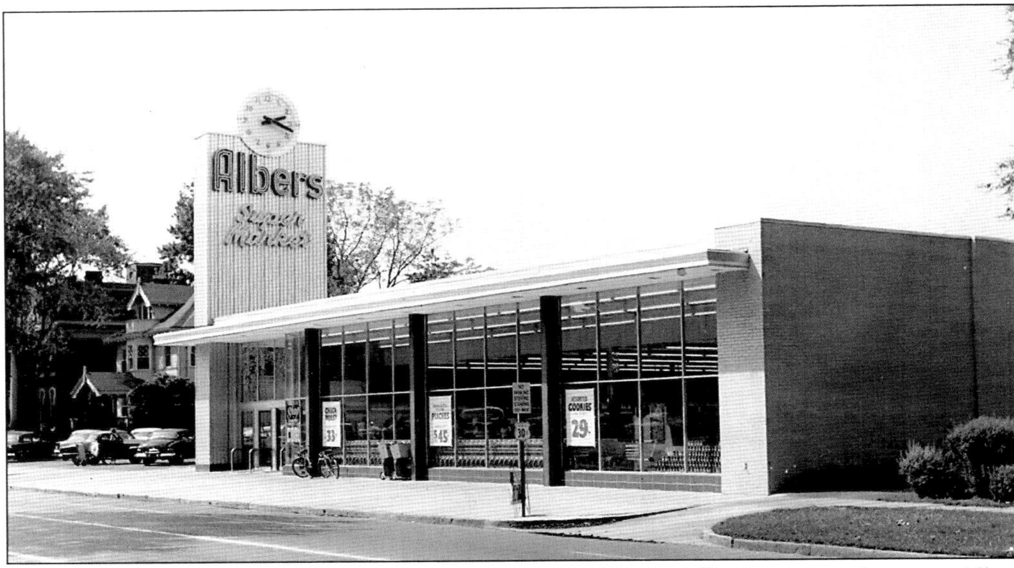

ALBERS SUPERMARKET, EAST CENTER STREET AT NORTH GREENWOOD STREET. Albers Supermarket first opened on East Center Street (between Vine and High Streets) in September 1942. In 1953, the chain bought Temple Israel's building (formerly known as the Owens Residence) on East Center Street, and constructed the first modern-format grocery store in Marion. In addition to featuring all of the modern amenities, the site also provided plenty of parking for shoppers. Albers Supermarket closed in May 1974; the site was also operated by the Great Scot chain for a number of years. (Photograph courtesy of Hughes Photography, John Rall, president.)

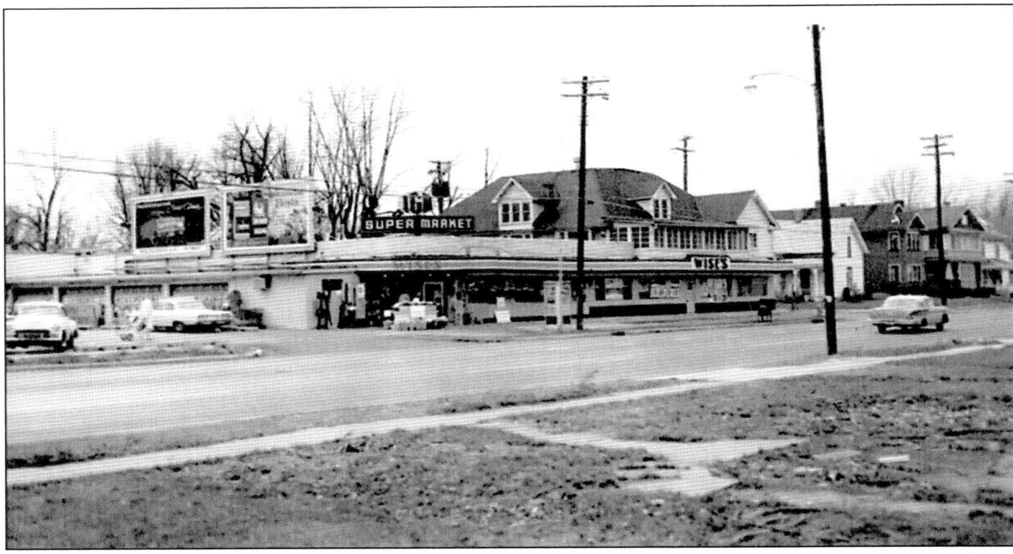

WISE'S IGA, EAST CENTER STREET AND REED AVENUE, 1964. Opened as a neighborhood market in 1910, the Wise family's store grew to meet the demands of Marion's growing middle class on the east side of the city. Despite the competition posed by the appearance of chain stores, Wise's remained popular until a fire destroyed its rambling building in 1964. (Photograph courtesy of Carol Robinson.)

Two

ATTENDING TO THE PEOPLE'S BUSINESS

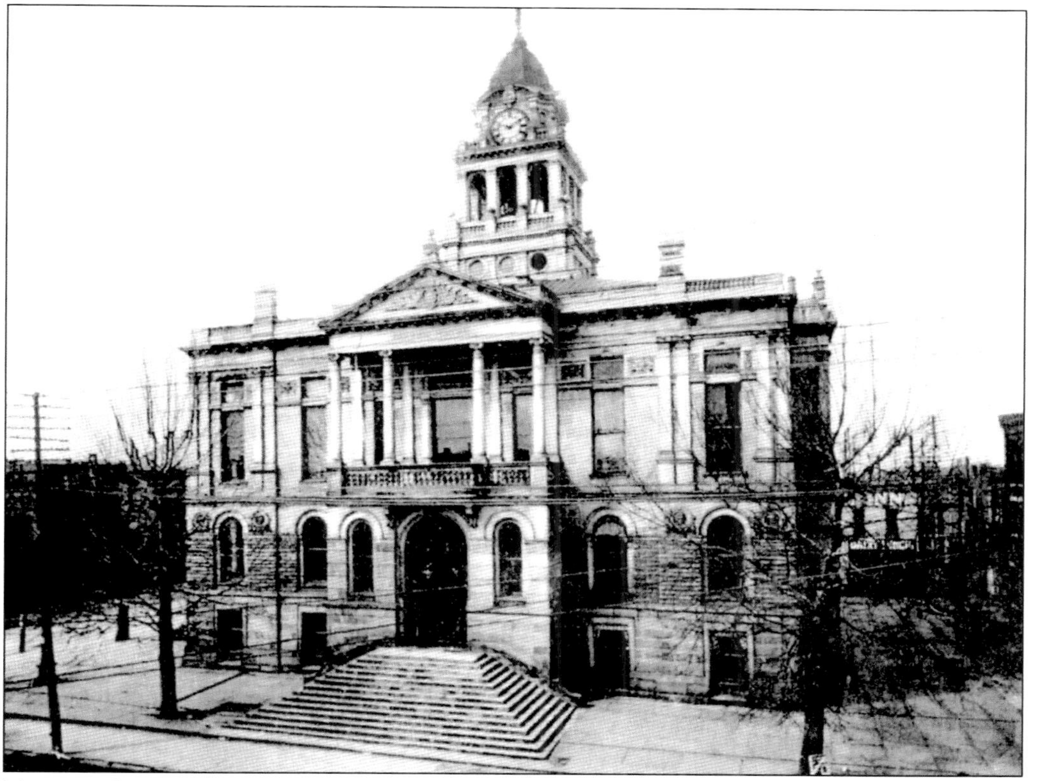

MARION COUNTY COURTHOUSE. Built between 1884 and 1885, the present Marion County Courthouse was designed by architect D.W. Gibbs. Difficult to classify, no single formal design theme dominates the building. However, the eclectic Victorian-era building does favor the Italian Renaissance Revival style. The buff-colored sandstone courthouse has undergone numerous renovations, some more sensitive than others, with the exterior of the building fairing best. (Photograph courtesy of the author.)

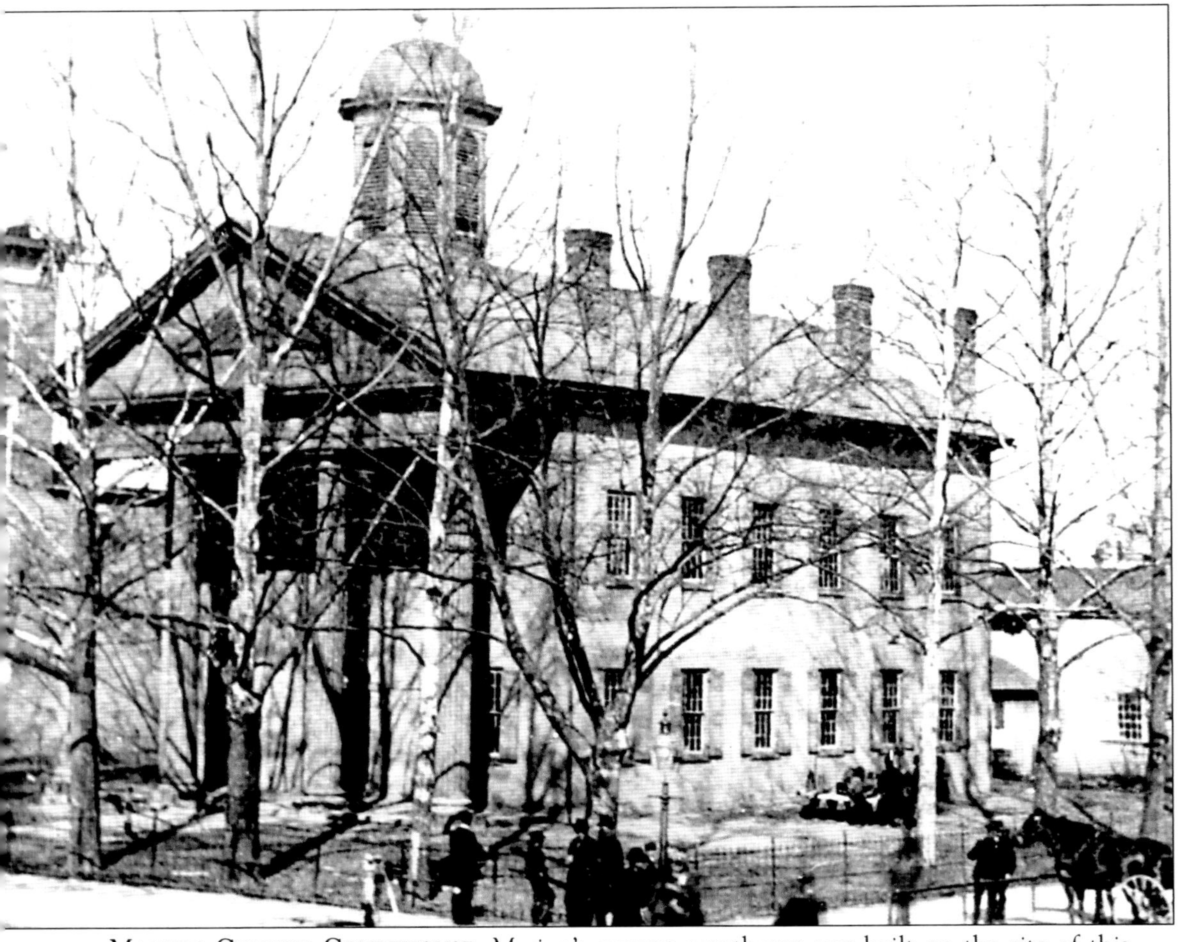

MARION COUNTY COURTHOUSE. Marion's current courthouse was built on the site of this building, which served the county from 1833 until 1883. The Greek Revival-style building was dominated by four classical Doric columns; its bell tower was uniquely American in origin.t was here in 1839 that the case involving Bill Mitchell was tried. Mitchell had come to Marion in the fall of 1838 declaring himself to be a free black man. He was well liked and welcomed by the community. In the summer of 1839, eight men from Kanawha County, Virginia, arrived, claiming that "Black Bill" was the runaway property of one of the men, Adnah Van Bibber. The matter went to trial with Judge Ozias Bowen presiding. As a black man, Mitchell was not allowed to testify on his own behalf; the eight Virginians were the main witnesses against him. Finding that Van Bibber had not proven clear ownership, Judge Bowen ruled Bill Mitchell a free man. The Virginians were displeased and disrupted the court, brandishing knives and taking Bill against the will of the court. Angry citizens gathered and began a riot outside the courthouse. They pelted the Virginians with rocks as they emerged from the building. They, along with Bill, were directed by Justice of the Peace John Bartram out of harm's way to his offices across the street. The citizens armed themselves with weapons from the arsenal, and with Associate Judge Thomas Anderson brandishing a pistol, they forced their way into the office. This distraction allowed Bill to escape through the back of the building. Bill made his way to freedom in Canada with the help of Abolitionists. News of the trial, riot, and outcome became fodder for national newspapers and broadsides and brought Marion into the limelight. (Photograph courtesy of the Marion County Historical Society.)

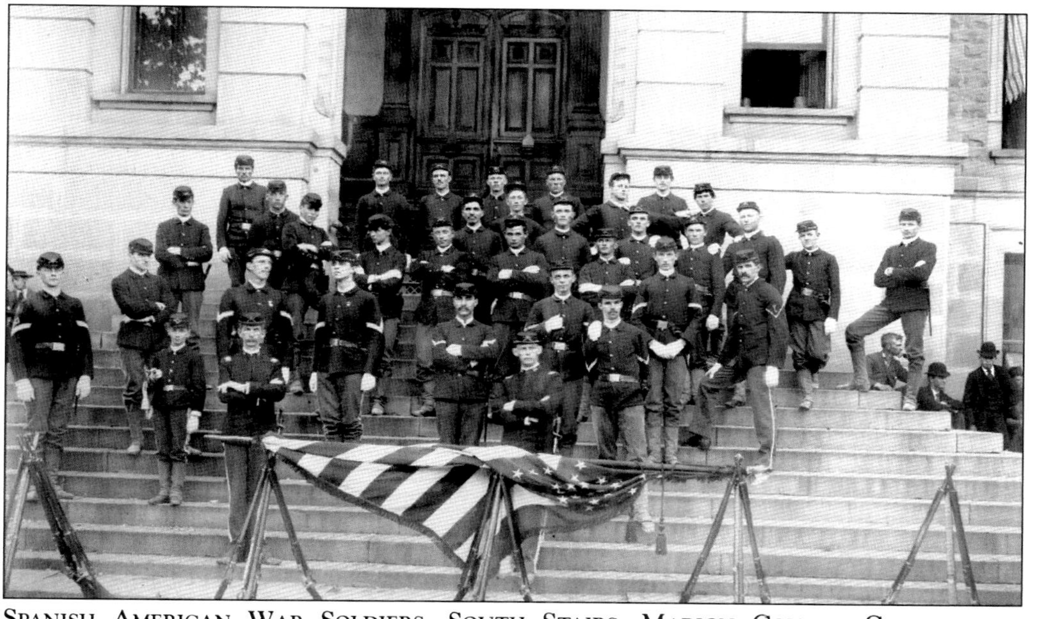

SPANISH AMERICAN WAR SOLDIERS, SOUTH STAIRS, MARION COUNTY COURTHOUSE. Marion County was represented in the Spanish American War by Company G, Fourth Ohio Infantry, United States Volunteers. Company G, comprised of 105 volunteers and three officers, returned from the war in January 1904. Charles Francis Brown, uncle of Hoover Brown, is located in the fifth row from the top, on the far right. (Photograph courtesy of the Marion County Historical Society.)

MARION COUNTY COURTHOUSE, BELL TOWER DETAIL. Crowning the Marion County Courthouse is a statue referred to locally as "Lady Justice." Placed atop the bell tower, the statue reigned over the courthouse until the mid-20th century when she was removed during work on the belfry. Unattended on courthouse grounds, Lady Justice was kidnapped by pranksters. The statue was buried under a barn floor when the search effort heated up. Twenty years later, a deal was made that resulted in the return of the statue for a complete restoration funded by the Marion County Bar Association; thus Lady Justice returned to her position of watching over downtown Marion. (Photograph courtesy of the Marion County Historical Society.)

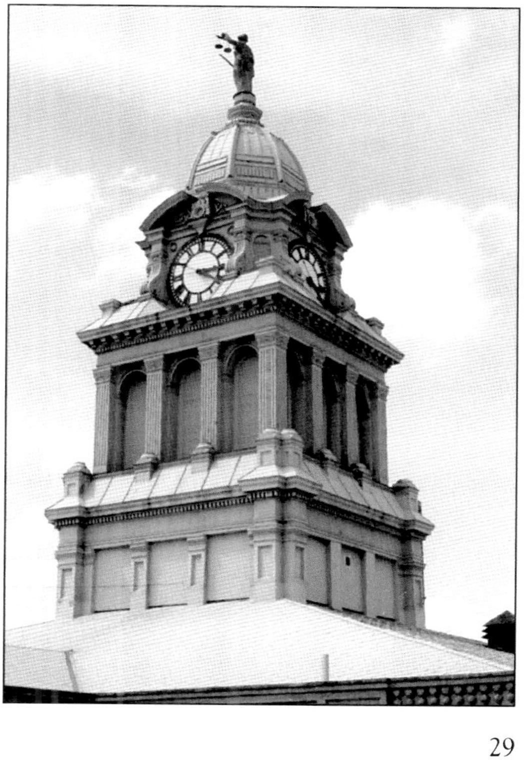

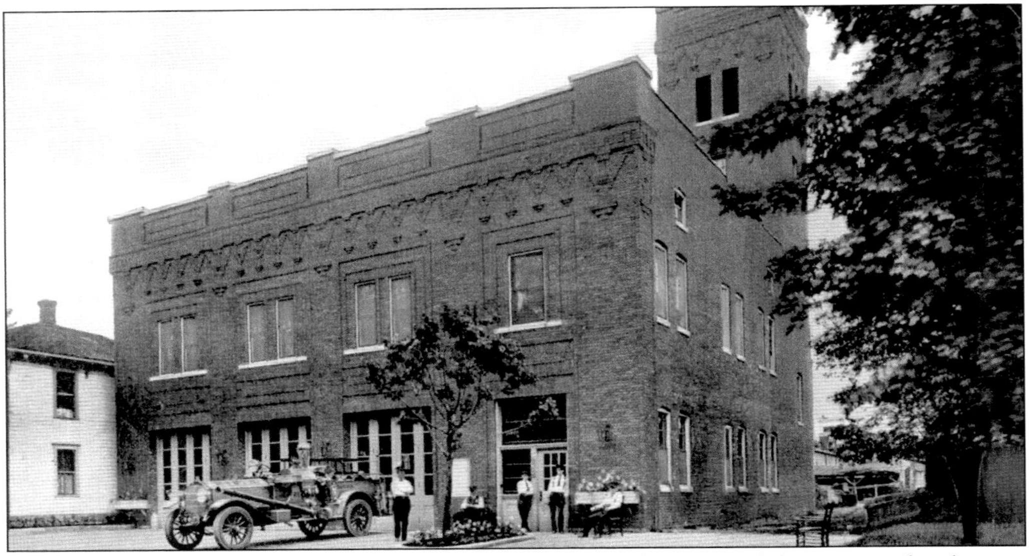

1912 Central Fire Station. Funds to construct a modern central fire station for the city of Marion were approved in 1912. Located at 186 South Prospect Street, the station could not only accommodate the newly motorized fire trucks, but also contained a stable for the horses that were in service through the 1920s. The station was built on the site of the Michael Brigle residence; to the immediate south was the home of Isaiah C. Jones, a longtime Marion volunteer firefighter who was reportedly delighted to have his friends as next door neighbors. Now known as Fire Station No. 1, the structure continues to serve the City of Marion. (Photograph courtesy of the author.)

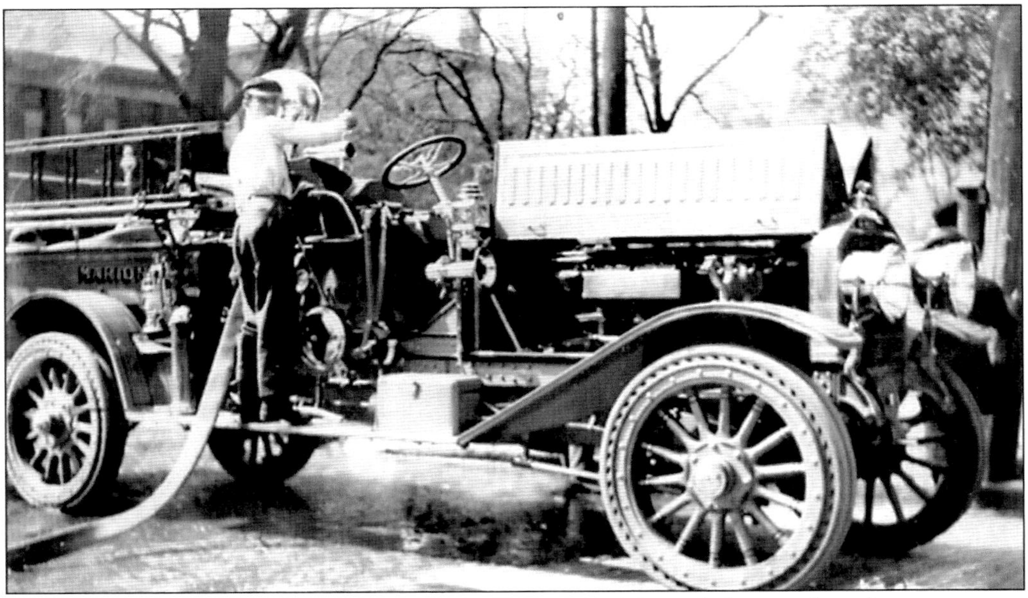

First Fire Truck, Marion City Fire Department. Marion's first modern fire engine was a marvel in its day. The truck could carry firefighters, hoses, and equipment, as well as act as a pumper. The vehicle also featured two solid rubber tires per wheel, both for traction and for reliability. (Photograph courtesy of Trella Romine.)

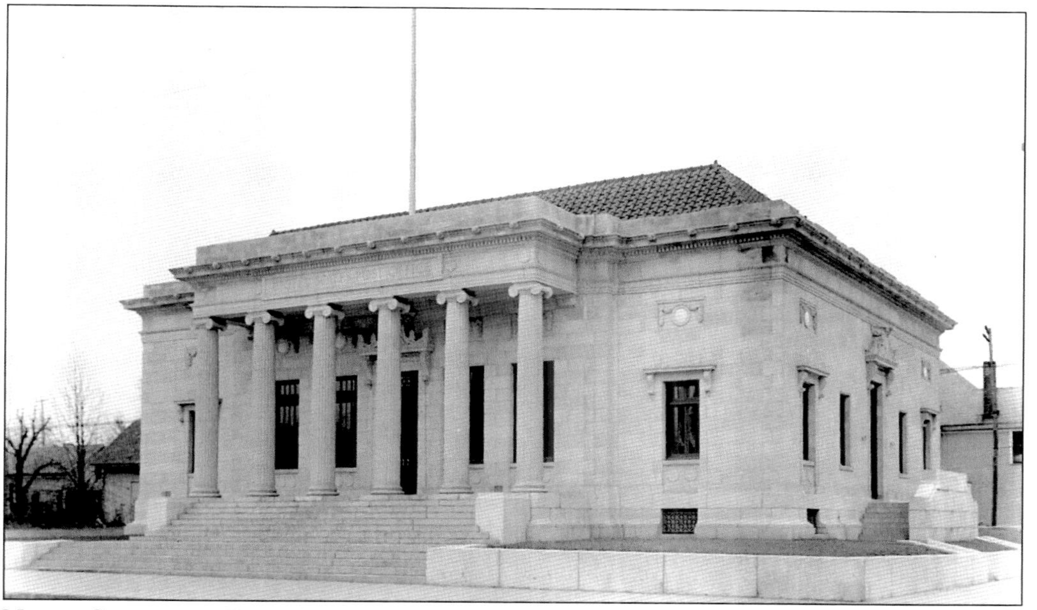

NEWLY COMPLETED POST OFFICE AND FEDERAL BUILDING. Completed in December of 1910, Marion's new Post Office and Federal Building sat imposingly on the corner of East Church and South State Streets. The building is now home to the Marion County Historical Society's Heritage Hall and Museum. (Photograph courtesy of the Marion County Historical Society.)

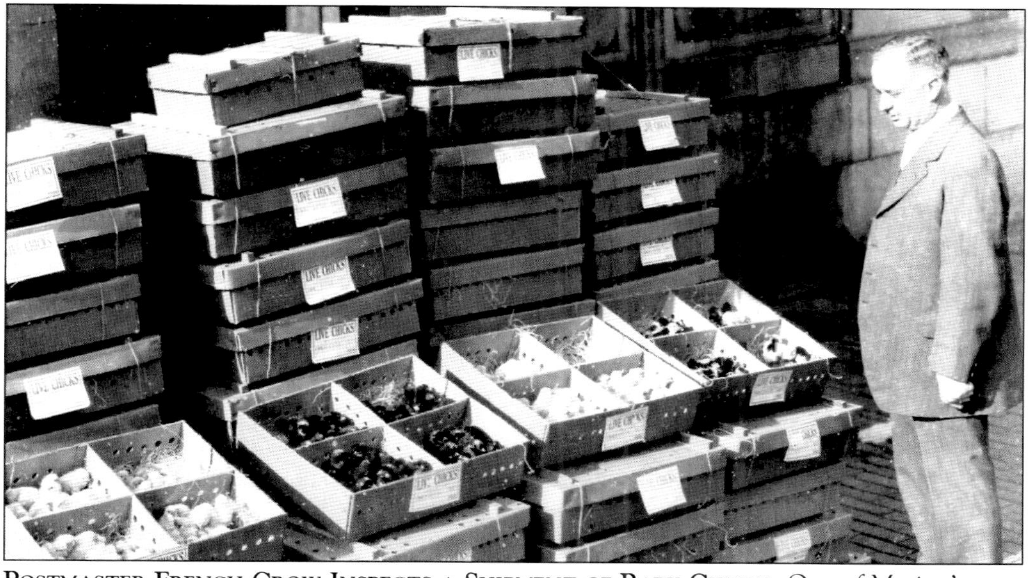

POSTMASTER FRENCH CROW INSPECTS A SHIPMENT OF BABY CHICKS. One of Marion's most prominent leaders in the early 1900s was Marion native French Crow. Born to Joseph and Lydia Crow in 1876, Crow's unusual birth name, French, was his mother's maiden surname. Crow established his Marion law practice after graduating from Case Law School in Cleveland. Appointed Postmaster by Warren G. Harding, Crow remained in that position until 1934. French Crow died in California in 1956 and is buried in Marion Cemetery. (Photograph courtesy of Shelby Needham.)

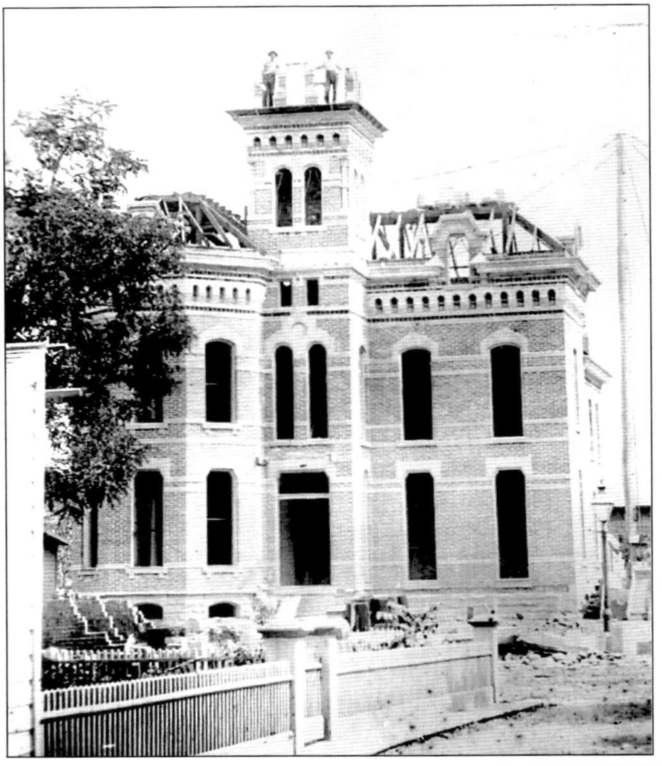

Marion County Sheriff's Residence and Jail, North State Street, 1878. During the 19th century, many of Ohio's counties, including Marion, combined a residence for the county sheriff with the jail. The sheriff and his family live comfortably, and the sheriff was close by in the event that he was needed in the jail section of the building. Shown during its construction on the east side of North State Street, the Victorian building served until a new jail facility was opened north of Marion on Likens Chapel Road. The 1878 building was demolished in 1968. (Photograph courtesy of the Marion County Historical Society.)

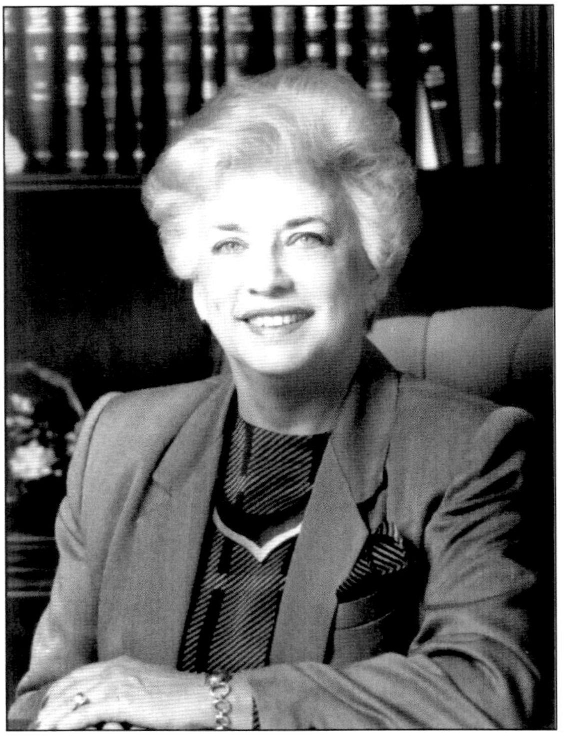

Mary Ellen Withrow, 40th Treasurer of the United States of America, 1994–2001. A native of northern Marion County, Mary Ellen Withrow (nee Hinamon) holds the distinction of being the first and only person to hold the office of Treasurer at all three levels of government—local, state, and federal. Withrow was elected to county office in 1976 and 1980, state office in 1982, 1986, and 1990, and appointed to the position of Treasurer by President Bill Clinton. Withrow remains active in Washington circles and is an inductee to the Ohio Women's Hall of Fame. (Photograph courtesy of Mary Ellen Withrow.)

Three

CARING FOR THE BODY, MIND, AND SPIRIT

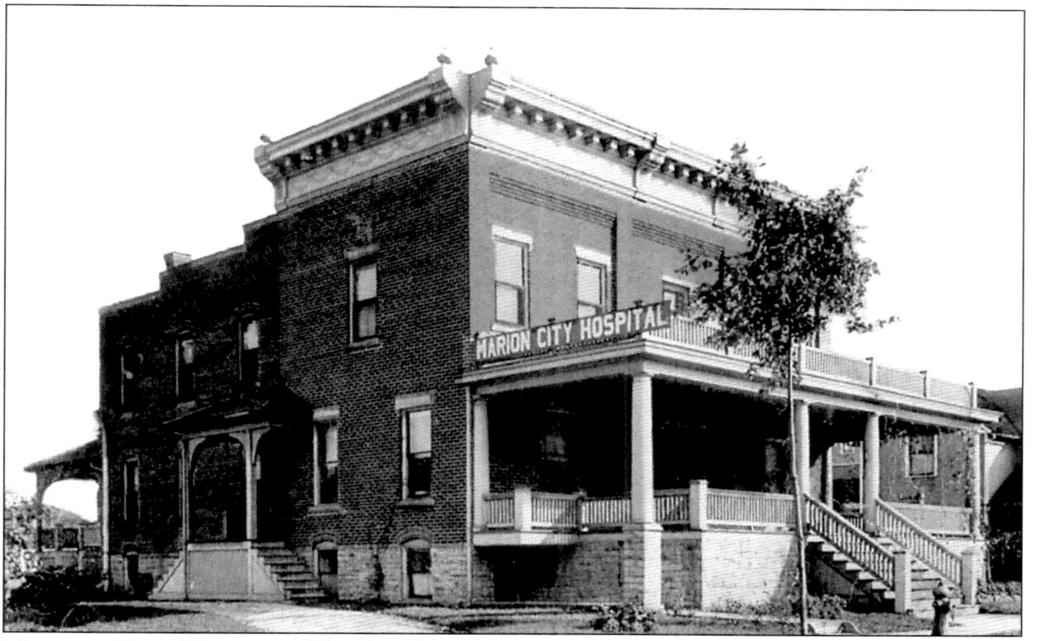

MARION CITY HOSPITAL. The first Marion City Hospital was located at 242–244 Blaine Avenue between West Church and Columbia Streets. During its operation, the Marion City Hospital promoted itself in an advertising letter as "a special hospital for the care and treatment of all surgical and emergency cases...accessible to all reputable physicians...massage and Swedish movement given as desired." Furthermore, the hospital was centrally located and equipped with "electric lights, 'annunciators' and fans, x-ray apparatus, heated by hot water, open porches and roof garden for convalescent patients, fire proof, elevators, and graduated nurses in charge." (Photograph courtesy of Robert Turner.)

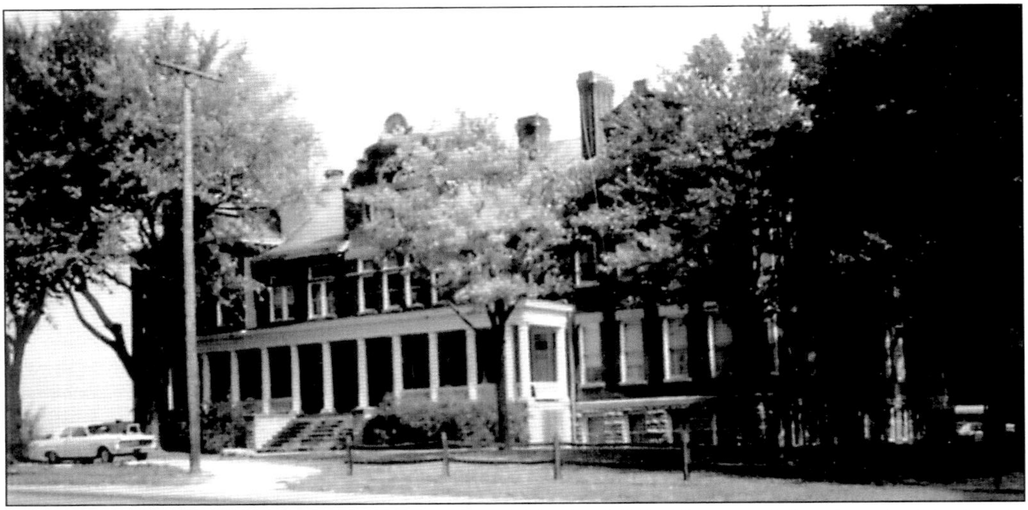

THE WADDELL CHILDREN'S HOME, 1900–1968. In 1900, Marion philanthropist Benjamin Waddell (pronounced wah-DELL) presented the Waddell Children's Home as a gift to the community. The facility was designed to provide shelter to Marion County children, in cases where their parents could not care for them, or when orphaned by the death of both parents. The Dutch Revival-style building was constructed on the site of the George Snyder farmstead. The institutional building was torn down in 1968 and replaced by Waddell Village, designed as a cottage campus, which continues the tradition of serving children who are displaced from their homes. (Photograph courtesy of the Marion County Historical Society.)

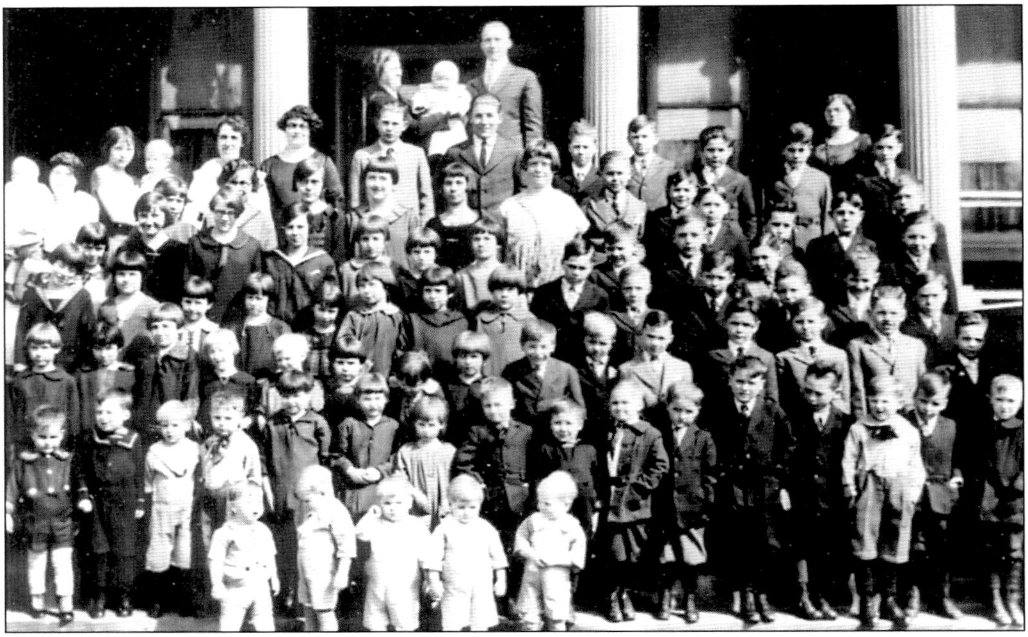

WADDELL CHILDREN'S HOME RESIDENTS. On a bright March day in 1926, Superintendent Carl F. Diegle posed with the residents of the Waddell Children's Home on State Route 4. Dressed in their best, one wonders if these youngsters found the homes that they all rightly deserved. (Photograph courtesy of Trella Romine.)

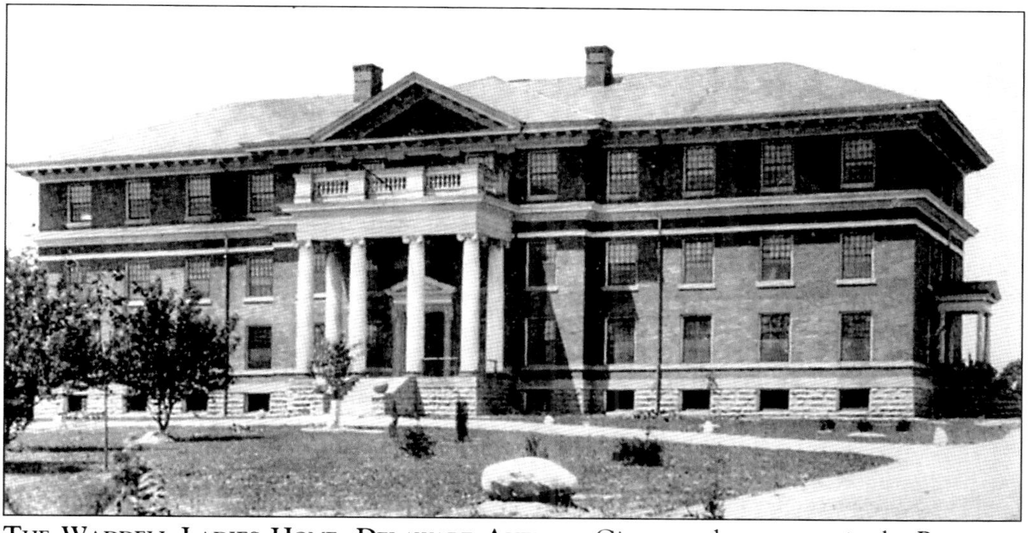

THE WADDELL LADIES HOME, DELAWARE AVENUE. Given to the community by Benjamin Waddell as a home for genteel ladies of advanced age, efforts by the City of Marion to secure the structure for a hospital facility began as early as 1916. The opening of Marion General Hospital in the building in 1920 represented the consolidation of the numerous private and primitive hospitals into one modern organization. Following the construction of the current Marion General Hospital in the 1950s, the building served as Marion City Hall until 1978. The Georgian Revival building is now privately owned. (Photograph courtesy of Trella Romine.)

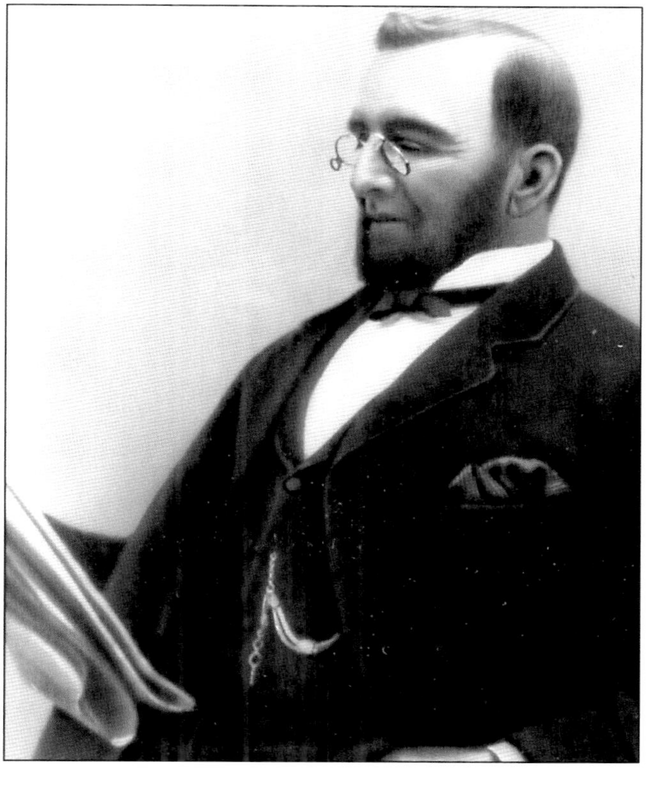

BENJAMIN WADDELL. Benjamin Waddell's name is synonymous with good works and charity in Marion County. A self-made man, Waddell first provided for the comfort of orphans, establishing the Waddell Children's Home on the site of the Snyder farm south of Marion. Replaced by a cottage facility, the grounds are now known as Waddell Village. Waddell also constructed the Ladies Home on Delaware Avenue. (Photograph courtesy of the Marion County Historical Society.)

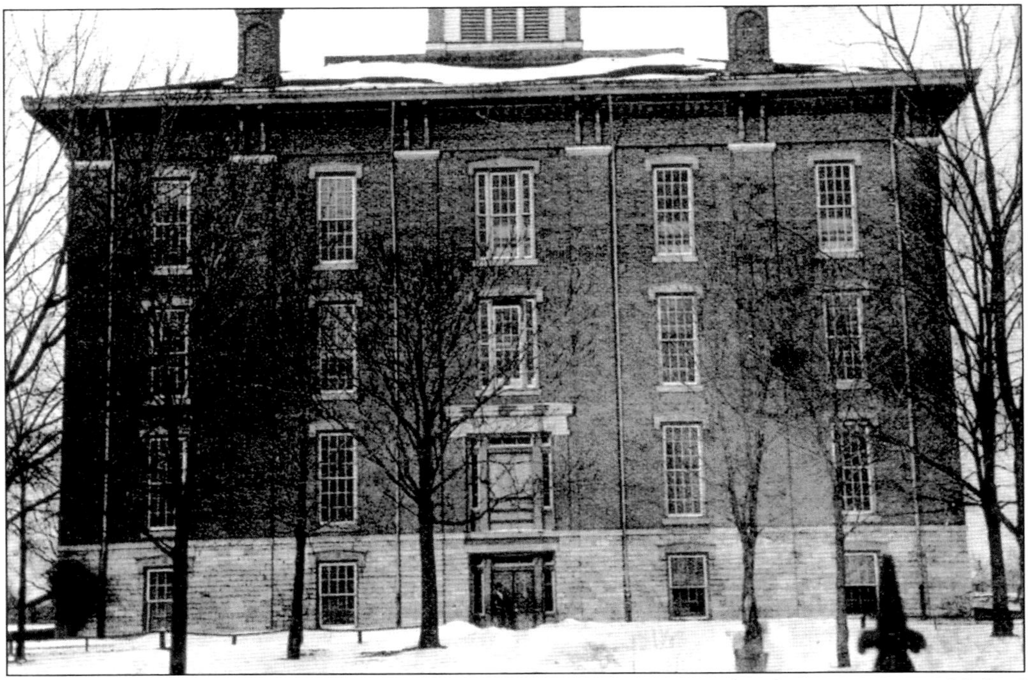

UNION SCHOOL, CENTER AND OAK STREETS. The Marion Union School System was established in 1851. In 1856, the school board authorized construction of the Union School building at the northwest corner of Center Street and Oak Street. Union School opened in 1858. (Photograph courtesy of the author.)

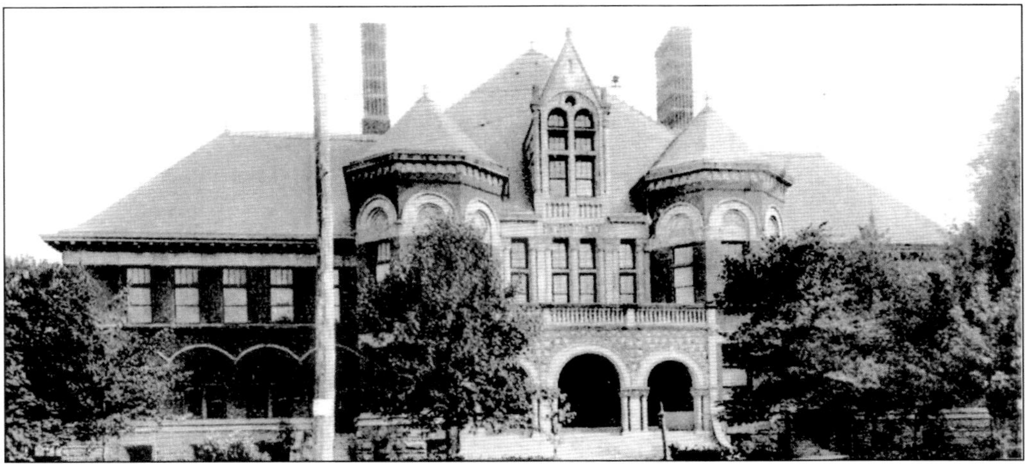

MARION HIGH SCHOOL. Built immediately in front of the Union School building, the Marion High School building of 1892 was perhaps the most ornate and picturesque building dedicated to education in Marion County. Built in the popular Richardson Romanesque style, the brick and polychrome stone building featured an exuberant main entrance comprised of arches, dual "bays," and a soaring dormer that led one's eyes up to the chimneys, which were comprised of tubular molded bricks. The high pitched roof of the 1892 building masked the presence of the Union School Building located immediately behind the new building. The Marion County Governmental Center now occupies the site. (Photograph courtesy of Gary Barnhart.)

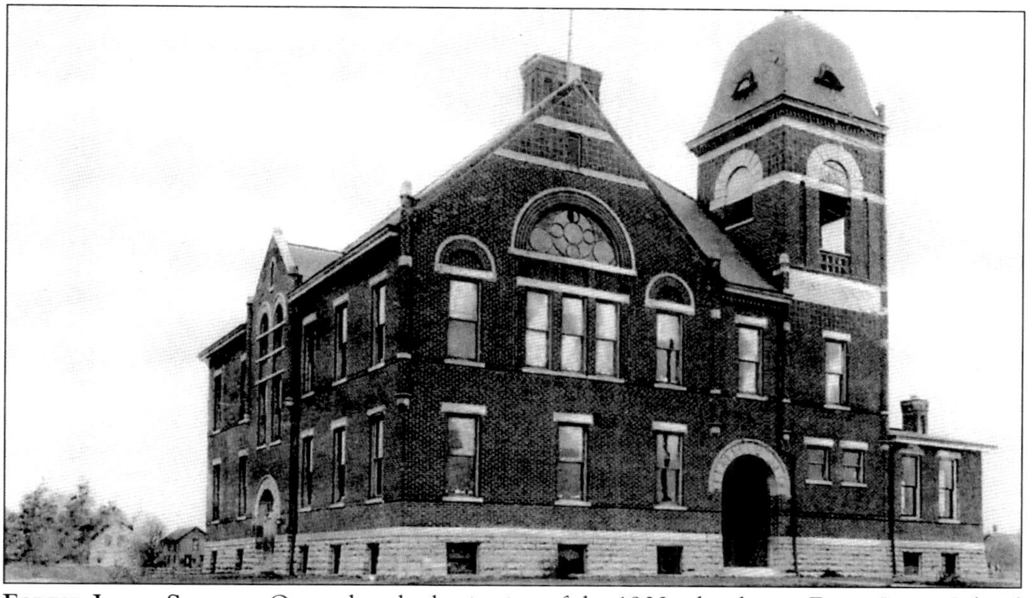

FOREST LAWN SCHOOL. Opened at the beginning of the 1900 school year, Forest Lawn School was located on East Church Street, between Reed Avenue and Forest Lawn Boulevard. The school was the first built in the city school district to be wired for electricity. Forest Lawn School served its student body until 1953, when Vernon School on South Grand Avenue was converted from a junior high school to an elementary. The Marion Public Schools Administration Building was later built at the corner of Forest Lawn Boulevard and Church Street. (Photograph courtesy of Gary Barnhart.)

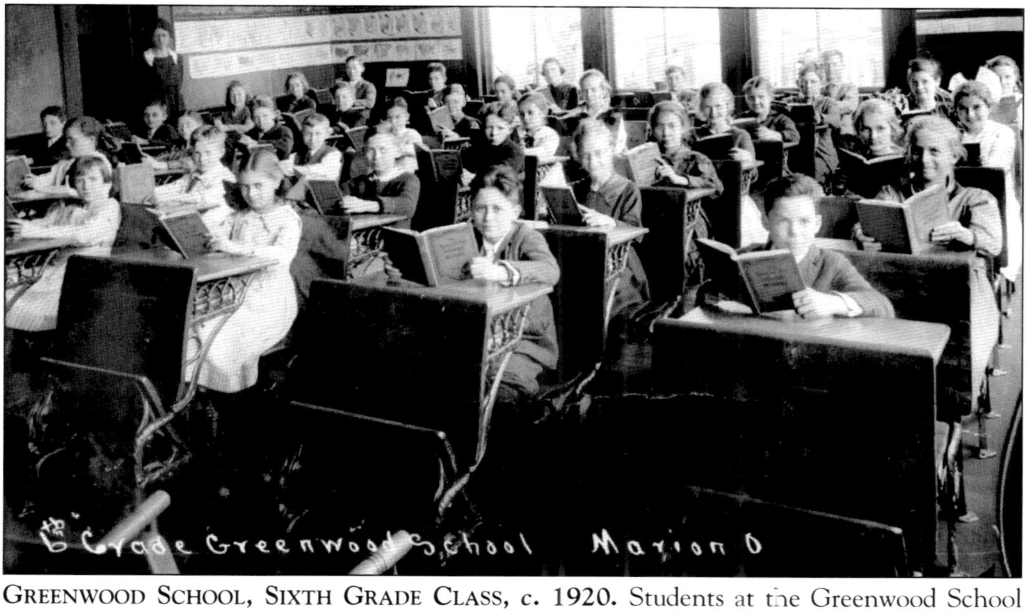

GREENWOOD SCHOOL, SIXTH GRADE CLASS, c. 1920. Students at the Greenwood School smile for a class photograph. Margaret Lusch is seated in the second seat from the right in the second row. George Bensley is seated in the third seat from the right in the fourth row. The two married in 1930. (Photograph courtesy of Susan Clevenger Vierow.)

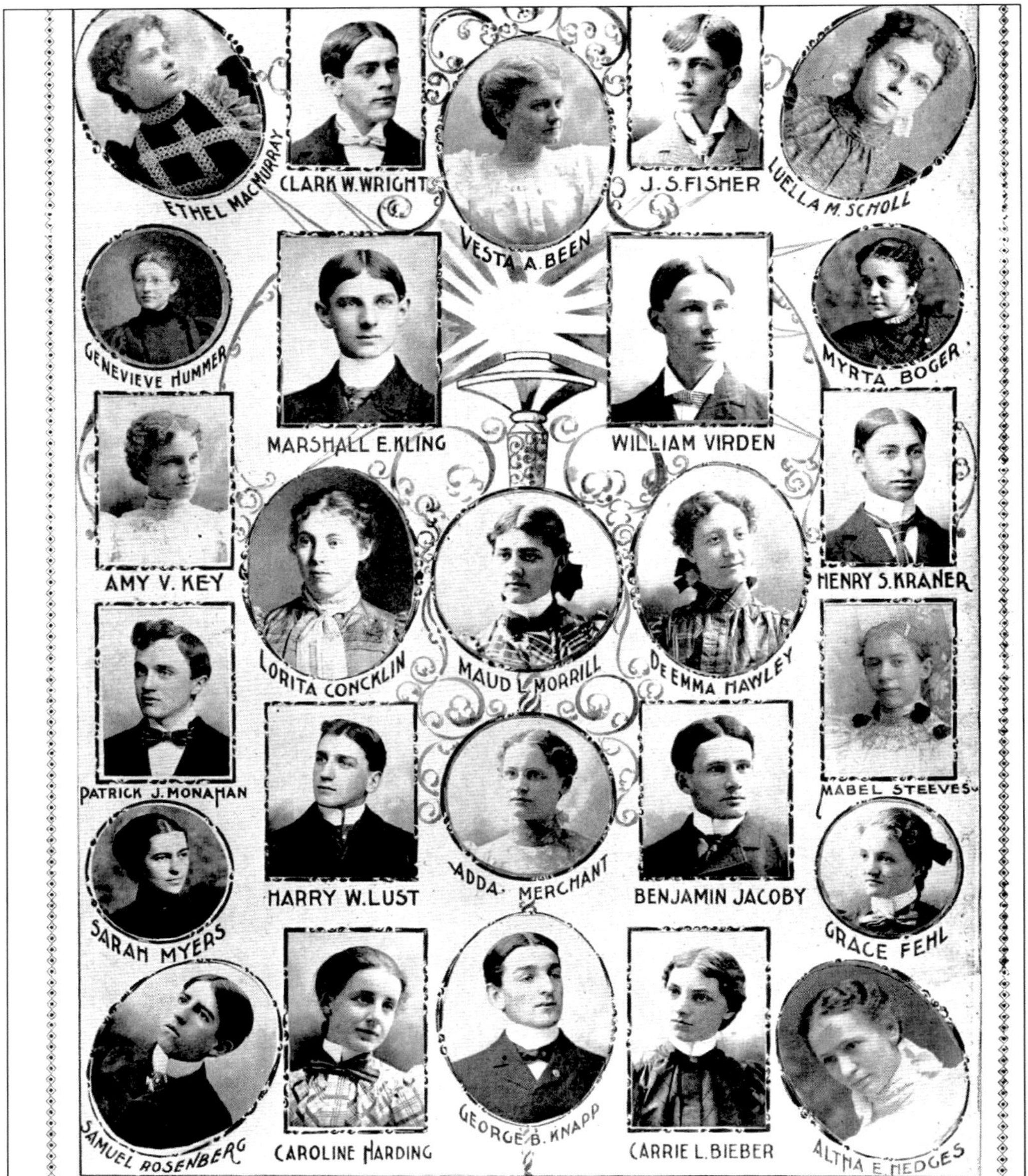

MARION HIGH SCHOOL CLASS OF 1898. Graduating from Marion High School in 1898 were two students, related through difficult circumstance, if nothing else. Caroline Harding was the youngest sister of *Marion Star* publisher Warren G. Harding. Marshall E. (DeWolfe) Kling was the son of Florence Kling Harding and her first husband Pete DeWolfe. Upon divorcing DeWolfe and marrying Harding, Florence placed her son in her father's (Amos Kling) care, and the boy was raised as his son. While Marshall was welcome in his mother and step-father's home, the relationship was strained at best. Still, the young man dreamed of being a newspaper editor like his step-father, and titled his senior paper, an ode to the newspaper reporter's duties, "Scoop." (Photograph courtesy of the author.)

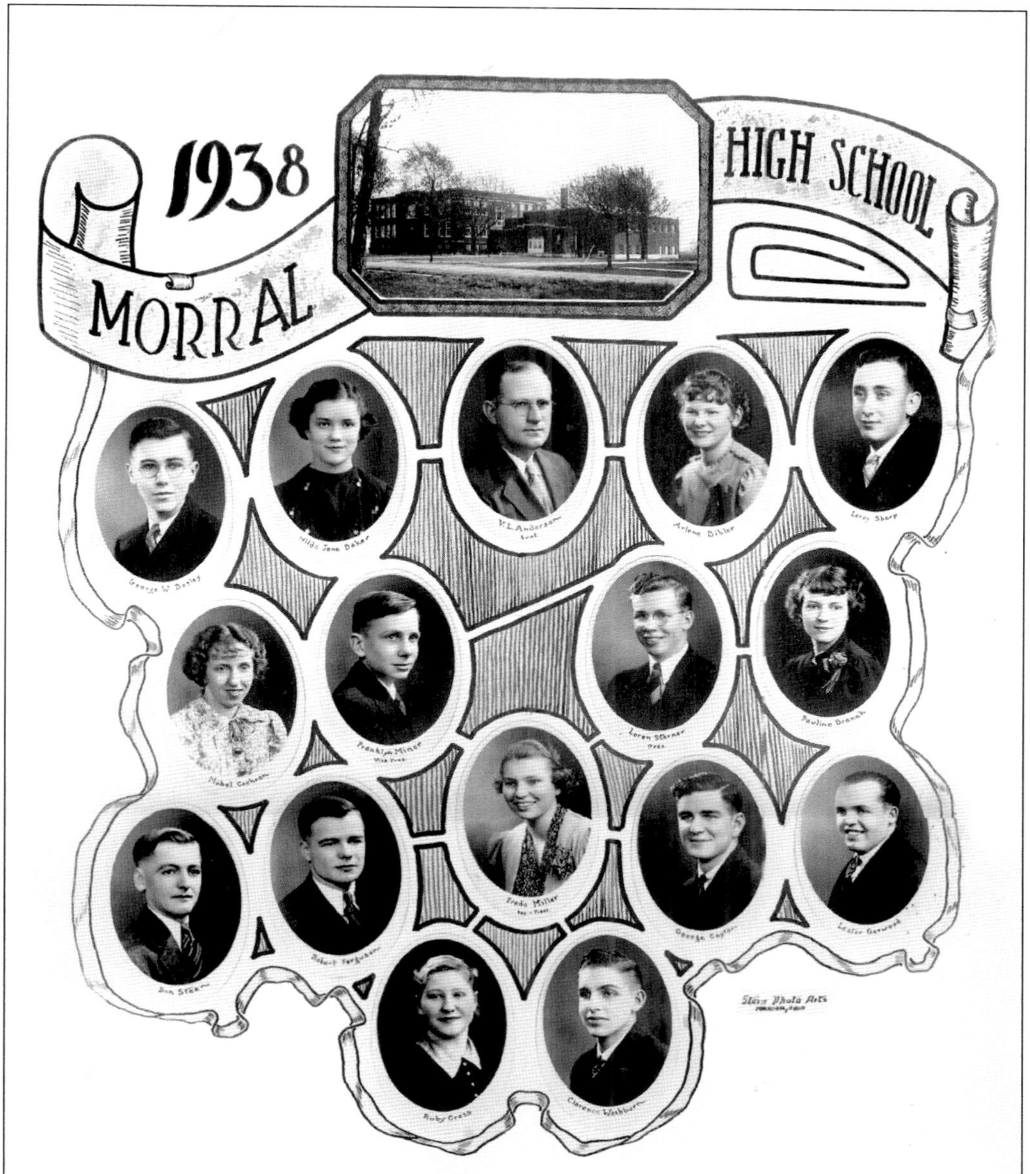

MORRAL OHIO HIGH SCHOOL CLASS, 1938. Like other townships in Marion County just prior to World War I, Salt Rock Township consolidated its rural school system into modern facilities at Morral, the largest community in the township. The Morral system was then consolidated again in the 1950s into the Ridgedale School District. The Morral School building served students in the area until 2004, when it was retired. (Photograph courtesy of the Marion County Historical Society.)

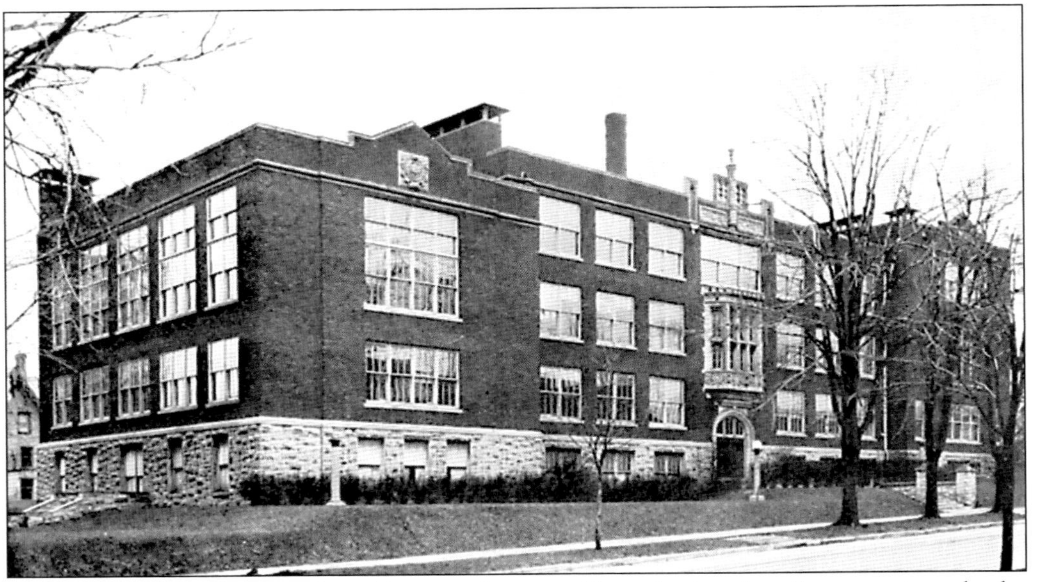

MARION HIGH SCHOOL, WEST CHURCH STREET. Conceived to handle approximately the same student population housed at the existing Marion High School facility, Marion's new high school opened in 1916. Immediately, it was apparent that the new building's size was inadequate to handle the rapidly growing student population within the city system. By 1925, the Marion City School System was planning a second high school on the city's west side (Edison) to handle the overcrowding. Renamed Marion Harding High School in 1920, this building also served as Baker Middle School, and finally as "the Freshman Building," before its demolition in the 1980s. (Photograph courtesy of the author.)

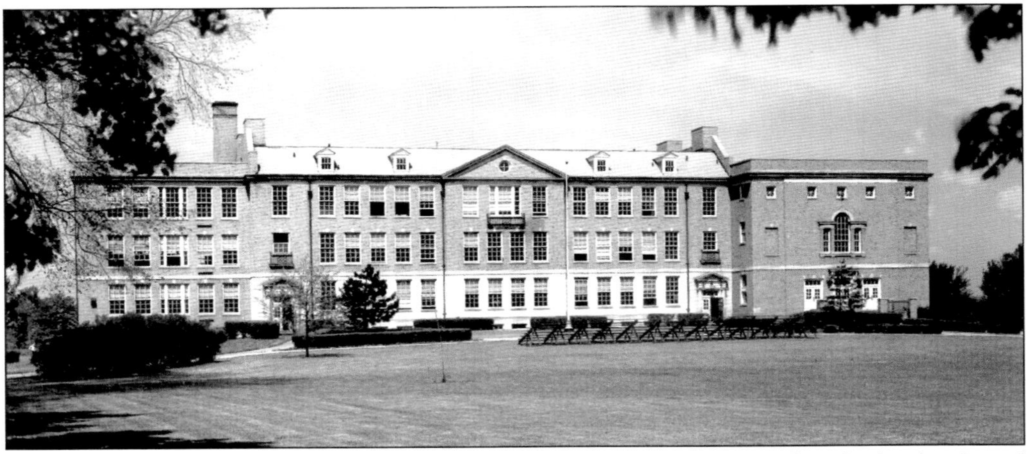

EDISON HIGH SCHOOL. Edison High School was built to handle the swelling high school-aged population that occurred in the 1920s in Marion. The Georgian Revival building, constructed of brick laid in a Flemish Bond pattern, was one of the most graceful in the Marion City System. Edison was also the only school in the system to have an auditorium built for that specific purpose. After the opening of Harding High School in 1953, Edison served as both a junior high and middle school. With the modernization and realignment of school buildings, Edison was closed at the end of the 2004 school year; its contents were sold at auction, and the building razed that July. (Photograph courtesy of the Marion County Historical Society.)

PLEASANT SCHOOL DISTRICT BOND ISSUE. Pleasant School District alone is the sole survivor of the original township school system in Marion County. While other townships opted to merge into the county-consolidated systems, Pleasant Township residents opted to go it alone. This particular bond issue was passed to enable Pleasant to modernize and enlarge its school in the 1930s. All of Marion County's school districts have enjoyed popular support—residents have understood that children benefit from good schools, and that good schools result in strong communities. (Photograph courtesy of the author.)

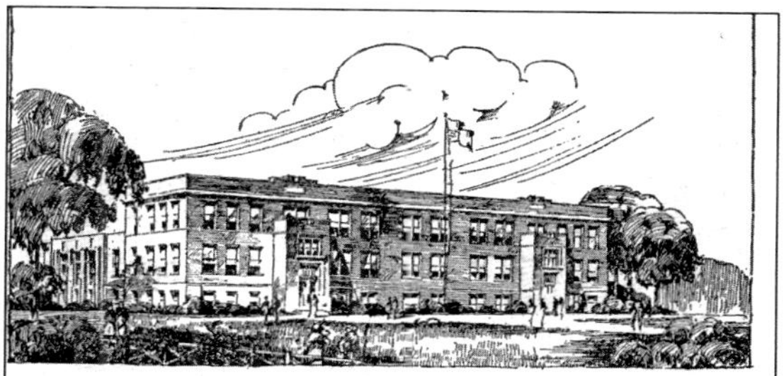

SCHOOL BUILDING WITH PROPOSED ADDITION
Pleasant Twp., Marion Co., Ohio.

A FEW REASONS WHY WE NEED THIS ADDITION

THE present building is entirely inadequate for our needs, it being utterly impossible to do our children justice with our present High School plant and to furnish them with equal advantages enjoyed by adjoining districts in the county. We must overcome the crowded situation prevailing in the grade school and provide for the future expansion and development of this department.

We need the Auditorium for social center uses, to provide community assemblies for lectures, farm bureau meetings, demonstrations, student entertainments, moving pictures and entertainments of various kinds.

The gymnasium is necessary for the physical development of our pupils and for athletic contests and recreation. The Auditorium and Gymnasium are for the benefit of the adults as well as the pupils.

VOTE YES ON THE BOND ISSUE

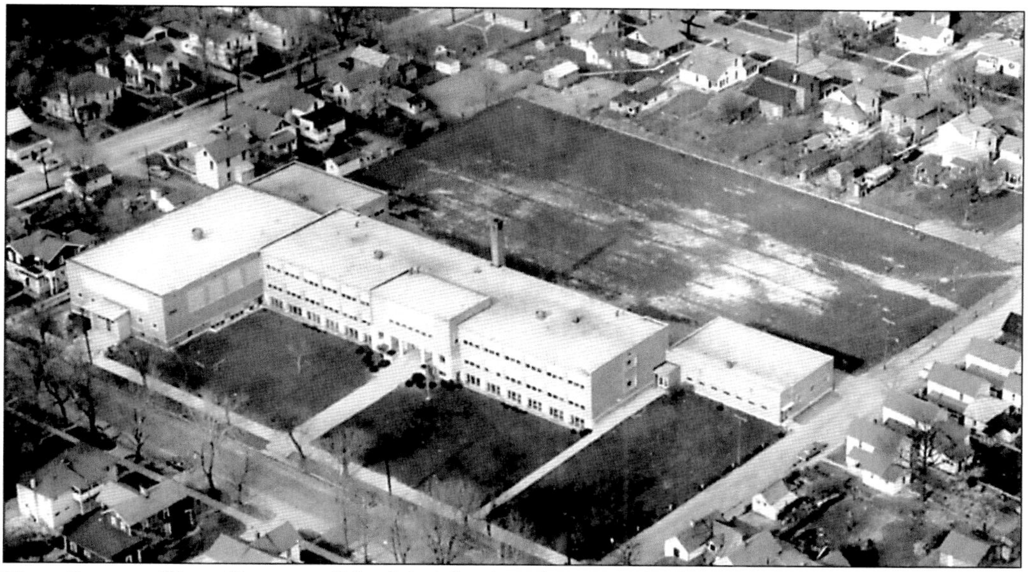

TAFT JUNIOR HIGH SCHOOL. Scheduled for demolition in the late summer of 2004, Taft Junior High School was one of the buildings realized after passage of Marion's landmark postwar school construction levy. Built on the site of the old State Street School building, the new building was opened as State Street Junior High before being renamed in honor of the Ohio Taft family. Taft's final year as a middle school was 2004, after which students in grades sixth through eighth transferred to Grant Middle School. Closing events included an alumni band concert and tours of the building. (Photograph courtesy of the Marion County Historical Society.)

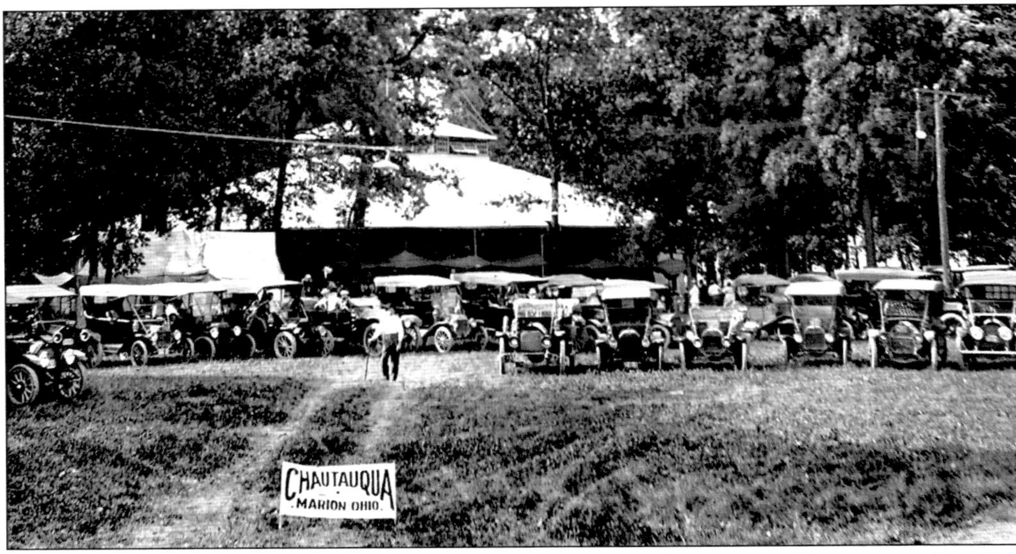

CHAUTAUQUA PAVILION, GARFIELD PARK. Marion's round, open-air Chautauqua Pavilion was built at Garfield Park on Marion's east side in 1912. The Chautauqua series brought noteworthy individuals to Marion to speak, sing, or perform, with the series designed to be both instructional and entertaining in nature. Campers pitched tents and made a week of it with their families. While heavily used by the community long after the Chautauqua events ended in the 1920s, the pavilion had one major drawback—it lacked a constructed floor. Thus, when it rained, guests could find themselves up to their ankles in mud. Host to high school graduations and the 1939 Miss Ohio Pageant, the pavilion was torn down in the 1950s. (Photograph courtesy of the Marion County Historical Society.)

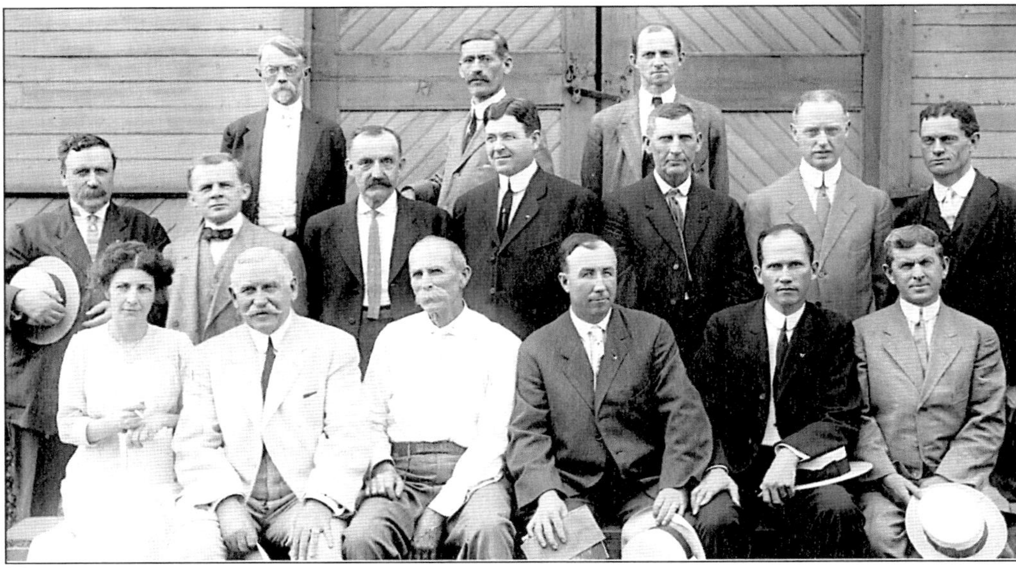

MARION COUNTY CHAUTAUQUA OFFICERS AND COMMITTEE MEMBERS. Selected from the local community, Marion's Chautauqua leadership ensured that programs were lively, as well as educational. Dr. Charles Sawyer is in the back row, on the far left. (Photograph courtesy of the Marion County Historical Society.)

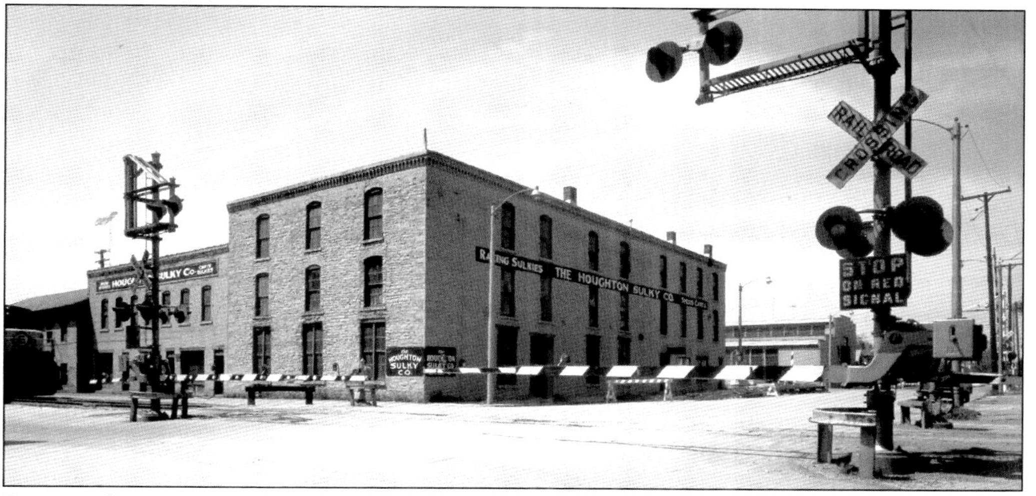

FORMER CENTENARY METHODIST CHURCH, LOOKING NORTHWEST FROM STATE AND MILL STREETS, 1965. The original portion of the Houghton Sulky building was built as Centenary Methodist Episcopal Church before the introduction of rail lines into Marion. Built of stone, Centenary Methodist Episcopal faced what is now Huber Street. Eventually unfit for worship services due to the trains that began to pass directly in front of the building, the structure was enlarged and converted to manufacturing space by the Huber Manufacturing Company. Artisans with the Houghton Sulky Company, which currently occupies the structure, still handcraft the finest horse-drawn vehicles in the United States. The State Street overpass has blocked this view since 1967. (Photograph courtesy of the Marion County Historical Society.)

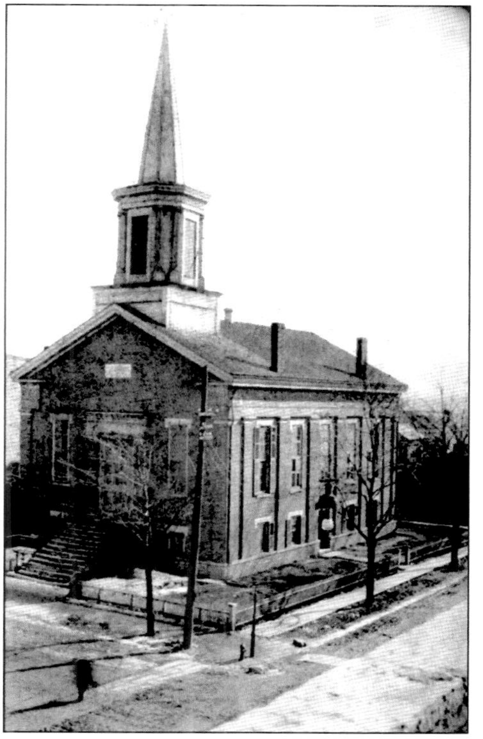

METHODIST EPISCOPAL CHURCH, SOUTHEAST CORNER OF CENTER AND STATE STREETS. Built in 1854, this was the second home of Marion's Methodist Episcopal Church, replacing Centenary Methodist Episcopal Church. The layout of both church buildings placed the sanctuary above street level, as was common at the time. Doing so symbolically lifted the congregation closer to "the heavens" during services: better air circulation and light were practical reasons for this type of layout. In 1890, the congregation completed Epworth Methodist Episcopal Church structure further east on Center Street. This structure was torn down and the site was developed for the Center State Block, which currently occupies this spot. (Photograph courtesy of the Marion County Historical Society.)

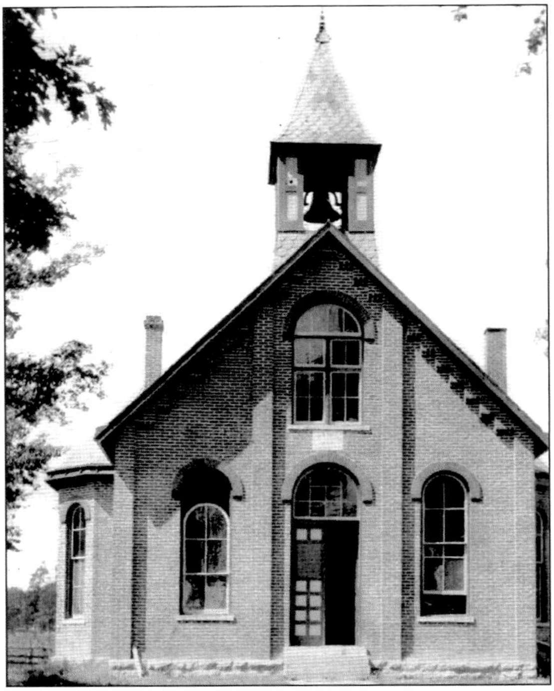

ROCKY FORK FREE WILL BAPTIST CHURCH, BRUSH RIDGE, GRAND PRAIRIE TOWNSHIP. Just as Richland Township in southern Marion County was known for its German Lutheran community, early Grand Prairie Township in northern Marion County was known for its active Baptist community. Led by Elder and Mrs. Louis Seitz, congregants of Rocky Fork included members of the Van Meter, Burtsfield, Mouser, Bretz, and Hinamon families. (Photograph courtesy of Rebecca Withrow Gooding.)

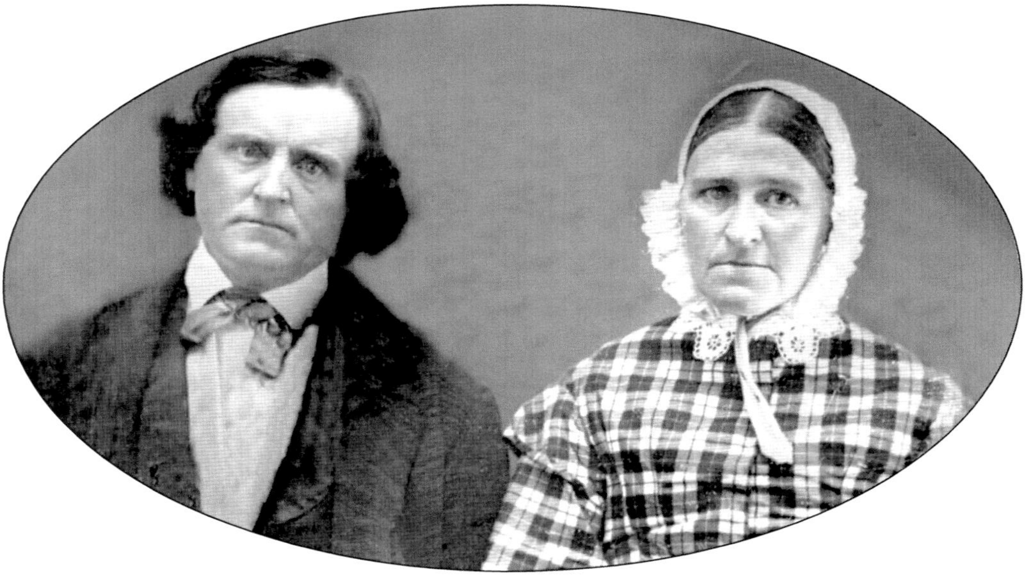

DAVID AND LUCY (THAYRE) MOUSER, 1850. One of Marion County's earliest and best-known citizens was David Mouser, pictured here with his first wife Lucy Thayer Mouser. A blacksmith by trade, Mouser operated his business on South Street, now West Church Street. The Mousers were also substantial landowners in the southwest quadrant of the emerging city and owned land in northern Marion and southern Wyandot County. The Marion Masonic Temple at South Main and West Church Street stands where the Mouser homestead stood until 1896. The Mouser's great-great-granddaughter, Mary Ellen Hinamon Withrow, served as Treasurer of the United States between 1994 and 2000. (Photograph courtesy of Babette Dusang Jones.)

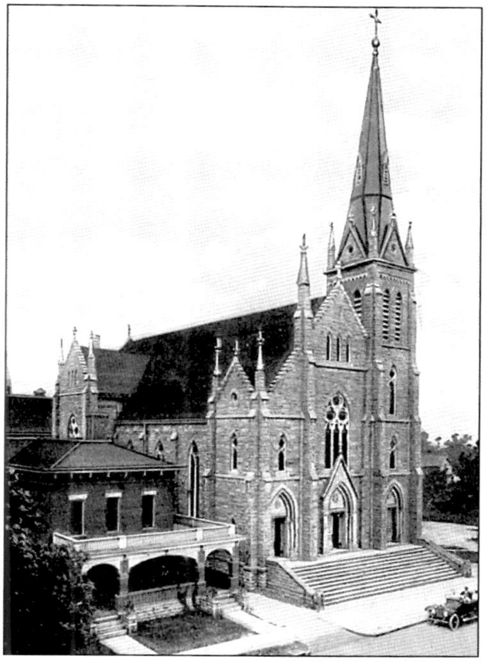

St. Mary's Church, North Main Street. Finding the former Centenary Methodist Church building unacceptable for worship services because of trains passing directly in front of the building, Marion's Catholic Community moved to North Prospect Street in the mid 1850s. By the 1890s, "old" St. Mary's could no longer hold the growing congregation. Work on the present St. Mary's Church on North Main Street began in 1891, and it was dedicated in 1895. Built of white sandstone that has mellowed with age, the towering spire of St. Mary's acts as one of Marion's north side landmarks. This image from the early 20th century shows the Italianate rectory prior to its enlargement from two to three stories. (Photograph courtesy of Robert Turner.)

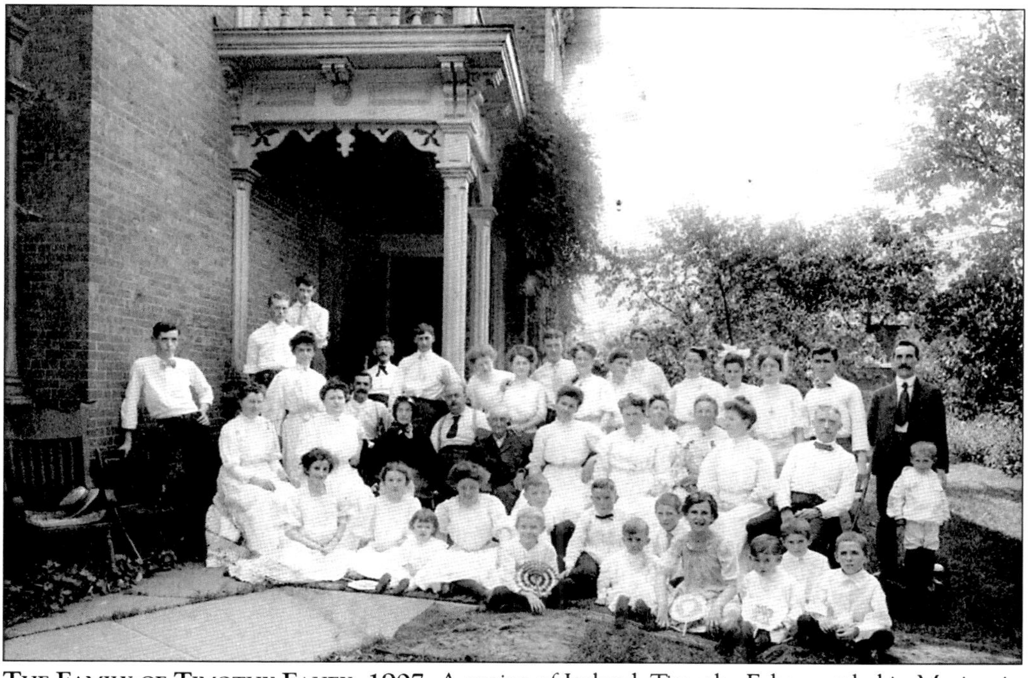

The Family of Timothy Fahey, 1907. A native of Ireland, Timothy Fahey settled in Marion in 1849. The parents of eight children, the Fahey's were strong supporters of the Catholic Community in Marion, and it was Timothy Fahey who helped to spearhead the construction of both downtown St. Mary's Church buildings, as well as St. Mary's School, built opposite his home on North Prospect Street. Fahey's legacy lives on in Marion through the banking company that bears his name. (Photograph courtesy of the Marion County Historical Society.)

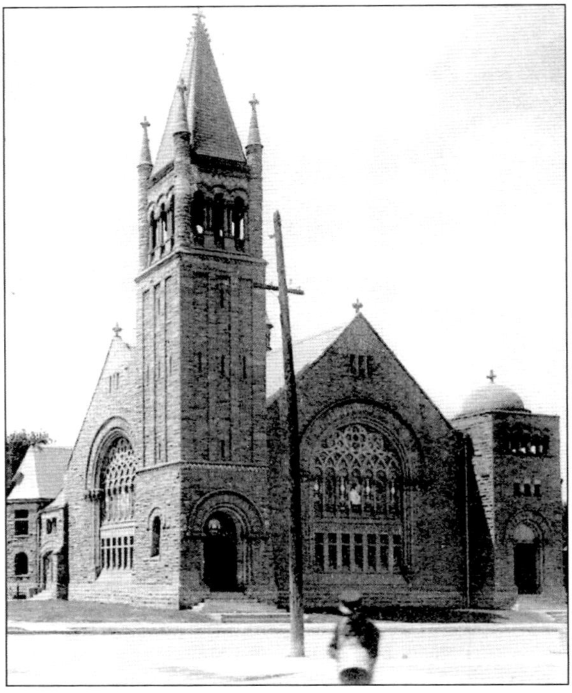

FIRST PRESBYTERIAN CHURCH. Built in 1893–4, Marion's downtown Presbyterian Church congregation held its first service in its landmark building in the fall of 1894. The structure is designed in the Richardson Romanesque style that was popular in the late 19th century. One of the unfortunate outcomes of downtown Marion's system of one-way streets is that the approach to the building does not allow this view, looking west from Church Street. (Photograph courtesy of Robert Turner.)

EPWORTH METHODIST CHURCH. One of Marion's most enduring physical and spiritual landmarks is Epworth United Methodist Church at the intersection of East Center Street and South Vine Street. Dedicated in 1891, the structure was one of the largest houses of worship in Marion County when built. (Photograph courtesy of the author.)

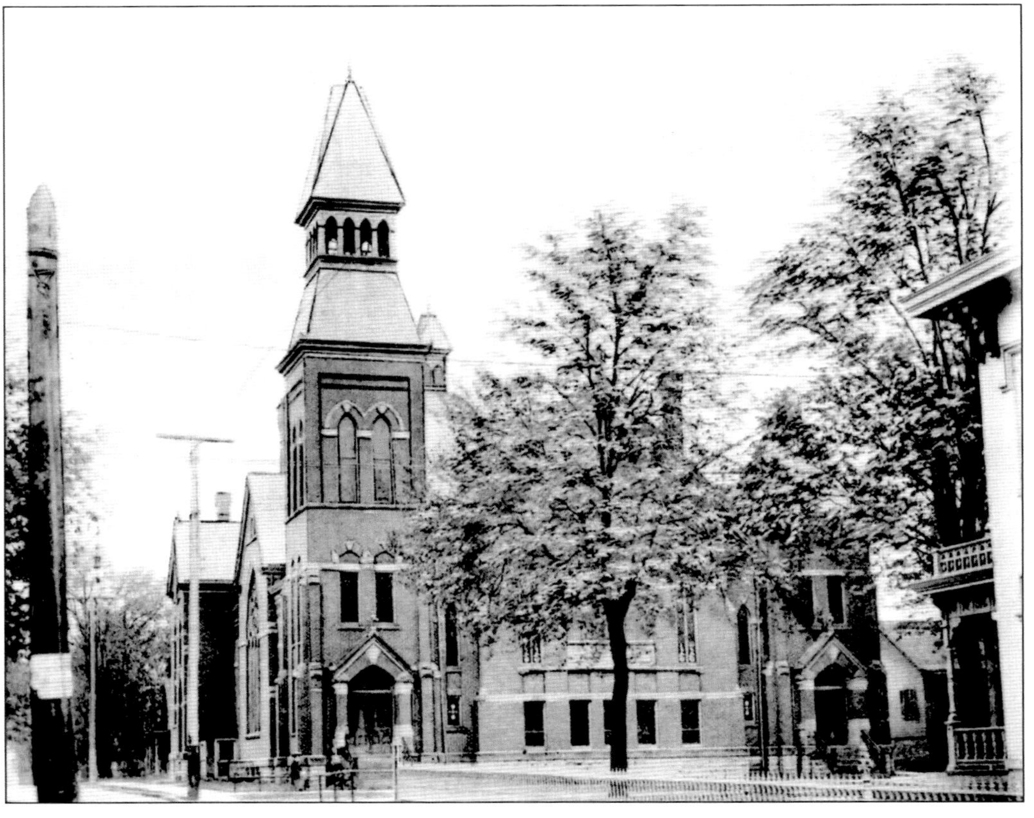

GERMAN METHODIST CHURCH. German immigrants heavily influenced Marion County during the mid-19th century. To meet the needs of the Methodist flock, the German Methodist Church was completed in 1869 at the southwest corner of West Church Street and South Prospect. The structure served the congregation until 1913–1914 when it was replaced by the current red brick church building. In 1918, the name of the congregation was changed to Prospect Street Methodist Episcopal Church. With the 1968 national union between the Methodist Episcopal Church with the Evangelical United Brethren (E.U.B.), the congregation's current name became Prospect Street United Methodist Church. (Photograph courtesy of the author.)

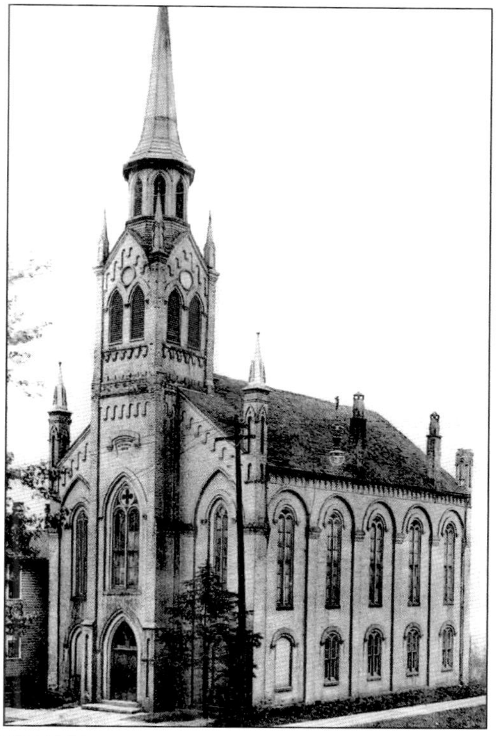

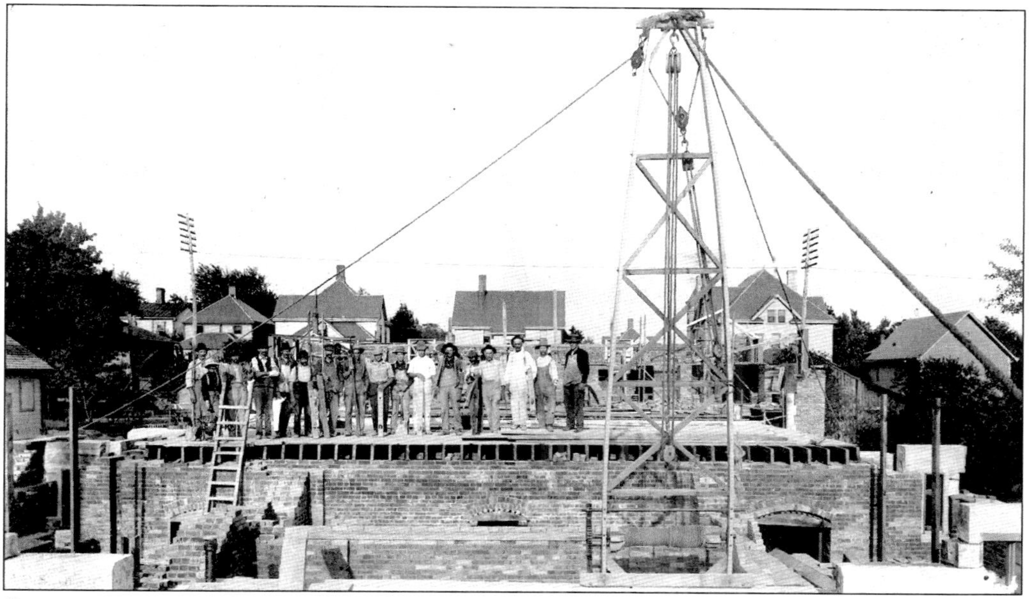

CONSTRUCTION OF TRINITY BAPTIST CHURCH. In 1900, the leaders of the Free Will Baptist Church on East Center Street began to plan for their congregation's new home. Securing the services of the highly regarded Cleveland architect Charles F. Schweinfurth, the cornerstone for the new church was laid in the late summer of 1908. With the merger of the First Baptist Church congregation, the united bodies emerged as Trinity Baptist Church. (Photograph courtesy of Gary Barnhart.)

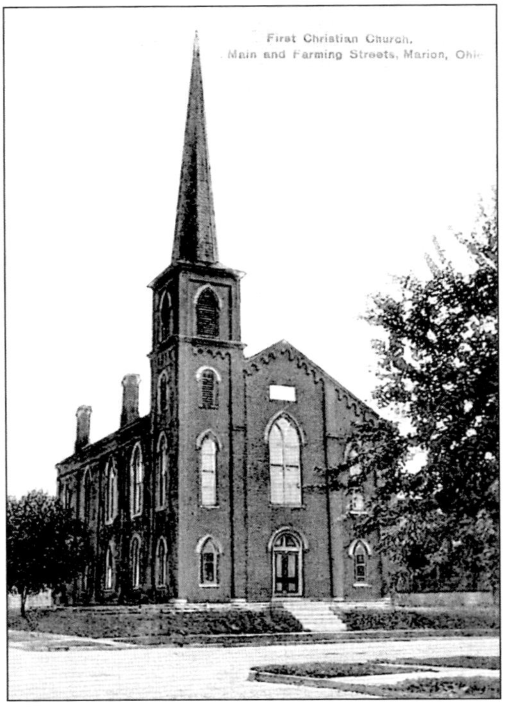

FIRST CHRISTIAN CHURCH, NORTH MAIN STREET. Marion's First Christian Church was organized at a meeting held in the Marion City Hall building in 1876. T.D. Garvin was the first minister. In 1880, the congregation moved to this structure on North Main Street where it resided until the early 1960s. After moving to its current location on Richland Road, the bell tower of the building was removed, its window bays were covered in plywood, and the building was converted for use into a lodge hall. (Photograph courtesy of Gary Barnhart.)

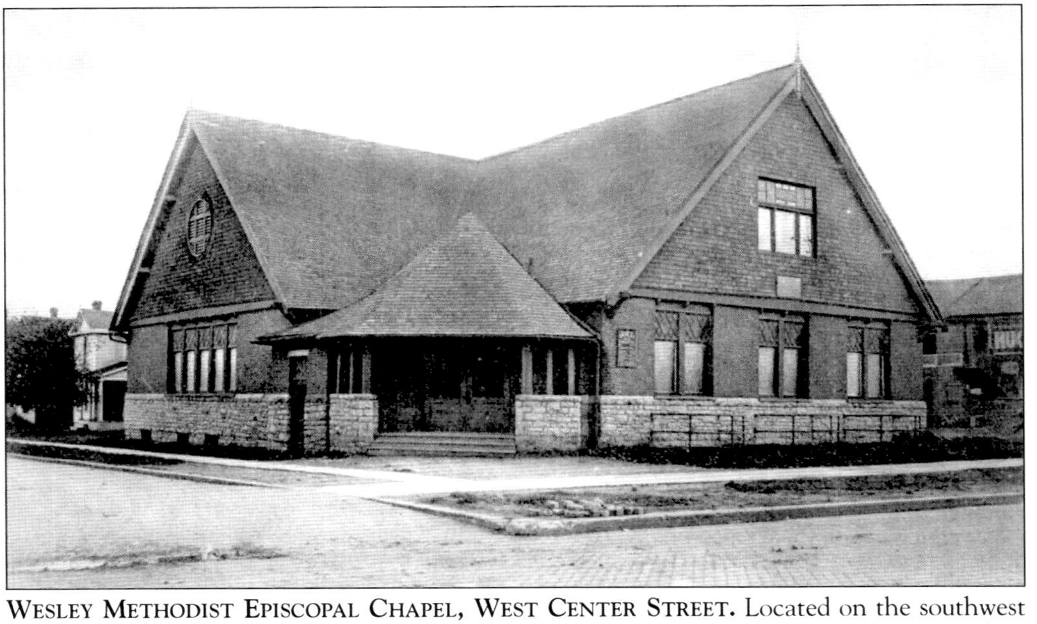

WESLEY METHODIST EPISCOPAL CHAPEL, WEST CENTER STREET. Located on the southwest corner of West Center Street and Olney Avenues was this shingle-style church, occupied by the Wesley Methodist Episcopal congregation. Unlike other churches in Marion, the Wesley Chapel structure did not have a formal bell tower. Built of brick on the first floor and wood shingle on the second floor and roof, the small church was replaced by a more formal church building further south on Olney Avenue. Wesley Chapel was razed and its site converted to commercial use. (Photograph courtesy of the author.)

Four

THE HARDINGS AND KLINGS OF MARION

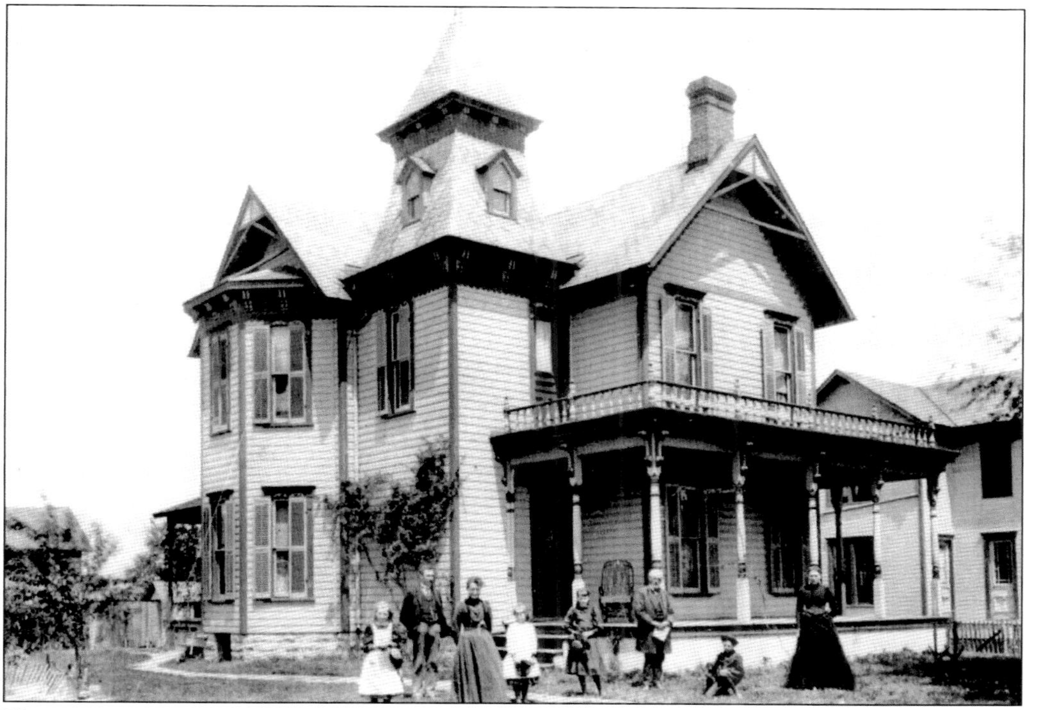

HOME AND FAMILY OF DR. GEORGE TRYON HARDING, 500 EAST CENTER STREET. After establishing himself in Marion, Dr. George Tryon Harding acquired this home at 500 East Center Street in 1885. This photograph, taken about 1887, shows (left to right) Mary, Warren, Charity (Chat), Carolyn, Daisy, Dr. George Tryon Harding, George ("Deke"), and Mrs. Phoebe Harding, who, like her husband, was a licensed doctor in Ohio. In 1923, the body of the Harding's son, President Warren G. Harding, was placed in the home's bay window for public viewing the evening before the funeral. The house fell into a state of disrepair and was torn down in the early 1950s; now, a professional building occupies the site. (Photograph courtesy of Carol and Gary Robinson.)

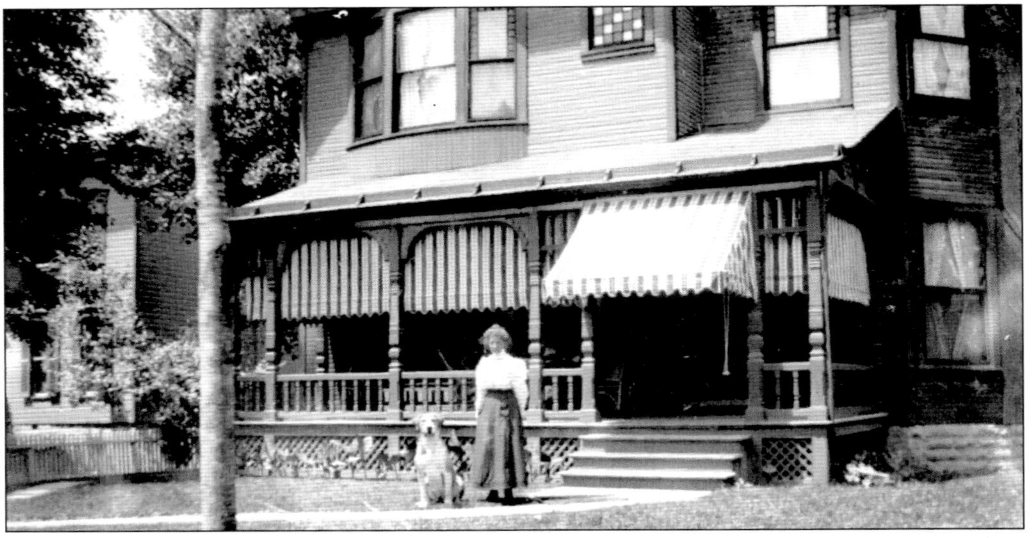

FLORENCE HARDING AND JUMBO AT HARDING HOME, c. 1895. Florence Kling Harding poses with the family dog, Jumbo, in front of the home that she and Warren Harding built on Mt. Vernon Avenue in Marion. The house, designed in the Eastlake style has its original front porch, which was replaced with a design by noted Columbus architect Frank Packard. Mrs. Harding had long admired the bandstand-style front porch of the Wollenweber residence up the street; Mr. Packard obliged in his design. During his presidency, Mr. Harding decided that Packard would design the home that they would retire to after his term ended, a plan that was left unfulfilled. (Photograph courtesy of the Marion County Historical Society.)

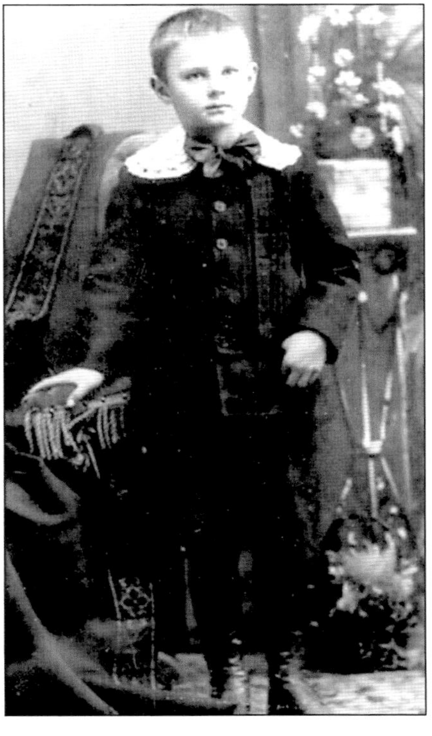

MARSHALL EUGENE KLING. This c. 1885 image shows young Marshall Kling in the early years of his bleak life. Born Marshall E. DeWolfe, the boy was given to his maternal grandfather by his mother. His grandfather, Amos Kling, would see to it that the boy would be raised as a member of the Kling family. Marshall's mother, Florence Kling DeWolfe, would try to make her own way in the world as a piano teacher. Marshall's father, Henry Atherton (Pete) DeWolfe, was a chronic alcoholic, a trait passed down to his son. After his mother's marriage to Warren G. Harding, Marshall's infrequent contact with his mother continued but he remained in the Kling home. After graduating from Marion High School in 1898, he tried several careers, none of which provided success. After his emancipation as an adult, Kling reverted to the use of his father's surname DeWolfe. When Marshall DeWolfe died January 1, 1914, of tuberculosis and acute alcoholism, Florence Harding went to Colorado to honor his debts. Marshall DeWolfe's body was returned to Marion and buried with members of the DeWolfe family in Marion Cemetery. His grave is unmarked. (Photograph courtesy of Gary Barnhart.)

CLIFFORD KLING. Second child of Amos and Louisa (Bouton) Kling, Clifford Kling followed in his father's footsteps, operating businesses in Marion for many years. Clifford Kling died in Marion in 1937 and is buried in the Kling family plot in Marion Cemetery. The Kling's youngest son, Vetallis, was ostracized from the family following his marriage to Elnora (Nona) Younkins Hinamon, a Catholic widow who was employed by the Klings as a housekeeper in their East Center Street home. Vetallis and Nona Kling are buried in Marion Catholic Cemetery. (Photograph courtesy of the Marion County Historical Society.)

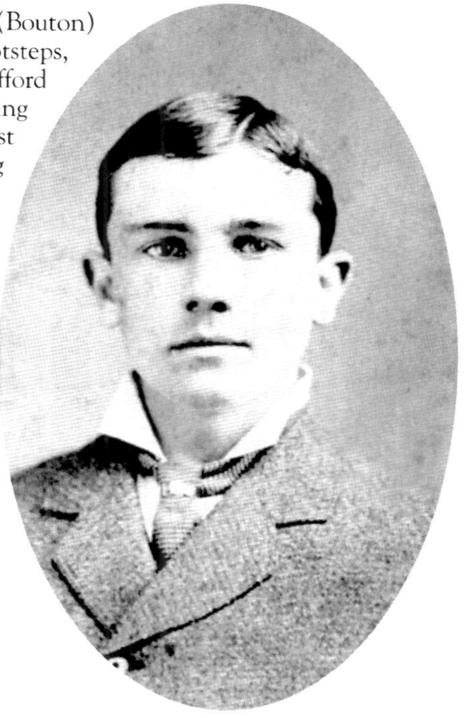

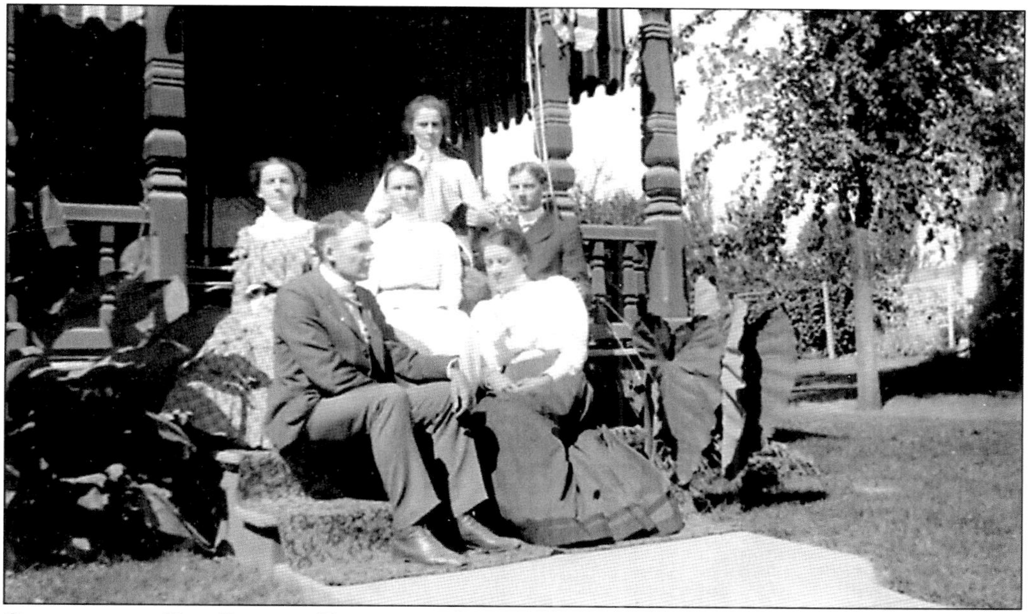

CHILDREN OF DR. GEORGE TRYON AND MRS. PHOEBE HARDING. Seated on the front steps of Warren and Florence Harding's new home on Mt. Vernon Avenue are (clockwise from top) Daisy Harding, George "Deke" Harding, Mary Harding, Warren Harding, and Carolyn Harding; Charity "Chat" Harding sits in the center. Phoebe Harding was often referred to as "Mrs. Dr. Harding" in her son's newspaper, the *Marion Star*. (Photograph courtesy of the Marion County Historical Society.)

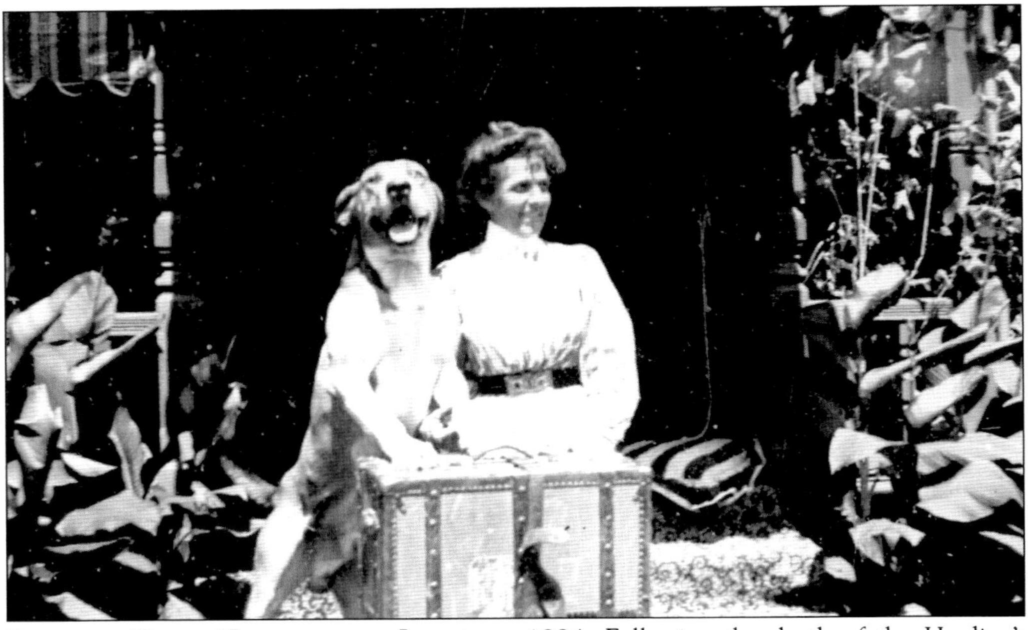

FLORENCE KLING HARDING AND JUMBO, c. 1894. Following the death of the Harding's dog Senator, the couple acquired Jumbo, a Mastiff mix, seen here hamming it up for the photographer with Mrs. Harding. Jumbo also doubled as Harding's guard dog against *Marion Star* readers who had a personal bone to pick with the publisher. Unfortunately, one such person decided to get back at Harding by poisoning Jumbo, who died after eight years in the household. (Photograph courtesy of the Marion County Historical Society.)

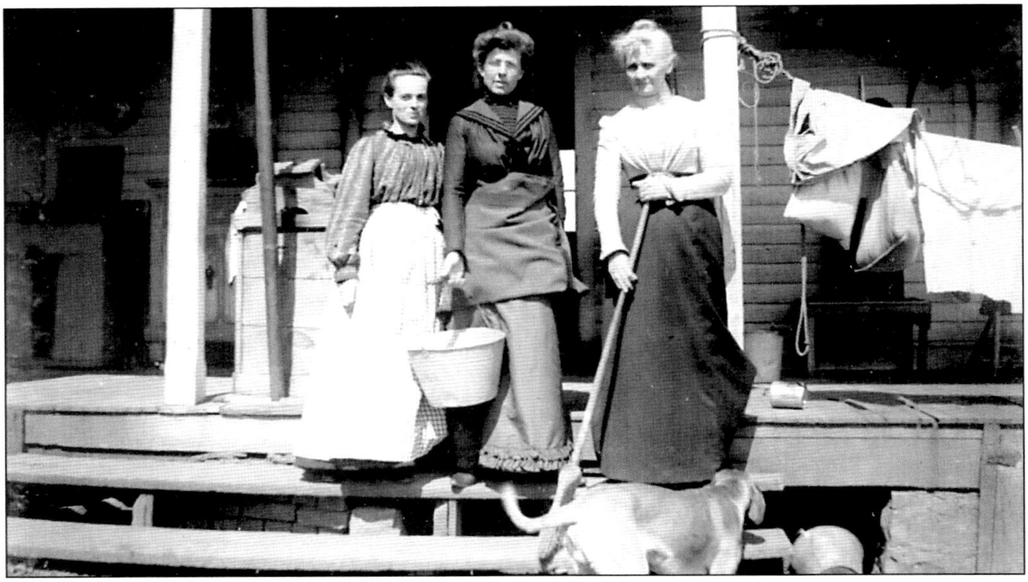

MRS. HARDING VISITS THE COUNTRYSIDE. Caught by the camera, Daisy Harding, Florence Harding, and Mildred Christian seem to have taken command of the house and the chores that came with it. No word was given as to whether the hound dog was welcome in the home or not. (Photograph courtesy of the Marion County Historical Society.)

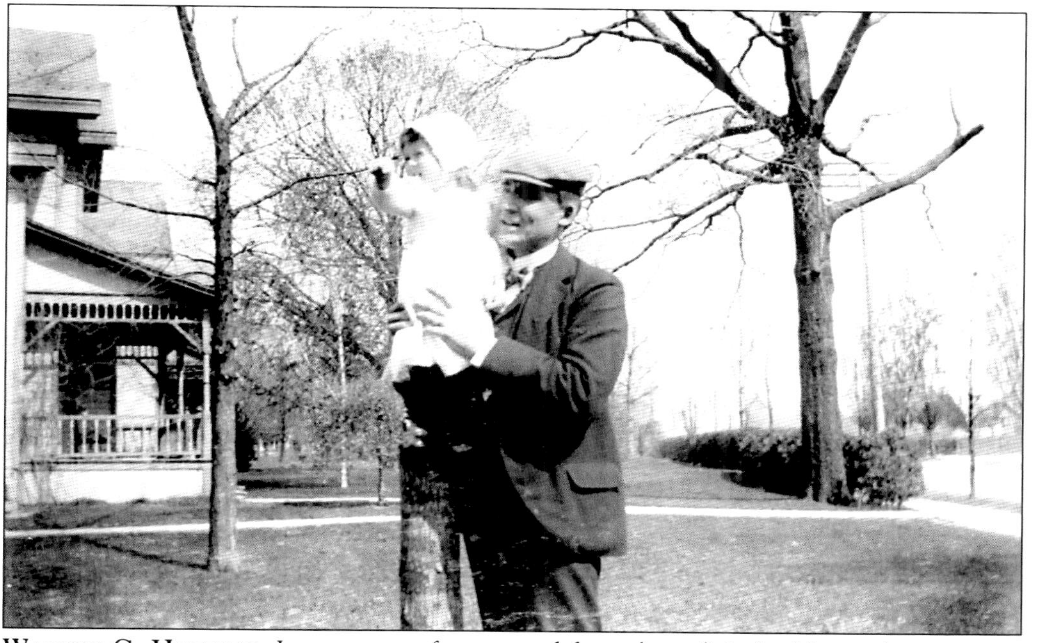

Warren G. Harding. In a moment far removed from the political tableaux that most are familiar seeing him photographed within, Warren Harding poses for the camera with the grandchild of his neighbor, George Christian, in the front yard of the Harding's Mt. Vernon Avenue home. (Photograph courtesy of the Marion County Historical Society.)

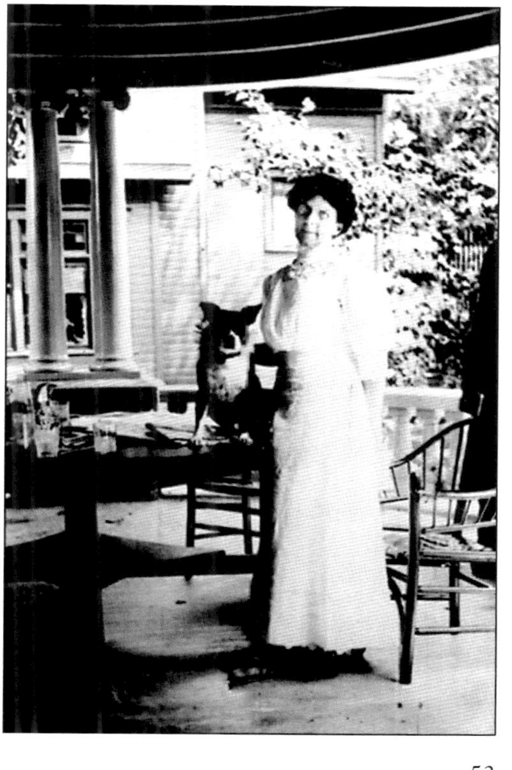

Florence Harding and "Edgewood Hub," Early 1900s. Following the death of their beloved Jumbo, the Harding's were given "Edgewood Hub," a pure-bred Boston Terrier by Mrs. Harding's son, Marshall. Known to the couple simply as "Hub" the dog was especially dear to Mrs. Harding, who lavished attention on him. Mrs. Harding stands on her newly finished front porch, designed to withstand the weight of well wishers. The Harding's were right in their decision; the well wishers of 1899 were nothing compared to the Front Porch Campaign of 1920. (Photograph courtesy of Gary Barnhart.)

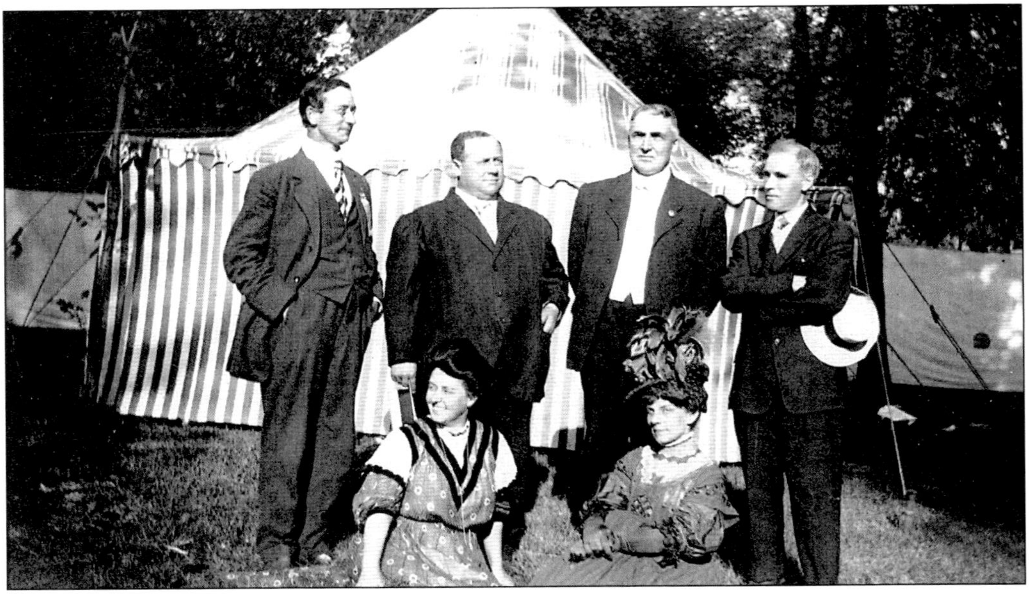

The Harding's Attend Marion's Chautauqua with the Phillips, c. 1905. In a moment of innocent yet telling fun, Warren and Florence Harding posed for a photograph with friends at the Marion Chautauqua at Garfield Park. The Hardings (standing, second from right, and sitting, right) and James Phillips (standing, far left) are ready for the photographer, while Phillips' wife, Carrie Fulton Phillips (seated, left), seems to have been preoccupied with happenings in the opposite direction from where her attentions should have been. (Photograph courtesy of Mike and Linda Perry.)

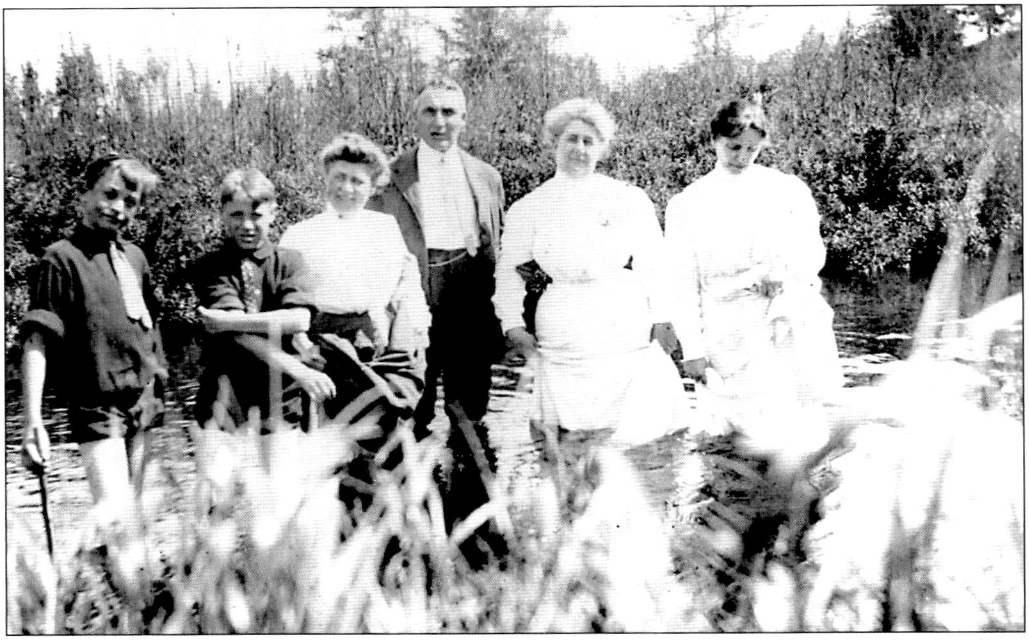

The Harding's Take a Wade. The Harding's, third and fourth from the left, take a wade in a pond with friends. (Photograph courtesy of the Marion County Historical Society.)

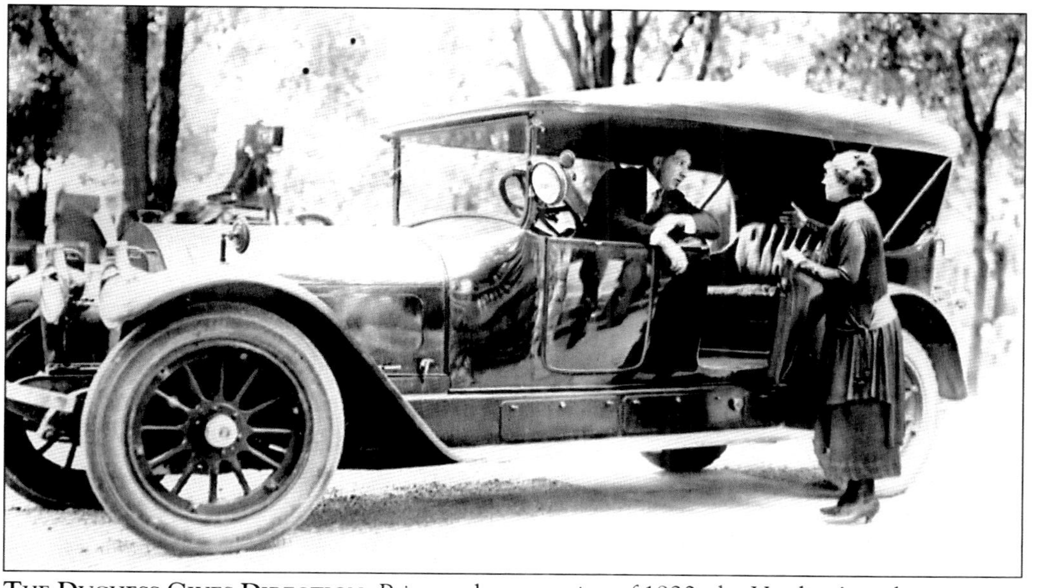

The Duchess Gives Direction. Prior to the campaign of 1920, the Harding's took possession of a new touring car, which due to circumstances was used sparingly. Both the senator and Mrs. Harding were avid motorists. Following the presidents death, Mrs. Harding sold the car, but complained about the low resale value realized from it. In the background of this image, one of the newsreel cameras of the day can be seen. (Photograph courtesy of Mike and Linda Perry.)

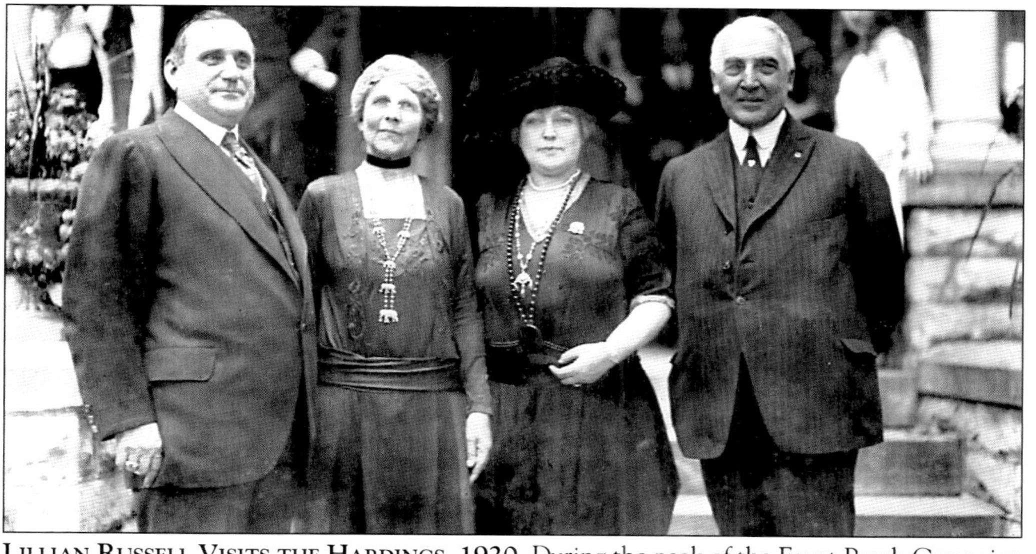

Lillian Russell Visits the Hardings, 1920. During the peak of the Front Porch Campaign of 1920, the Hardings were host to numerous luminaries of the day. One star of the era to visit was Lillian Russell (third from left), along with her husband Alfred Moore (first on right). As president, Harding appointed Russell to undertake a fact-finding mission to Europe and to report back on the status of public sentiment on the continent. When Russell died shortly after returning stateside in 1922, at the age of 62, she received full military honors at her burial, per the president's instructions. (Photograph courtesy of the Marion County Historical Society.)

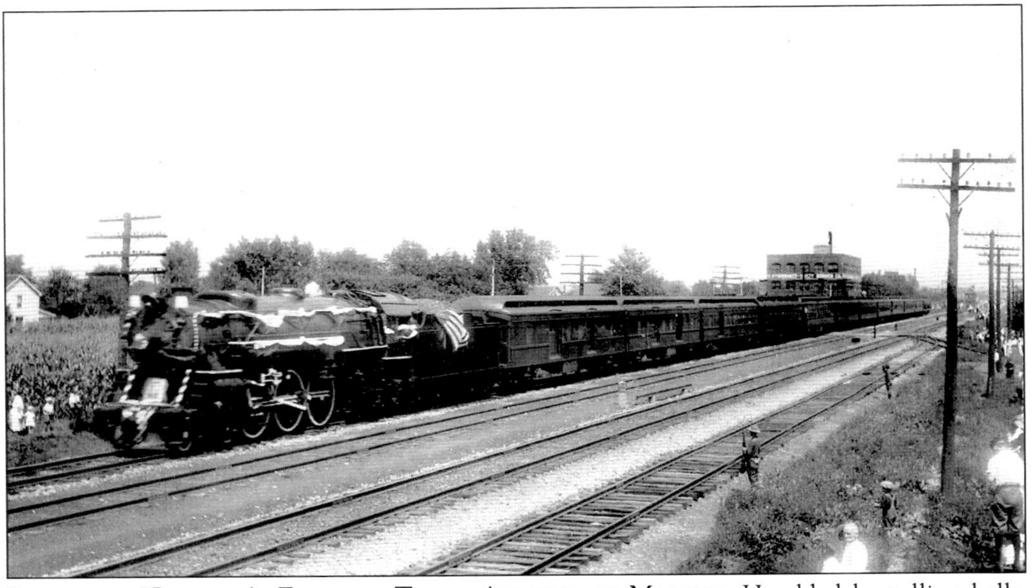

President Harding's Funeral Train Arrives at Marion. Heralded by tolling bells, the crepe-draped funeral train bearing the body of the deceased president arrived in Marion on August 9, 1923. In addition to the presidential car, "Superb," in which the first lady was riding, a dining car, seven Pullman cars, and two express cars filled with flowers comprised the train. Passengers aboard included members of the Harding cabinet, Dr. Charles Sawyer, George Christian, and Harding's brother, sisters, and their families. President Coolidge arrived by train in Marion the following morning. (Photograph courtesy of Babette DuSang Jones.)

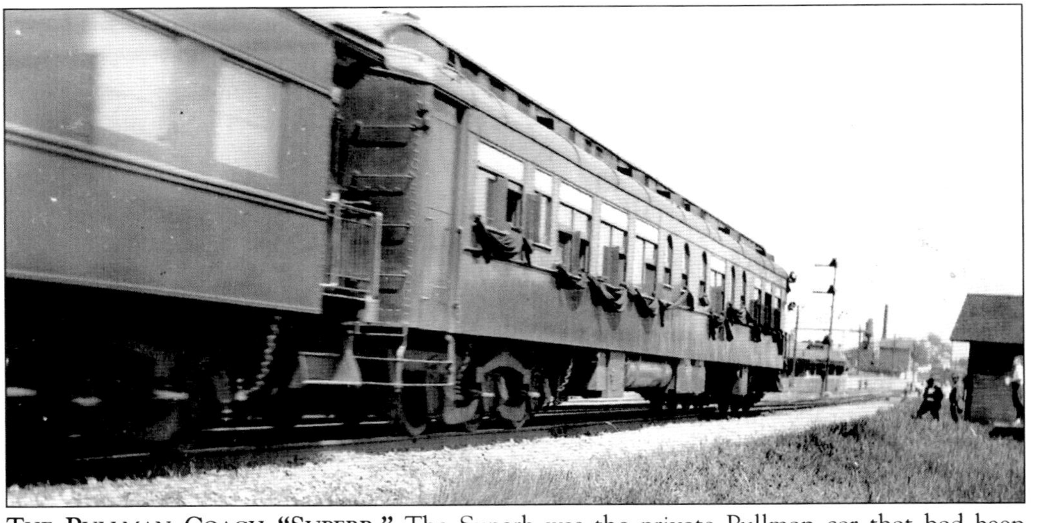

The Pullman Coach "Superb." The Superb was the private Pullman car that had been in use during the presidents final journey westward in 1923, the "Voyage of Understanding." Following the funeral, Mrs. Harding again boarded the Superb for the return trip to Washington to gather her personal effects and the president's papers. Mrs. Harding declined the Superb as a gift, wanting nothing more to do with it after arriving in Washington. Built in 1911, the restored Superb is the oldest surviving Pullman coach and is owned by the Southeastern Rail Museum in Duluth, Georgia. (Photograph courtesy of Babette DuSang Jones.)

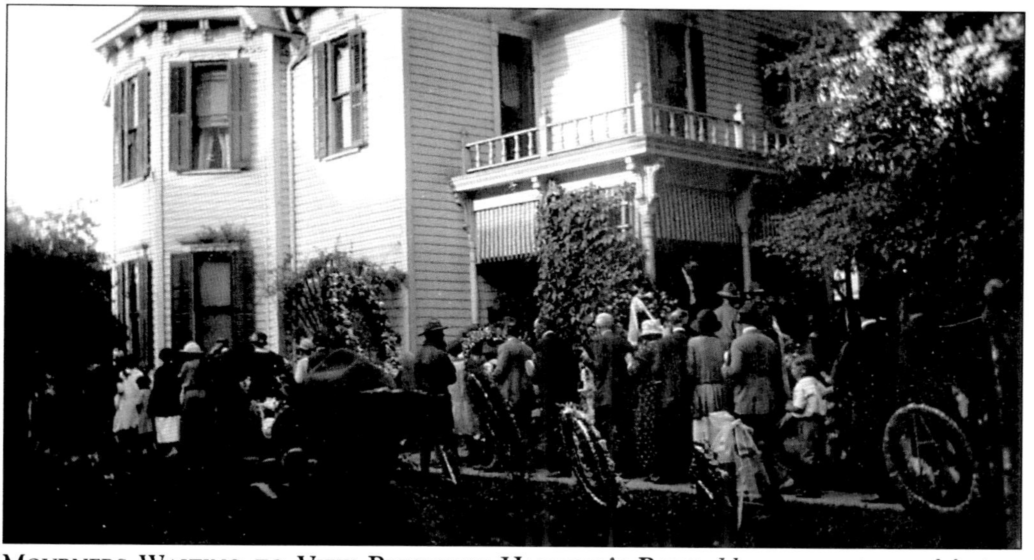

Mourners Waiting to View President Harding's Body. Upon returning to Marion, the body of President Harding was taken to his father's East Center Street home for public viewing. The half-mile long line of those wishing to pay their final respects stretched from Dr. Harding's home to the Marion County Courthouse. Florence Harding, who was staying on the second floor of the house, watched the mourners through a gap in the lace curtains and gave instructions not to close the doors "as long as they come, even if it takes all night." (Photograph courtesy of the Marion County Historical Society.)

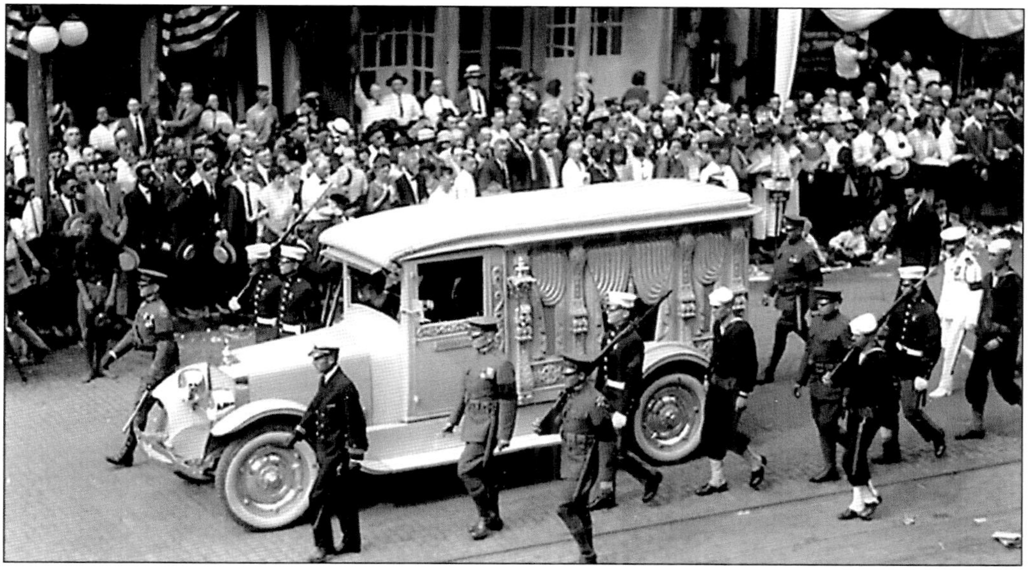

Hearse Bearing the Body of President Harding. From Marion's Union Station, the body of President Harding was carried to his father's home by a Locomobile-powered hearse featuring a custom hand-carved wooden body by Riddle Coach of Ravenna, Ohio. Two employees of the hearse's manufacturer, Joseph Kirk and Lawrence Geer, drove the hearse during the two day event in Marion. Following the funeral, the hearse was returned to the manufacturer, and then sold to an Indianapolis funeral director. (Photograph courtesy of Carol Robinson.)

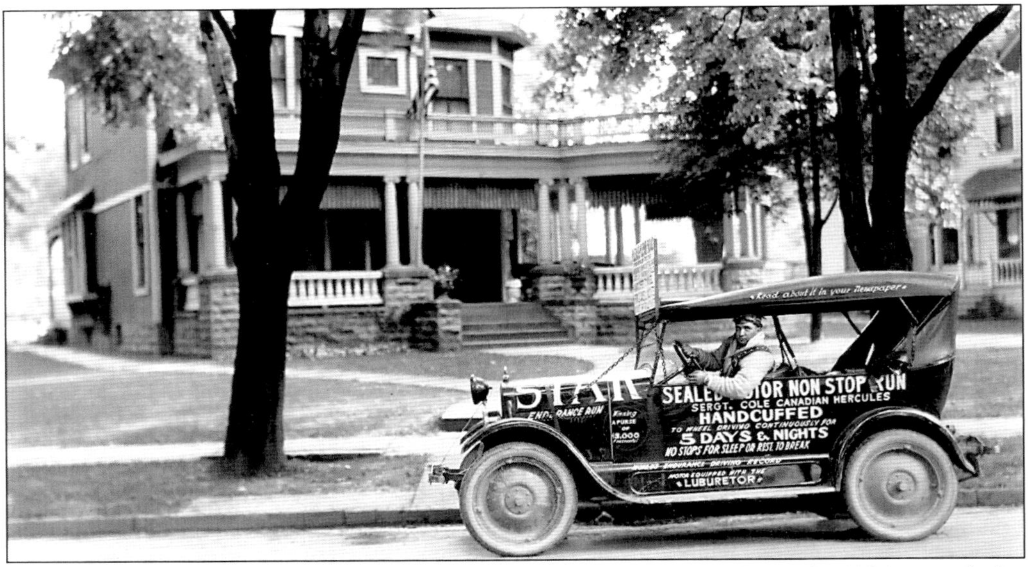

SERGEANT COLE AND THE STAR CAR IN FRONT OF THE HARDING HOME. In 1924, a car dealer in Zanesville, Ohio, wanted to prove that a Durant Motor Company's Star brand automobile was as durable as Ford's Model T. Sergeant Cole, a former Canadian Mounted Police officer, was handcuffed to the wheel of a used Star automobile and set about driving non-stop (except for refueling and for passing trains) for five days and nights. Cole's route took him from Zanesville to Marietta to Marion and back again, until 3,300 miles had been traversed. A nurse checked the driver at fuel stops and reported on his condition. Cole received one speeding ticket, in Norwich, Ohio, but completed the ordeal, winning $3,000 in the process. (Photograph courtesy of Mike and Linda Perry.)

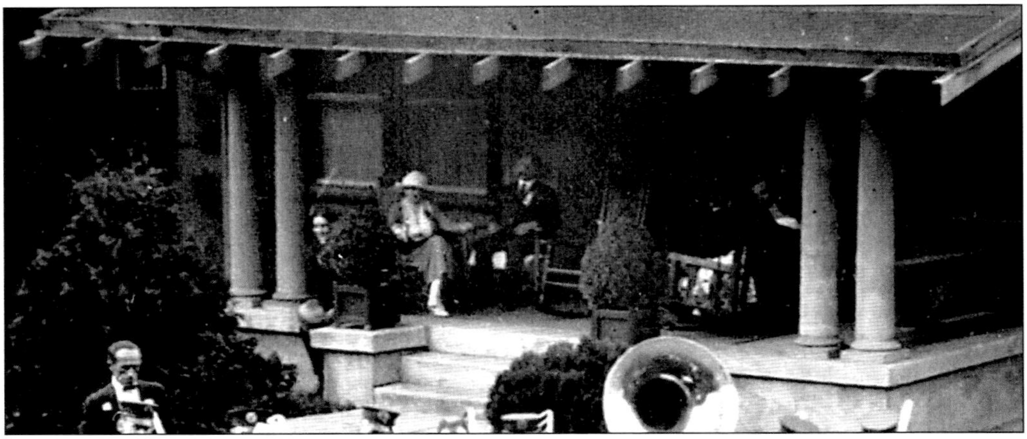

FLORENCE HARDING AT ROSE COTTAGE, SAWYER SANATORIUM, WHITE OAKS FARM. One of the last known pictures of former First Lady Florence Kling Harding was taken in early October 1924, during a band concert held on the Sawyer Sanatorium grounds. Mrs. Harding had wanted to retire to Washington, D.C.; however, she was pressured to return to Marion by Dr. Charles Sawyer after a kidney ailment flared up again. Mrs. Harding stayed on at the sanatorium, living in Rose Cottage, but yearned to return to the nation's capital. Florence Kling Harding died at Rose Cottage, Sawyer's Sanatorium in November 1924. (Photograph courtesy of the Marion County Historical Society.)

Five

The Sawyers in Marion

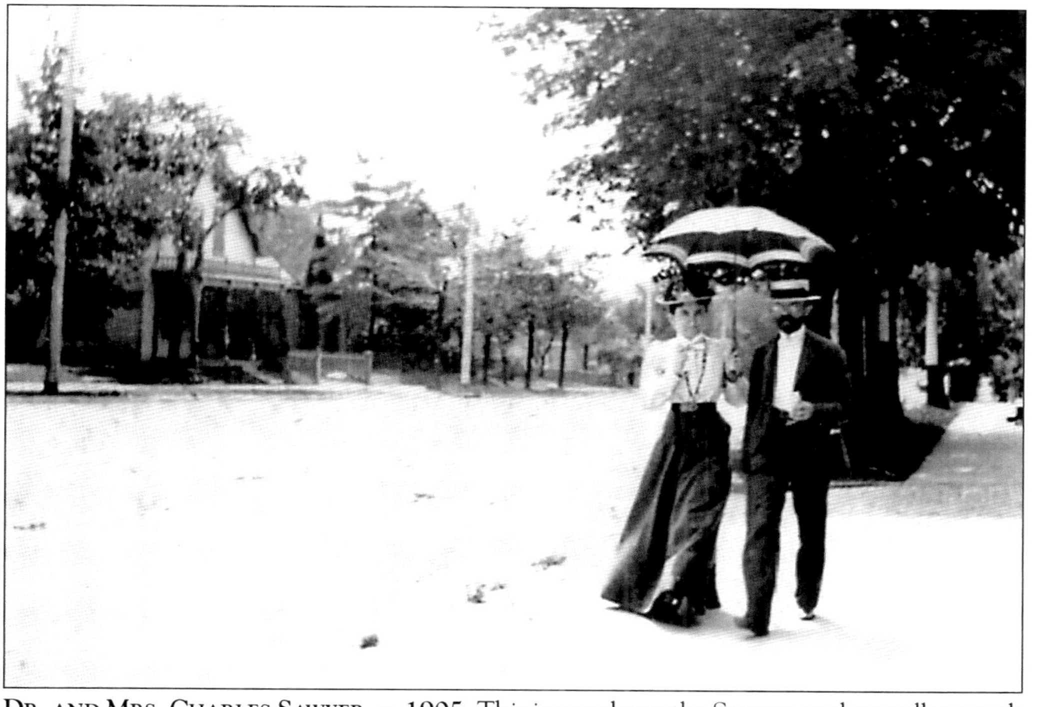

Dr. and Mrs. Charles Sawyer, c. 1905. This image shows the Sawyers as they walk towards downtown on South Prospect Street. The Sawyers were civically involved in Marion, as well as in their church, and thus were well known to the citizens in Marion and Marion County. A man on the move, Sawyer was already planning his next big business endeavor when this photograph was taken. (Photograph courtesy of the Marion County Historical Society.)

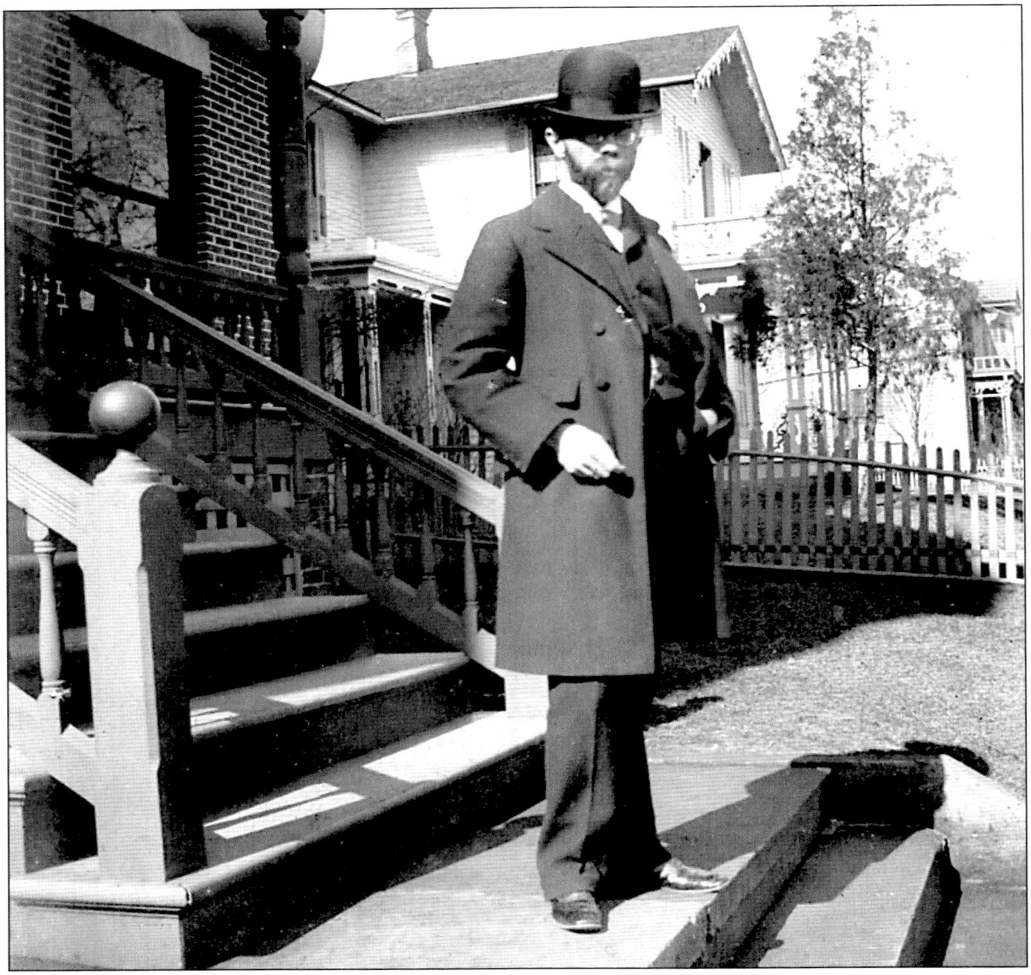

DR. CHARLES E. SAWYER. A native of Wyandot County, Dr. Charles Elmer Sawyer established his homeopathic practice of medicine in LaRue, Ohio, in 1881, having received his diploma from the Cleveland Homeopathic College in that same year. He later moved his practice to Marion in order to leverage the benefits of being located in a larger community. (Photograph courtesy of the Marion County Historical Society.)

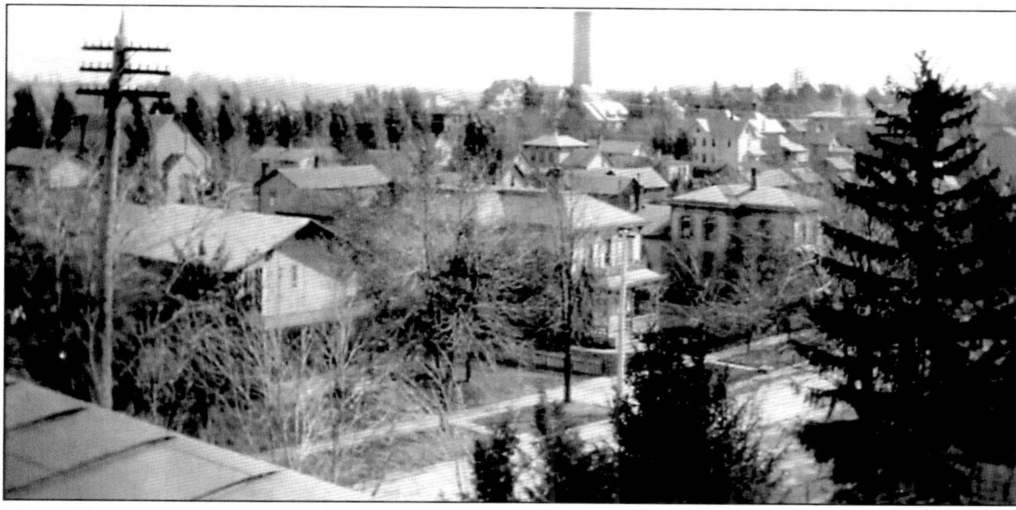

VIEW FROM THE ROOF OF SAWYER'S SANATORIUM. In 1895, Sawyer's South Main Street building offered unobstructed views of Marion. To the southeast, one would see residential South Main Street, the spire of the Lutheran Church at State and Columbia Streets, and the "Stand Pipe" atop Gurley Hill. The Stand Pipe was part of Marion's pressurized water system and has since been replaced with a modern water tower. (Photograph courtesy of the Marion County Historical Society.)

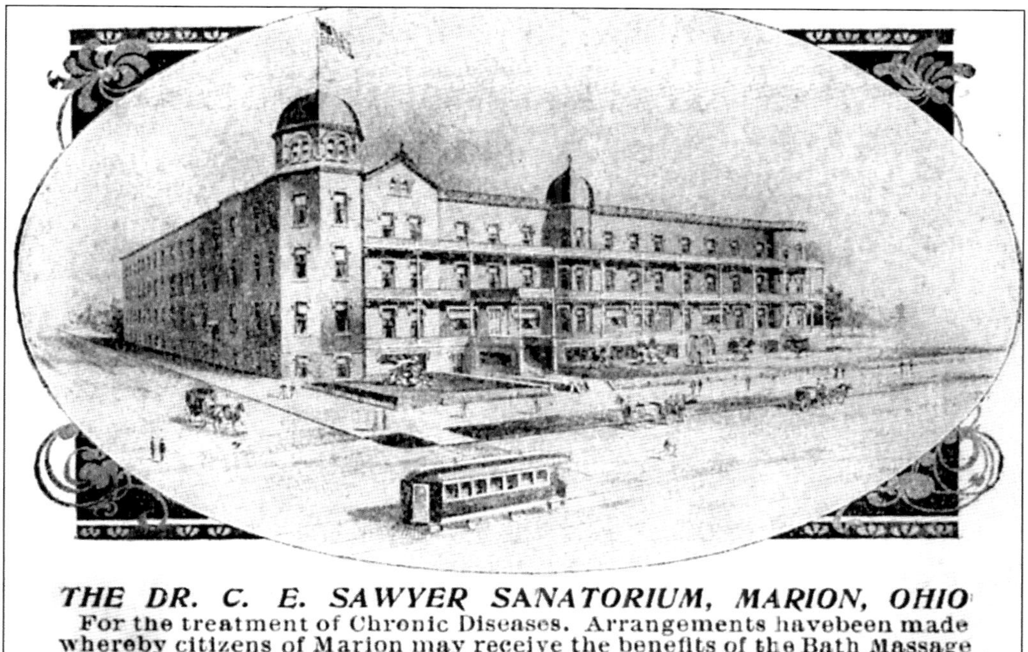

SAWYER'S SANATORIUM. By 1901, Dr. Sawyer operated two successful facilities, due in part to his aggressive advertising. In addition to the building in Marion, Sawyer also operated the Park View Sanatorium in Columbus. During this era in medicine, the widely accepted treatment for women's "hysteria" was the use of popular "electro-vibration" treatments, which Sawyer's fully modern facility could provide. (Photograph courtesy of the author.)

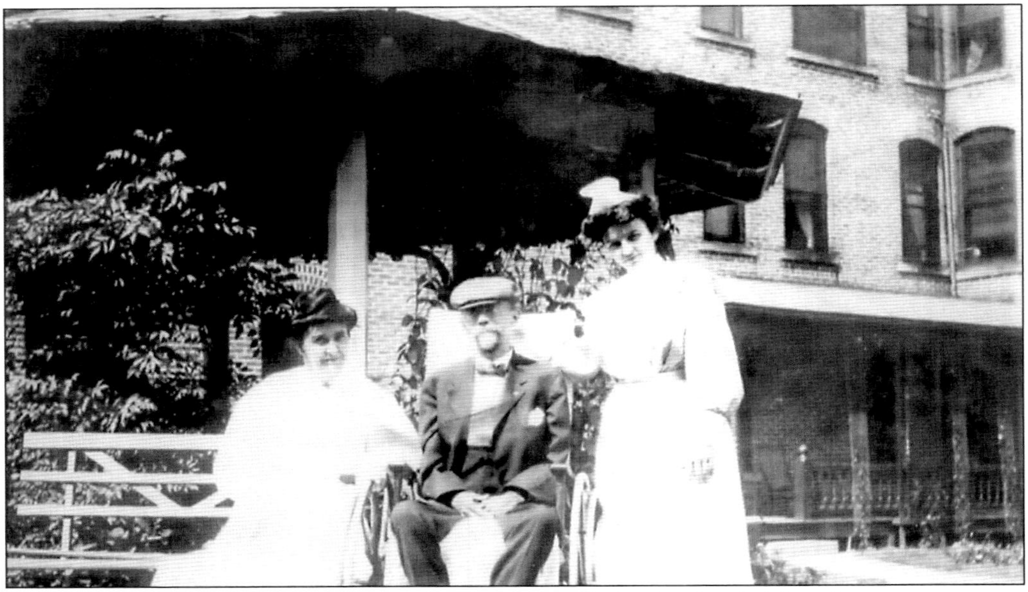

DR. AND MRS. CHARLES SAWYER AND A NURSE. While the South Main Street sanatorium was designed as a commercial block, the building also included a private back yard for patients' use. This photograph appears to have been taken in a moment of fun, as Dr. Sawyer poses with his wife and a nurse employed at the facility. (Photograph courtesy of the Marion County Historical Society.)

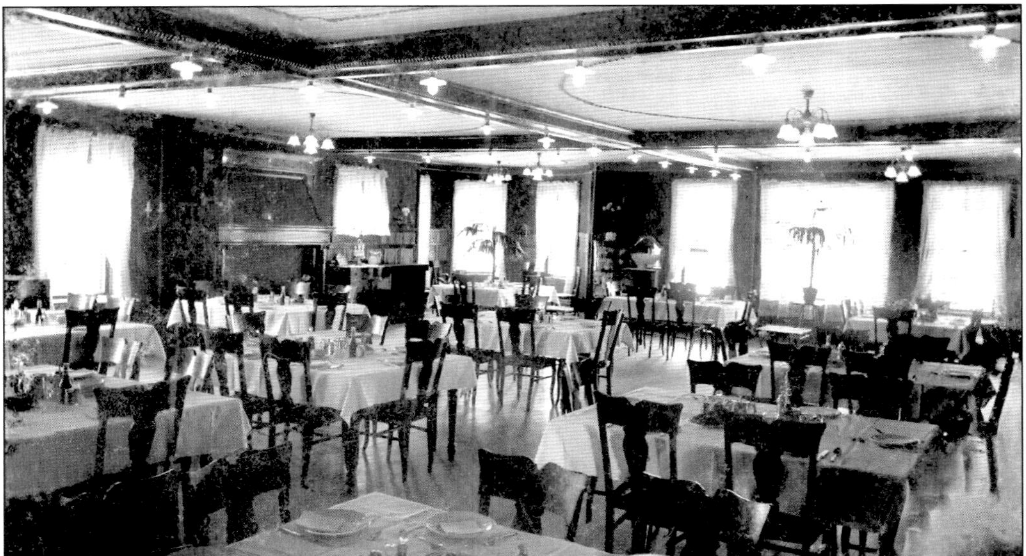

DINING ROOM, SAWYER SANATORIUM. Dr. Sawyer included a modern dining room for his patients and his guests when the northern addition was constructed. The dining room could easily accommodate 80 people and was often the site of private parties hosted by Dr. and Mrs. Sawyer. To further his claim that the sanatorium was modern, Sawyer used electricity extensively throughout the building, instead of the more commonly found gas jet and electric light combination fixtures. (Photograph courtesy of the Marion County Historical Society.)

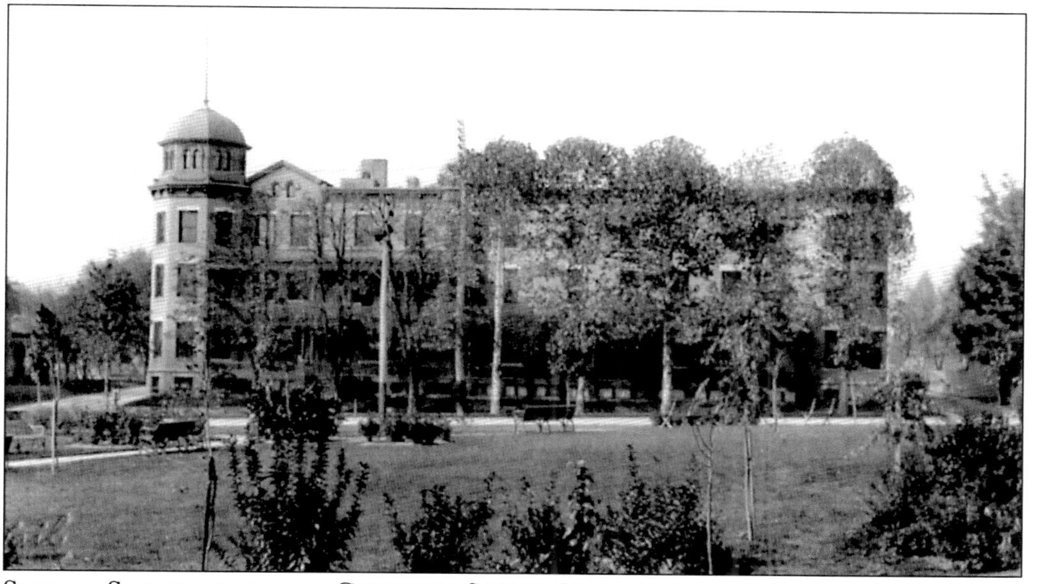

SAWYER SANATORIUM AND GARDENS, SOUTH MAIN STREET. Subsequent additions to Sawyer's downtown Marion facility almost tripled the square footage of the original section. The new building allowed for a greater variety of medical treatments, as well as housing for his patients. Sawyer purchased the lot across South Main Street and landscaped it for the pleasure of his patients. He later sold that lot to the city for the construction of Marion's Carnegie Library. (Photograph courtesy of the Marion County Historical Society.)

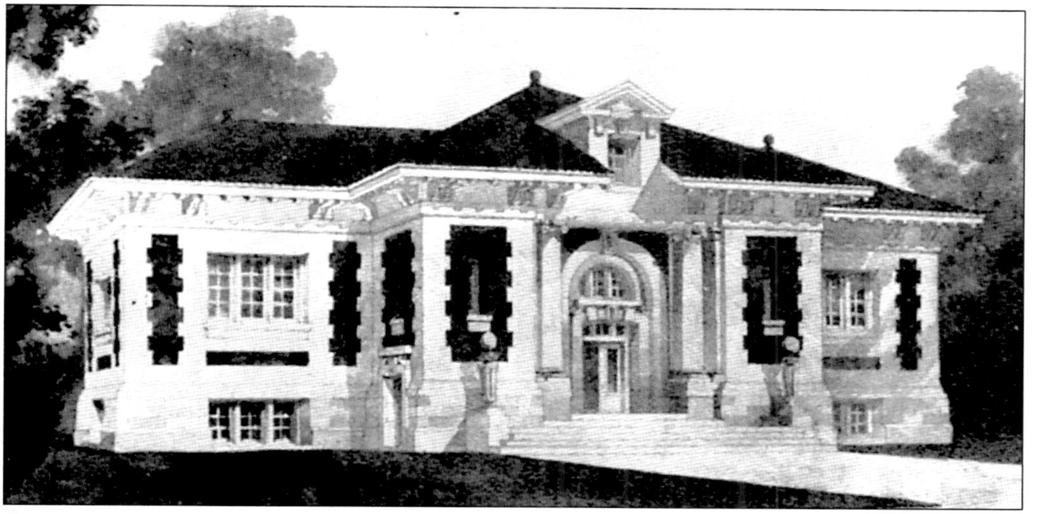

CARNEGIE LIBRARY BUILDING, SOUTH MAIN STREET. In 1905, Andrew Carnegie extended the sum of $25,000 towards the establishment of a permanent home to Marion's library. Sites for the proposed library included West Center Street, adjacent to Marion High School; East Church Street; and South State Streets. In the midst of the discussion, Dr. C.E. Sawyer offered a donation of the small park that he had installed opposite his South Main Street Sanatorium building, on the condition that once the building was erected that the grounds be maintained in a park-like setting. The city accepted Sawyer's offer, and work on the building begun. (Photograph courtesy of the author.)

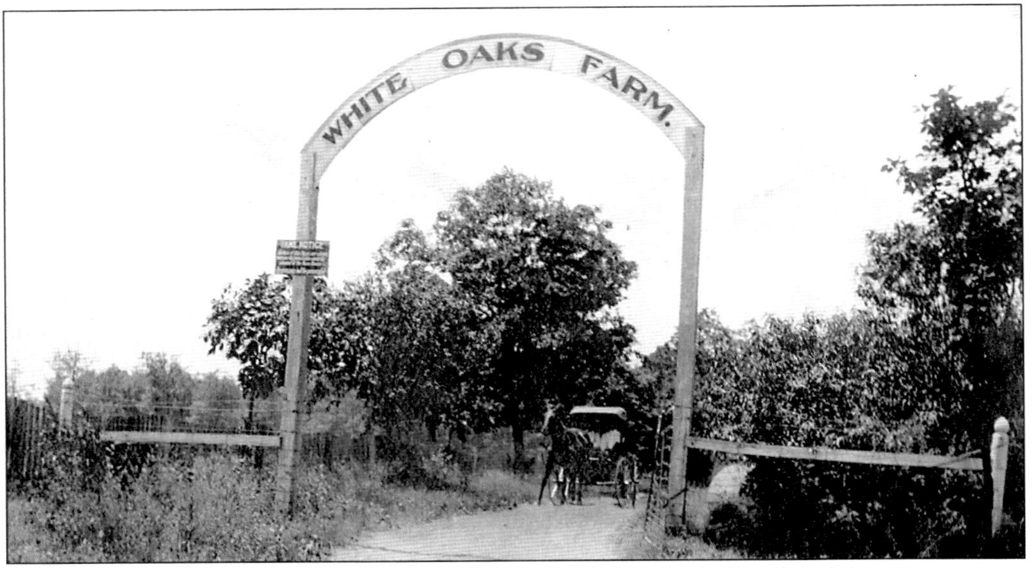

GATEWAY TO WHITE OAKS FARM. Located between White Oaks Road and the Green Camp Pike (now Bellefontaine Avenue), the White Oaks Farm was created by merging the James Jones, Uncapher, and Hudson family farms. The name for the farm was derived from numerous white oaks that populated the landscape. Always a working farm, Dr. Charles Sawyer's vision was to put a portion of the land to a different use. (Photograph courtesy of the Marion County Historical Society.)

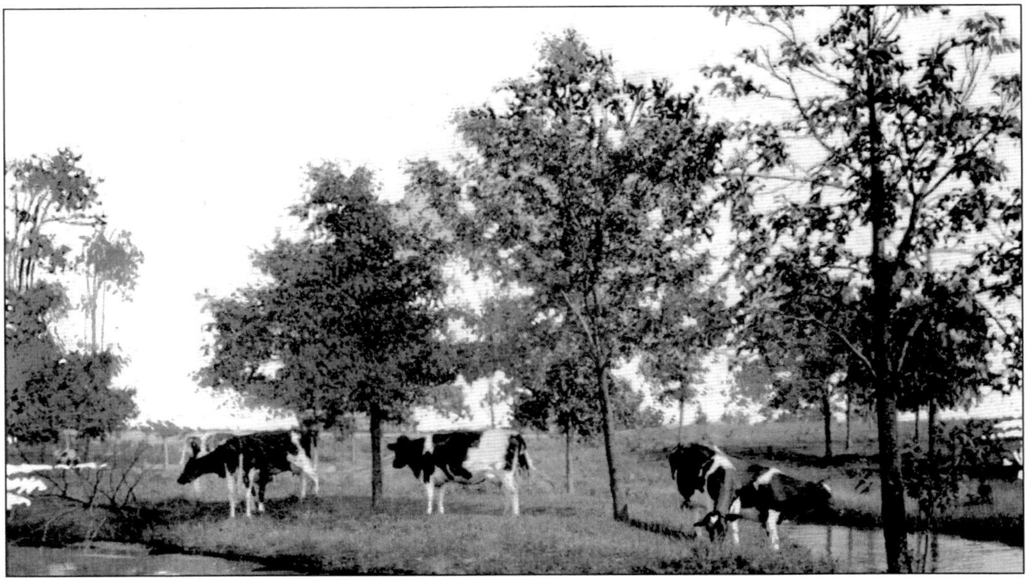

BUCOLIC WHITE OAKS. The Sawyer's began promoting White Oaks around 1905 as a haven from the cares of the world. Pastoral scenes were used in the advertising leading up to the construction of Sawyer's new vision for a restful sanatorium, where patients could relax and reap the full benefits that nature's bounty and modern medicine could provide. For a brief period, White Oaks Milk was sold by the Marion Pure Milk Company. (Photograph courtesy of the Marion County Historical Society.)

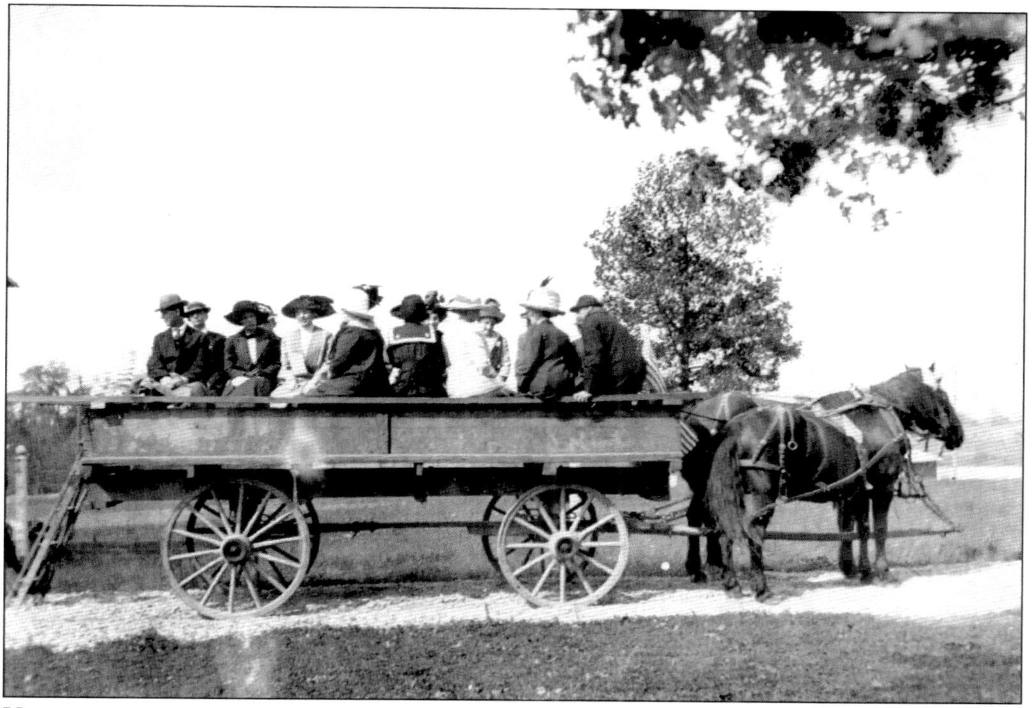

VISITORS AT WHITE OAKS FARM. After advertising the curative properties of the White Oaks Farm, the Sawyers began operating tours for the curious. Tours were also given of the sanatorium site during construction, as well as its extensively landscaped lawns and gardens. Tours inside the facility were discontinued after 1923. (Photograph courtesy of the Marion County Historical Society.)

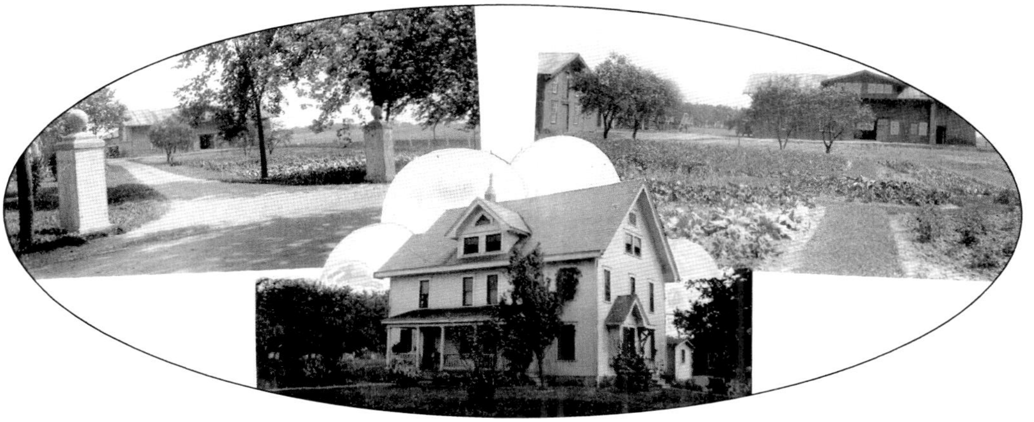

THE SAWYER'S RESIDENCE, GREEN CAMP PIKE. The Sawyer family built their home on the northwestern edge of the property, which still stands on what is now Bellefontaine Avenue. White Oaks Farm was a working farm; much of its produce and livestock were used in the operation of the sanatorium. While the house was more conventional in its design, the barn followed the overall craftsman style used for the sanatorium buildings. (Photograph courtesy of the Marion County Historical Society.)

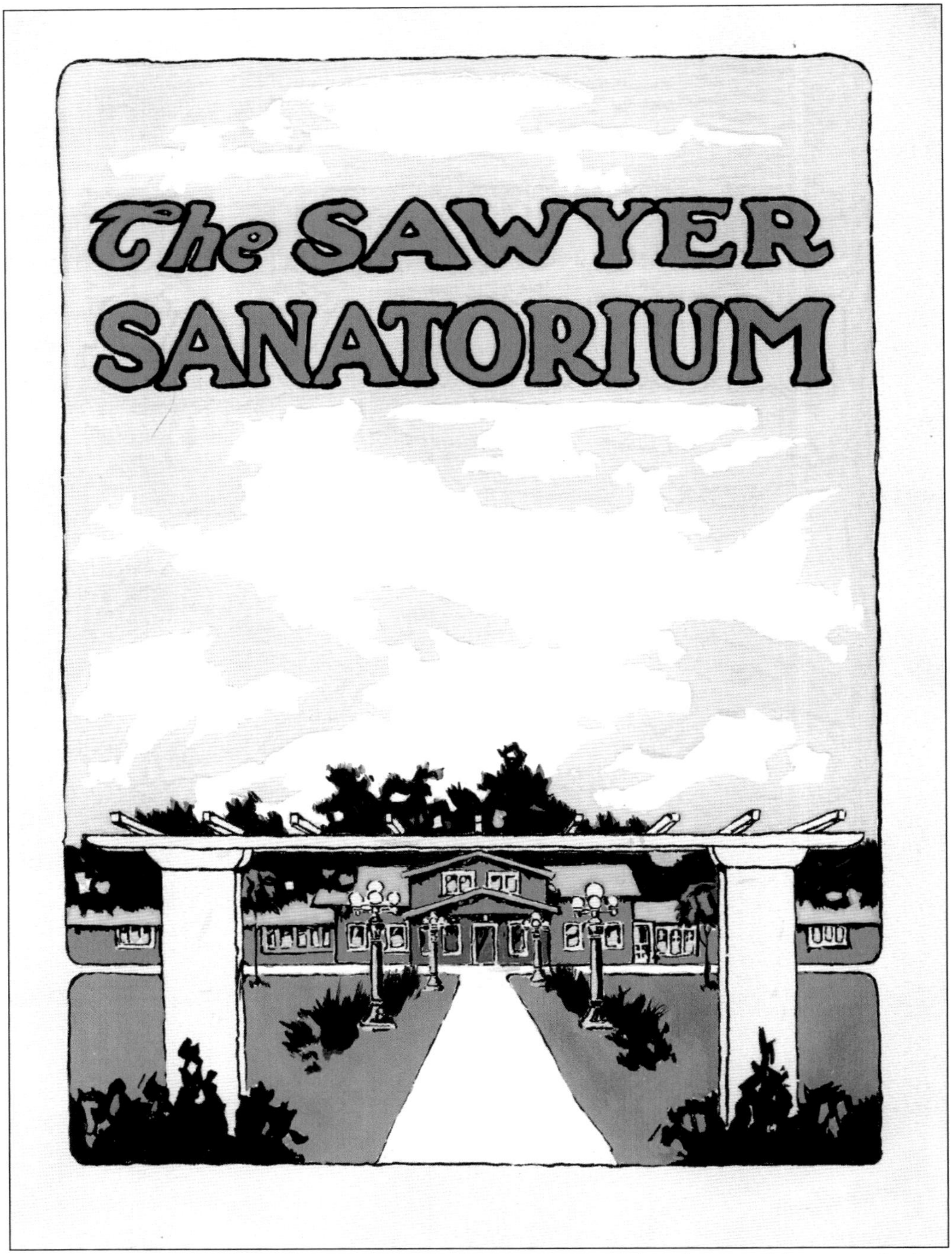

The Sawyer Sanatorium at White Oaks Farm. For the design of his new facility, Dr. Charles Sawyer embraced the "craftsman" principles established by Gustav Stickley and the Roycrofters. In 1908, the design of the buildings and the compound itself was shockingly modern, unlike anything seen before in Central Ohio. (Photograph courtesy of the Marion County Historical Society.)

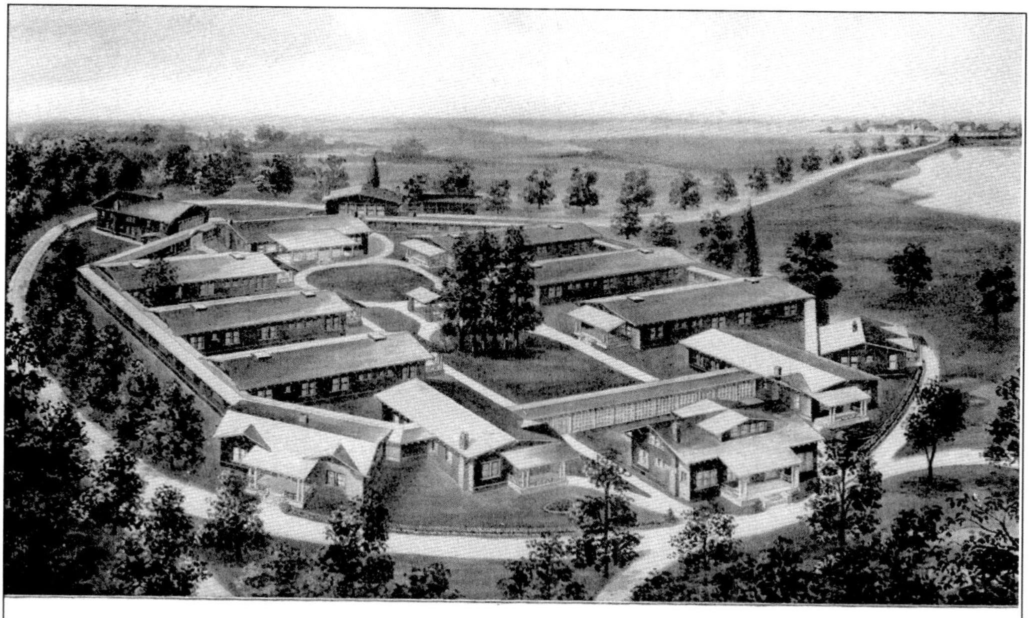

BIRDSEYE VIEW OF THE SAWYER SANATORIUM

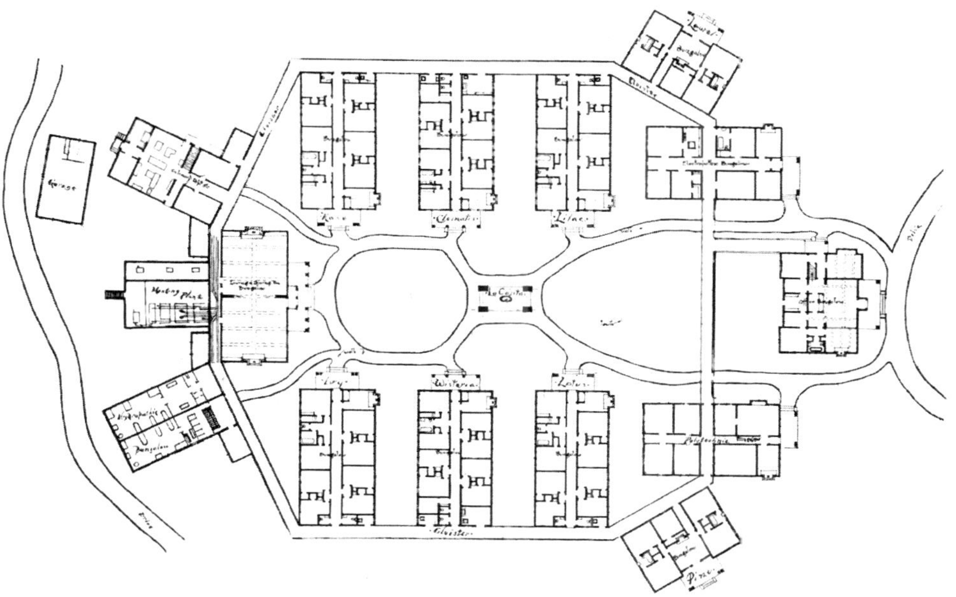

FLOOR PLAN OF THE SAWYER SANATORIUM

BIRDSEYE VIEW OF THE PLANNED SAWYER SANATORIUM AND WHITE OAKS FARM. Dr. Sawyer's plan for his White Oaks Sanatorium used 14 bungalows placed around a landscaped central courtyard, called "the Patio." An enclosed hall, called "the Cloister," encircled the compound and connected all of the buildings to one and other. The one-fifth-mile-long Cloister provided privacy for patients, as well as an exercise hall that was used in bad weather. To the immediate northwest of the sanatorium was Sawyer's private residence, the White Oaks Farm.

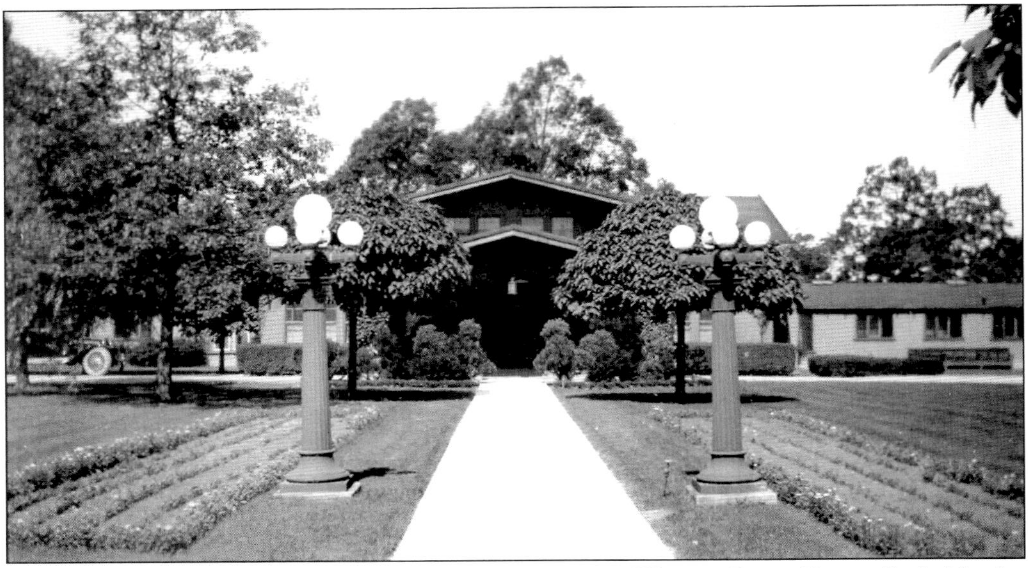

ADMINISTRATION BUILDING, SAWYER'S SANATORIUM, WHITE OAKS FARM. Probably the most familiar image of the Sawyer Sanatorium facility at White Oaks is this view of the administration building from White Oaks Road. Sawyer shrewdly licensed the view to Wiant's Bookstore in Marion for use on a picture postcard. The postcard ensured that an image of the facility would circulate well beyond Marion County and Ohio. (Photograph courtesy of the Marion County Historical Society.)

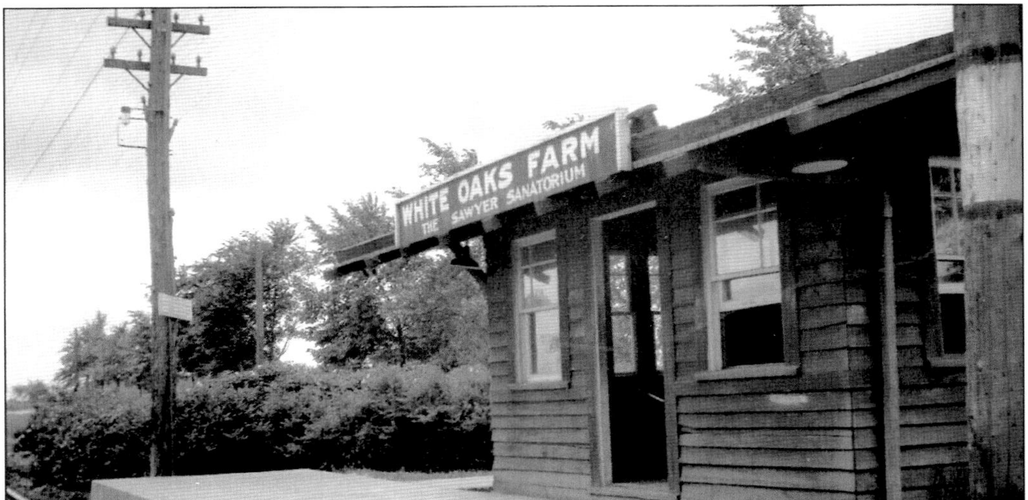

WHITE OAKS FARM RAILROAD STATION. One reason why Dr. Sawyer chose the White Oaks site was the location of the rail and interurban tracks along White Oaks Road, allowing patients (and prospective patients) easy access to the grounds. Sawyer also paid for a private siding that would allow wealthy patients who traveled via private rail cars the ability to park their cars while at the sanatorium. The railroad siding was used by Evalyn Walsh McLean (then the owner of the Hope Diamond) when she traveled to Marion in early November 1924 for what would be her last meeting with her friend, Florence Kling Harding. (Photograph courtesy of the Marion County Historical Society.)

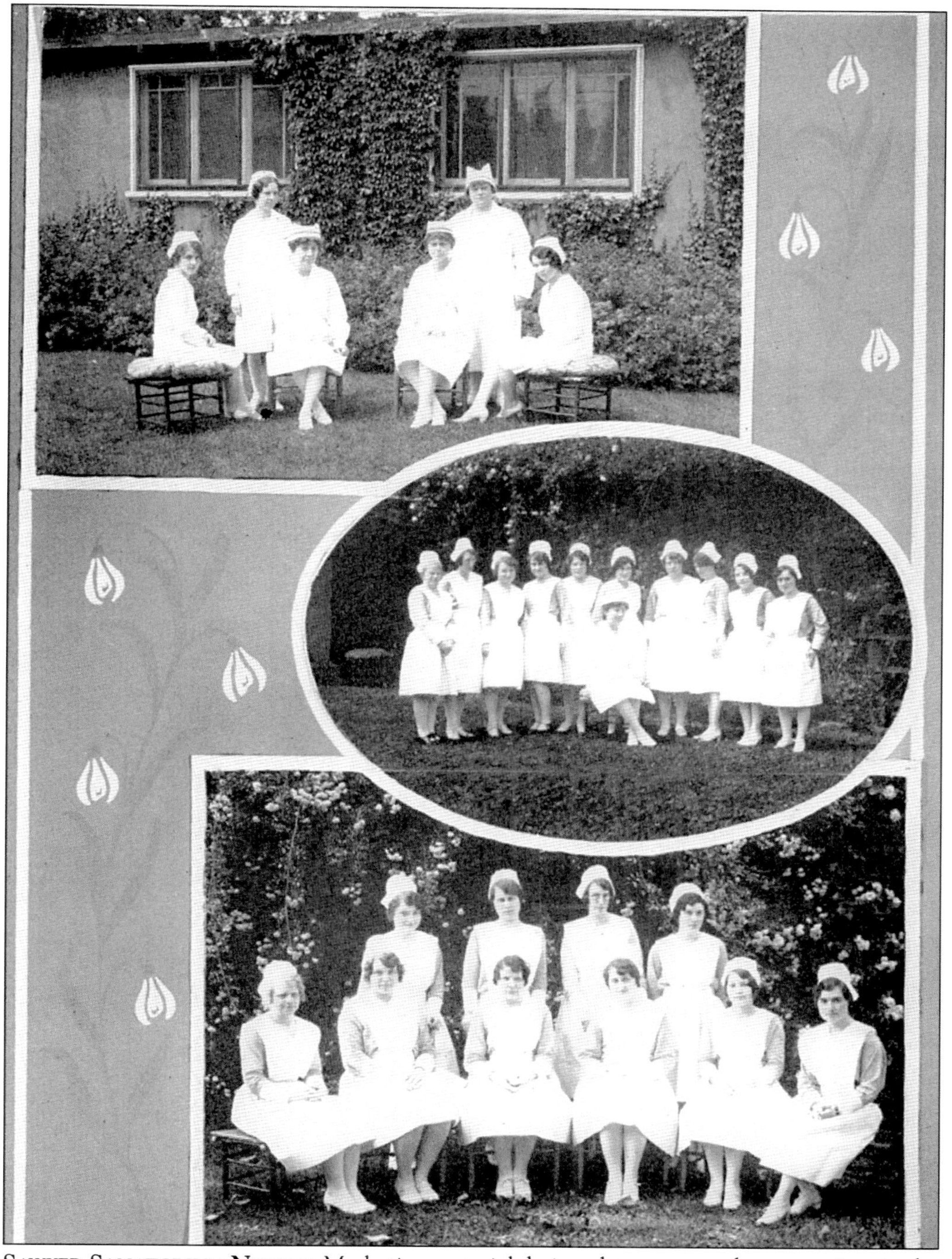

SAWYER SANATORIUM NURSES. Marketing material designed to promote the sanatorium in the mid 1920s lavished attention on the facility's trained nursing staff: "Our nurses are especially trained to treat and care for the special class of patients that we accept and they provide regulated care and nursing for all our patients." (Advertisement courtesy of the Marion County Historical Society.)

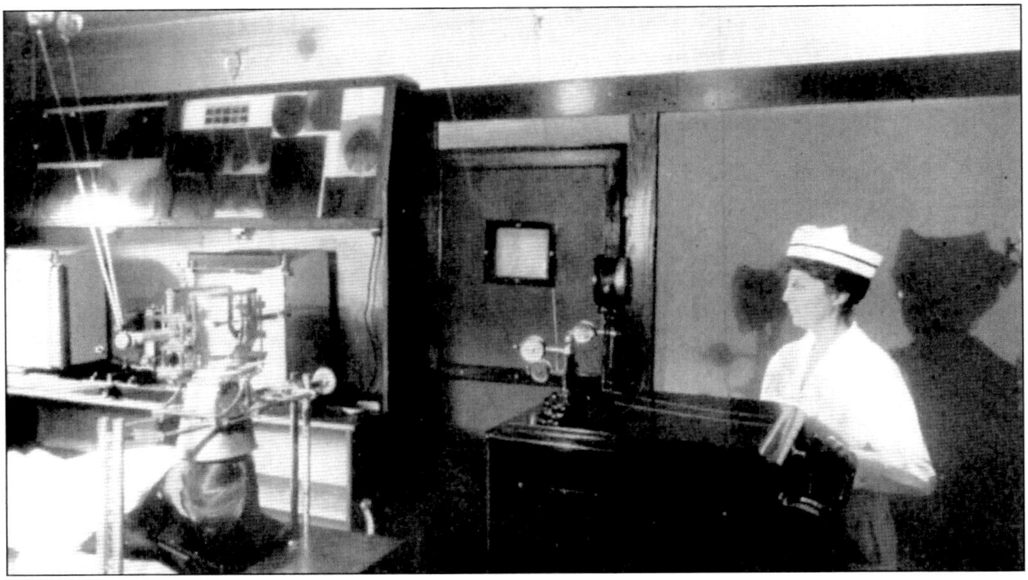

Modern Treatments in the 1920s. This 1920s demonstration photograph showing the X-ray facilities was meant to show the complete means employed to treat patients with nervous and mental illness conditions. In this photograph, the patient (face down on the table) is receiving direct x-ray "treatments" from the nurse at the control panel. (Photograph courtesy of the Marion County Historical Society.)

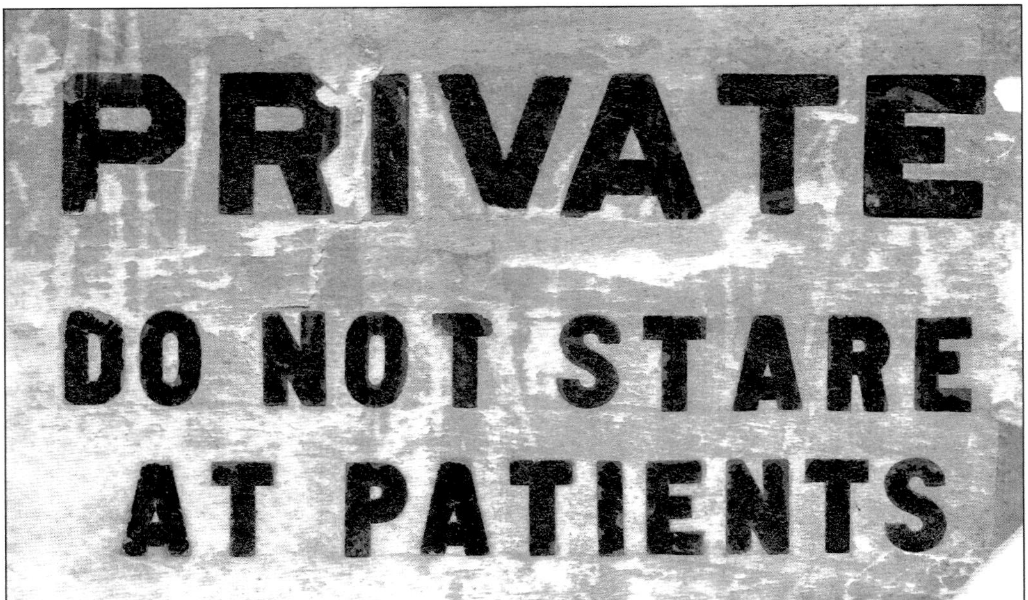

A Not So Gentle Reminder. Public tours of the new Sawyer Sanatorium were held Sundays from its opening in 1908 until 1923, after which, only the gardens were open. While curiosity seekers may have attempted to gawk at the patients, this warning sign, rescued by Gary Barnhart during the demolition of the White Oaks facility in the late 1960s, was a strong reminder of what would not be tolerated. (Photograph courtesy of the Gary Barnhart.)

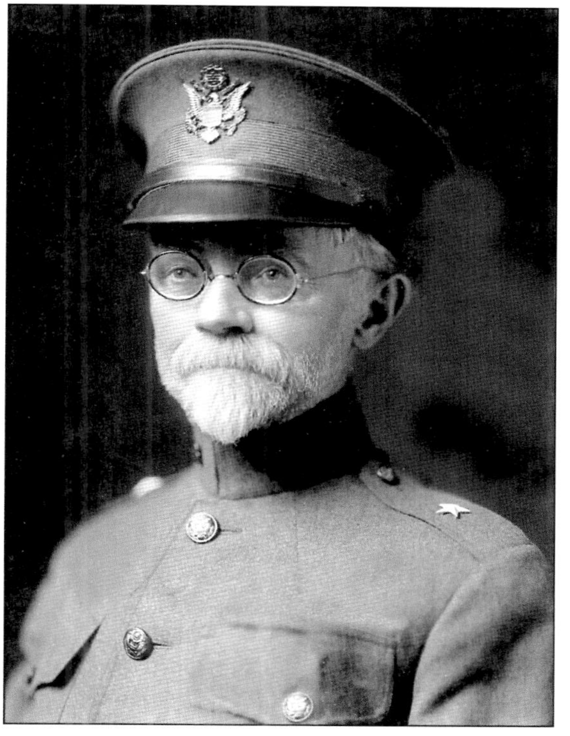

DR. CHARLES E. SAWYER, SURGEON GENERAL OF THE UNITED STATES OF AMERICA. After winning the 1920 presidential election, Warren G. Harding appointed his longtime physician and family friend, Charles Sawyer, Surgeon General of the United States. After Harding's death in 1923, the Coolidge Administration retained Sawyer; however, he resigned the post in 1924 and returned to Marion. Dr. Sawyer's final days were occupied with the Harding Memorial Association and the sanatorium. According to local historian Carroll Niedhart, during his tenure as the Harding's physician, Dr. Sawyer and his son Dr. Carl Sawyer never took payment for their services; in doing so, he and his son felt that they could never be blamed if something went wrong. Dr. Charles Sawyer died at White Oaks Farm on September 23, 1924. (Photograph courtesy of the Marion County Historical Society.)

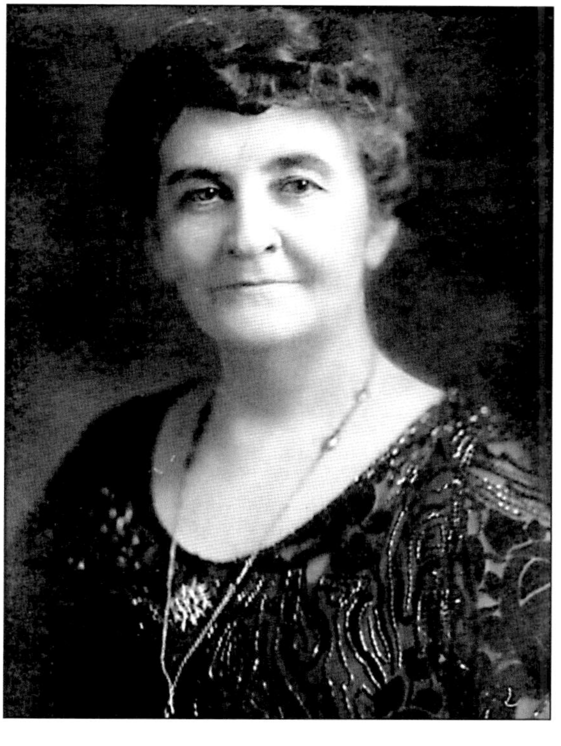

MAY BARRON SAWYER. Born in Ottumwa, Iowa, May Elizabeth Barron married Charles Sawyer in 1879. Less inclined to draw the public eye than her husband, Mrs. Sawyer nevertheless enjoyed a wide circle of friends, many from her years in Washington while her husband served as the Surgeon General in the Harding Administration. May Sawyer died in her home at the White Oaks Farm in 1945 and was buried next to her husband in Marion Cemetery. (Photograph courtesy of the Marion County Historical Society.)

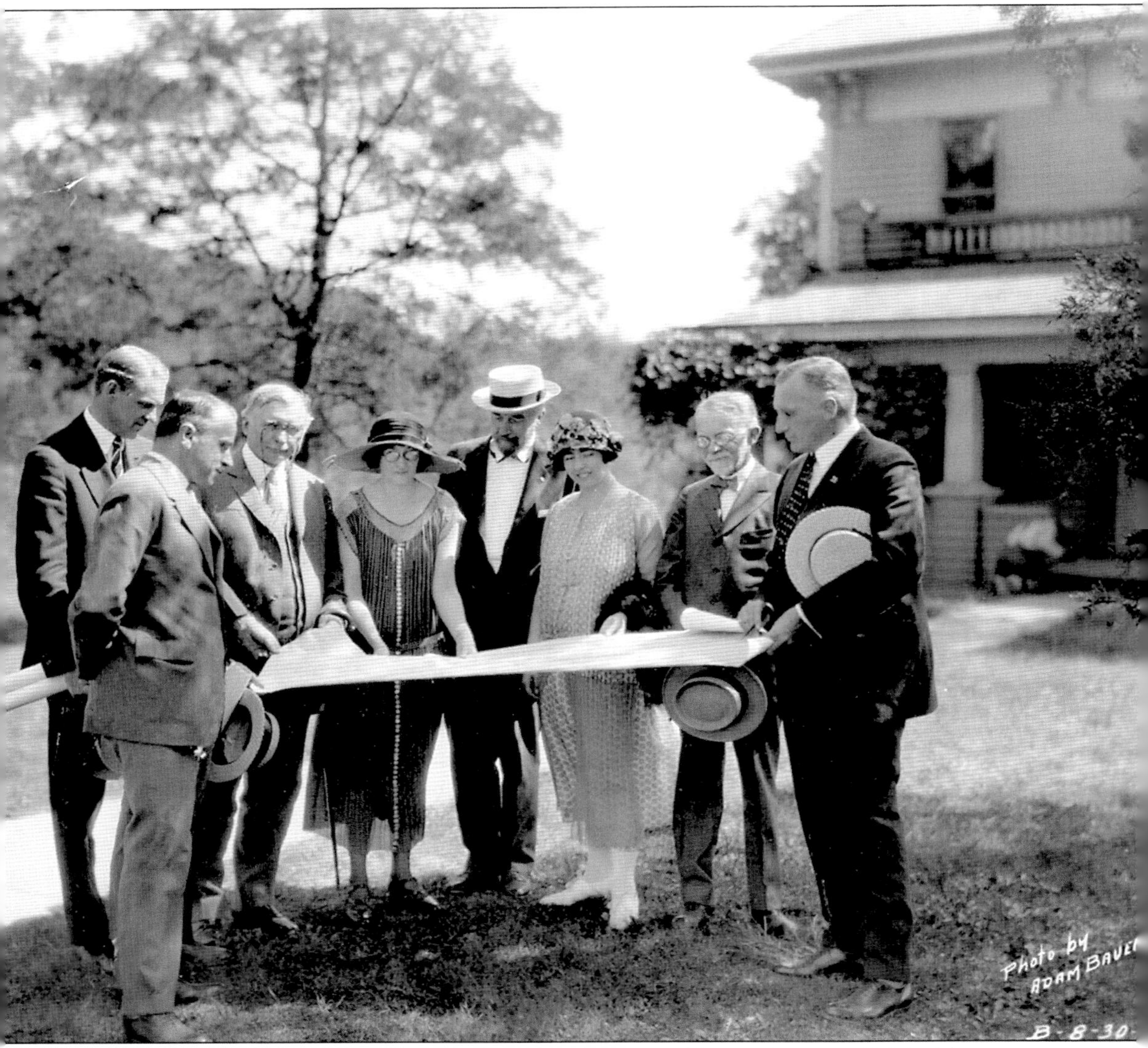

Harding Memorial Association Reviews Site and Plan, August 1924. After reviewing all of their options, the Harding Memorial Association chose the Fisher and Uncapher farms south of Marion for the Harding Memorial. Standing in front of the Uncapher home are members of the Harding Memorial Association. The association announced that they hoped to have the memorial built by 1926. However, former Surgeon General Dr. Charles Sawyer (second from right) died less then a month after this picture was taken, and then Mrs. Harding's death the following November, delayed the process, and a final plan and architect were not selected until June of 1925. (Photograph courtesy of the Marion County Historical Society.)

Six

WE REMEMBER ISALY'S

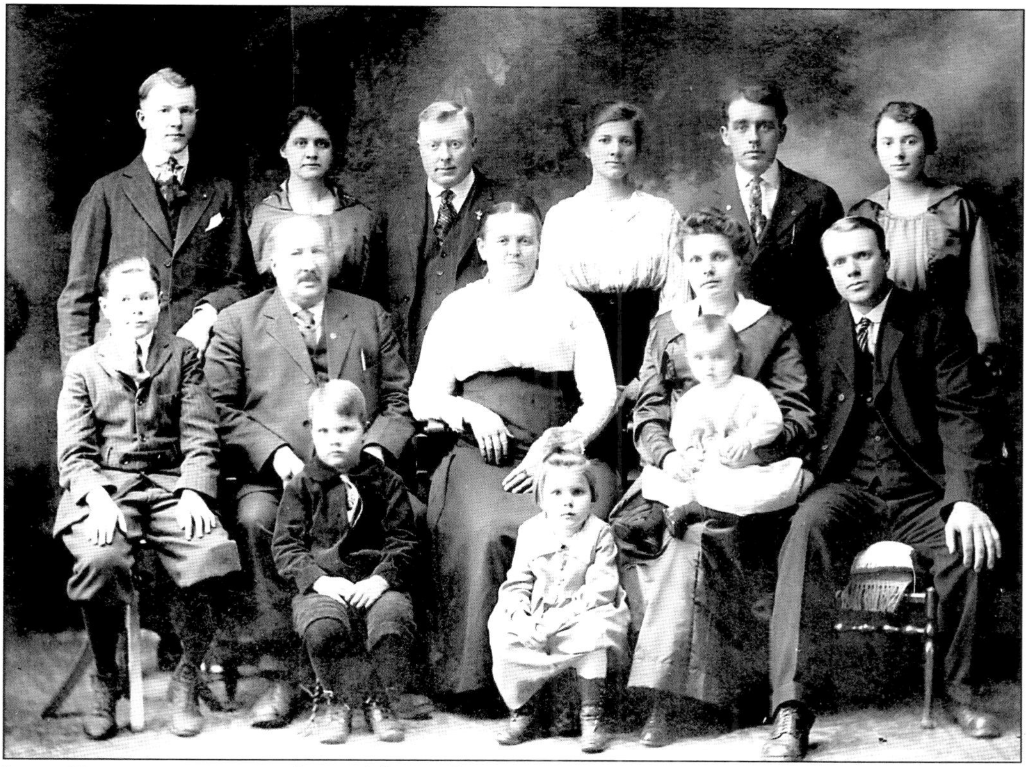

ISALY FAMILY, 1917. Members of the William and Louisa Isaly (pronounced EYEZ-lee) family pose for their portrait, left to right: (top row) Samuel Isaly, Nelle (wife of Chester Isaly), Chester Isaly, Selma Isaly Mahon, John Mahon, and Josephine Isaly; (middle row) Henry Isaly, William and Louisa Isaly, Bertie Jane Deardorff (wife of Charles Isaly), and Charles Isaly. The children pictured, Richard, Marian, and William, were the children of Charles and Bertie Isaly. (Photograph courtesy of Patty Isaly Fulakis.)

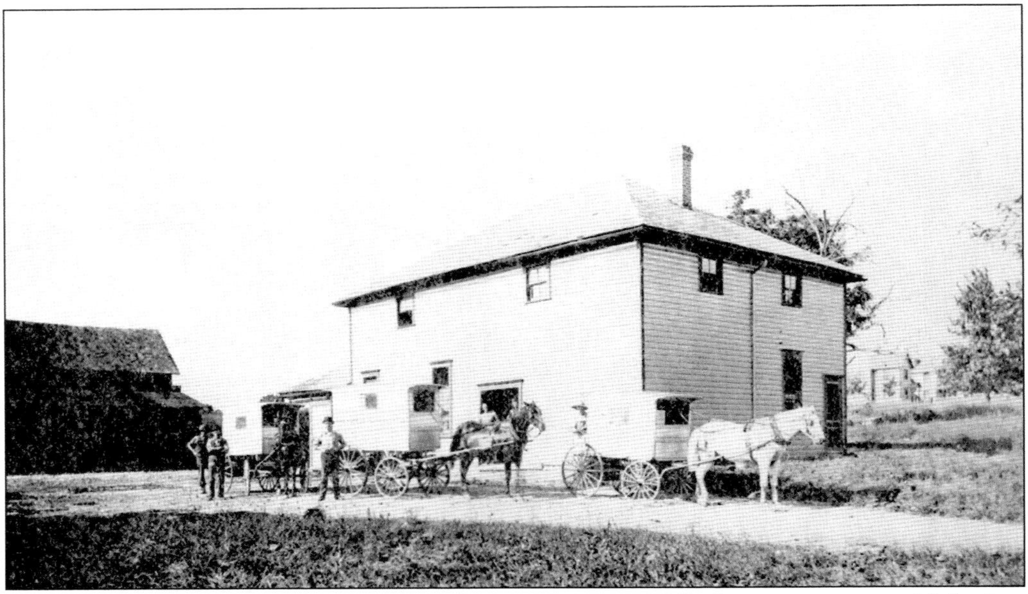

THE MARION PURE MILK COMPANY. The Marion Pure Milk Company was established in 1905 and operated a plant on Belmont Street. In 1914, the Milk Company and its assets were purchased by William Isaly of Mansfield, Ohio. Isaly appointed his son Charles to oversee the Marion operation. Under Charles Isaly, sales of the Marion facility tripled within two years. (Photograph courtesy of the Marion County Historical Society.)

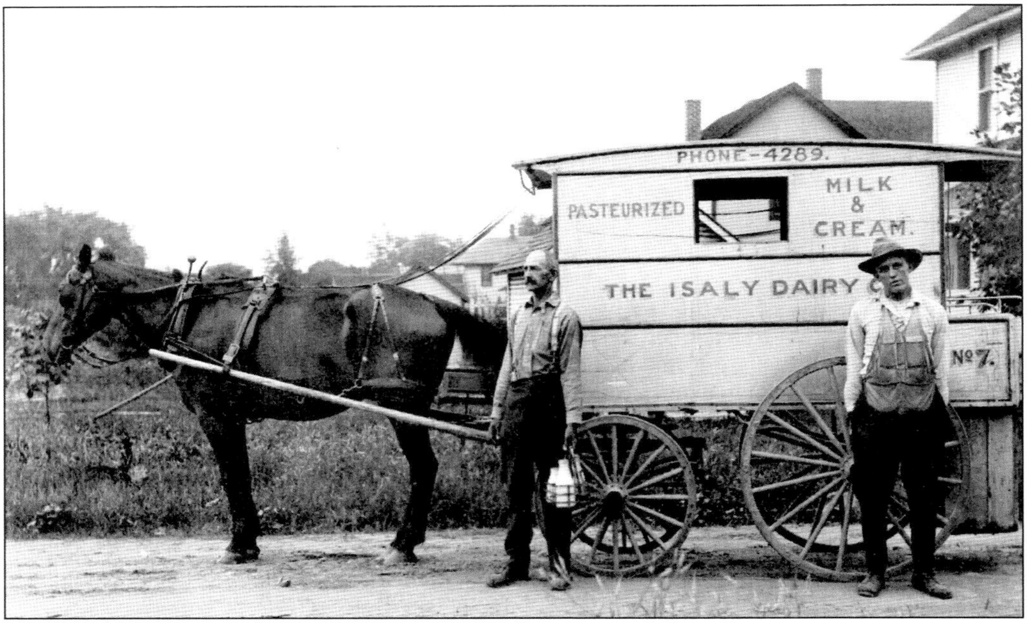

EARLY ISALY MARION DAIRY DELIVERY WAGON. While the Isaly family established itself in Marion after the introduction of the automobile, early milk routes were covered by horse drawn wagons. Originally, the company maintained the four milk routes established by the Marion Pure Milk Company. Eventually, the dairy would grow to serve over 40 such routes. (Photograph courtesy of Hughes Photography, John Rall, president.)

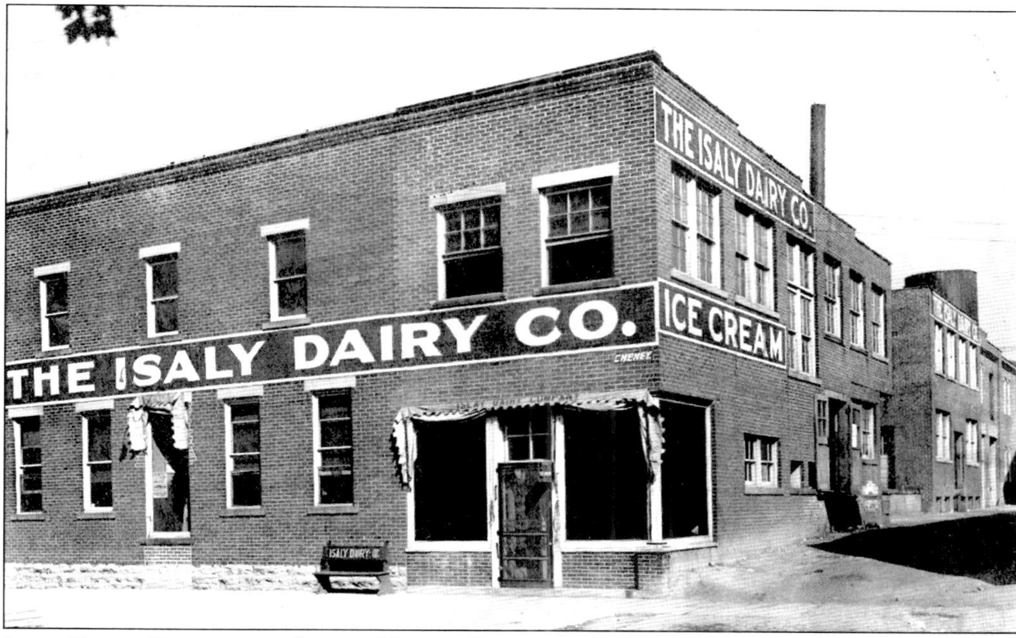

Isaly Dairy Plant and Store, North Prospect Street, 1914. Located on the east side of North Prospect Street, the Isaly Diary plant included two buildings, one for the production and direct sale of milk and dairy products and the other a stable to house the horses and mules used to pull the dairy wagons. The old plant was one of the first stops on Saturday evenings when local farmers brought their families into town; ice cream could be had for 2¢ a cone. In 1934, the dairy facility and store installed one of the first neon signs in Marion—an ice cream cone with the name "Isaly" written in script across it. (Photograph courtesy of Patty Isaly Fulakis.)

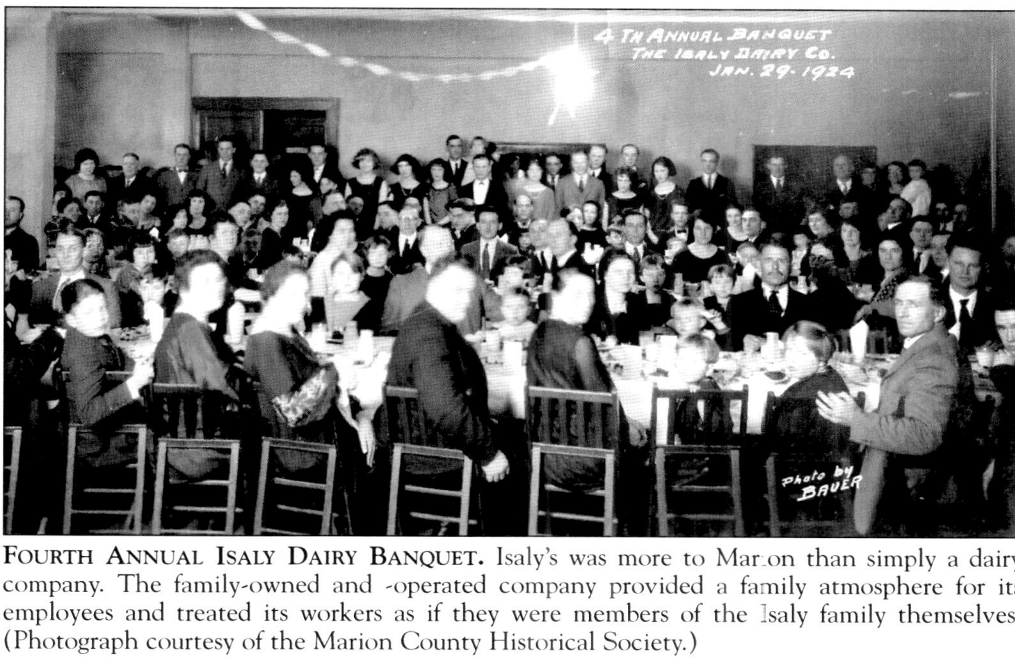

Fourth Annual Isaly Dairy Banquet. Isaly's was more to Marion than simply a dairy company. The family-owned and -operated company provided a family atmosphere for its employees and treated its workers as if they were members of the Isaly family themselves. (Photograph courtesy of the Marion County Historical Society.)

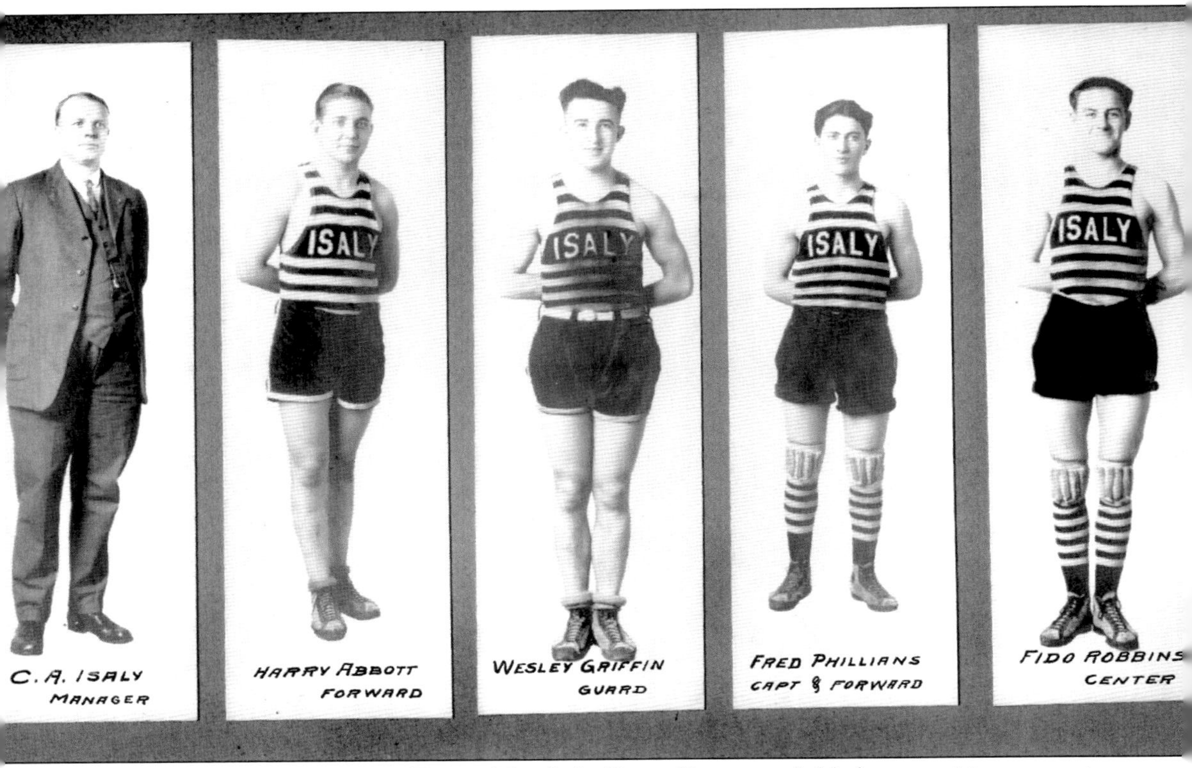

ISALY DAIRY BASKETBALL TEAM. The Isaly Dairy Company fielded competitive teams in a variety of sports in the 1920s. However, it was the basketball teams that garnered the most publicity. The Isaly team played other local business teams, as well as semi-professional and exhibition teams, including the Buffalo Silents, a team from New York State comprised of deaf and/or mute players. Reunions of the team players were held into the 1960s, with Charles

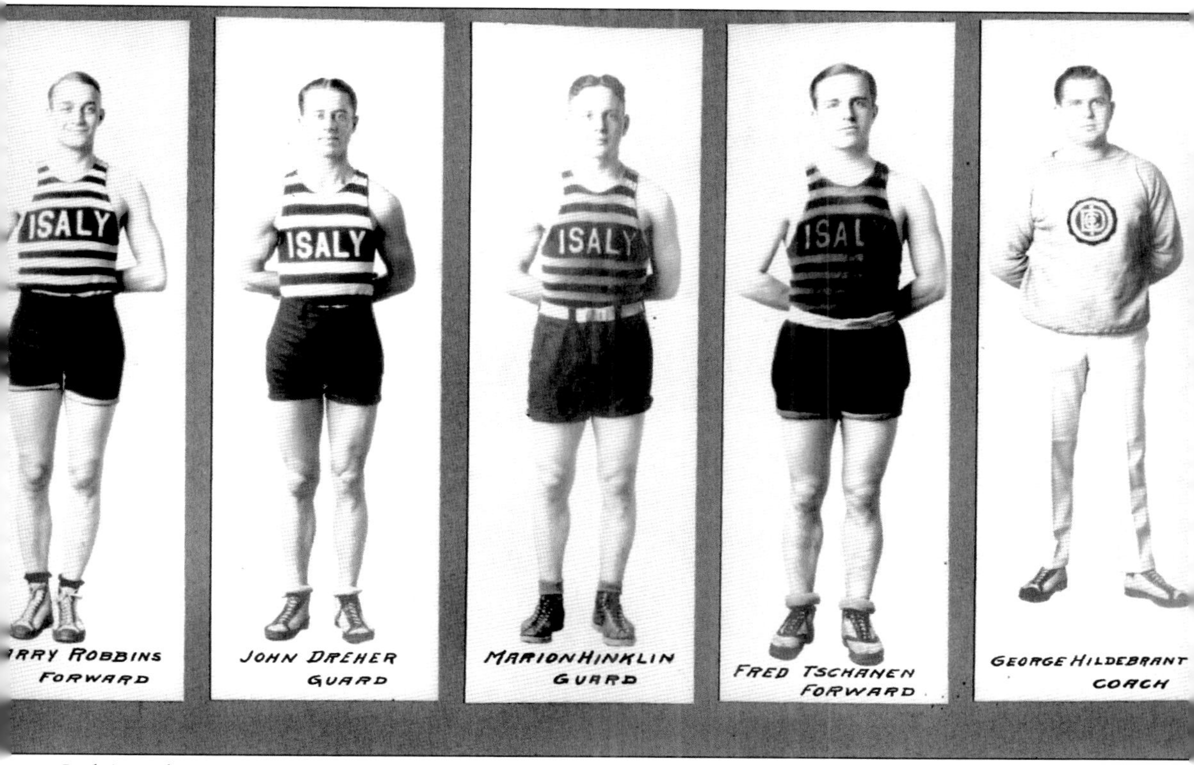

Isaly's widow Bertie Isaly often seated as the guest of honor. Left to right are Marion facility manager Charles Isaly, Harry Abbott, Wesley Griffin, Fred Phillians, Floyd "Fido" Robbins, Harry Robbins, John Dreher, Marion Hinklin, Fred Tschanen, and Coach George Hillebrandt. (Photograph courtesy of the Marion County Historical Society.)

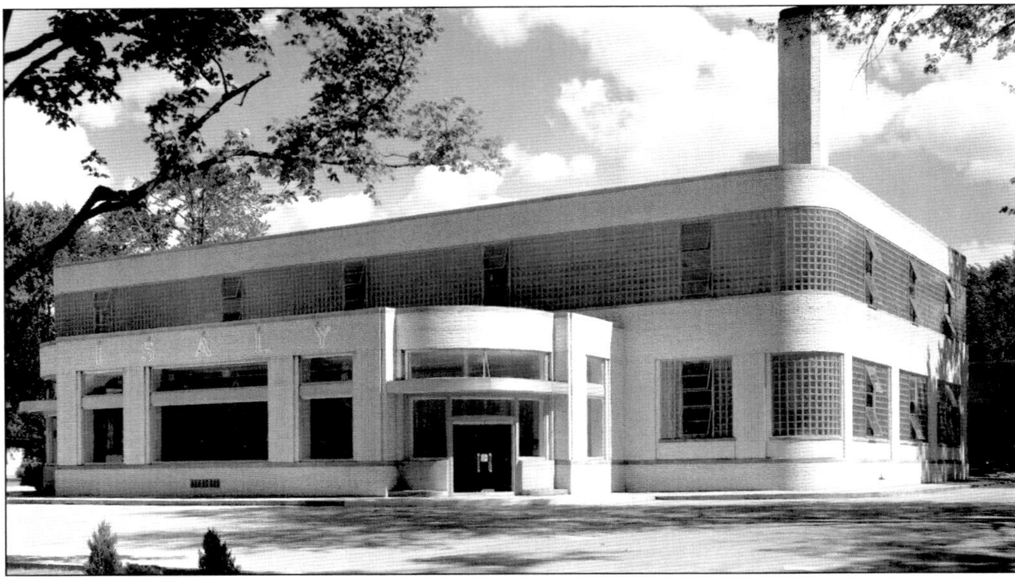

NEW ISALY DAIRY PLANT AND RETAIL STORE, EAST CENTER STREET. Plans for a modern Isaly Dairy facility in Marion were made in the late 1930s. Three private homes were acquired along East Center Street near South Greenwood Street, with two of the three homes razed in September 1940. The third house, built by Urias Seffner and long the home of the Hane Family, was retained and altered for use as a sign shop. Building material and steel shortages during World War II postponed construction of the diary until 1947. (Photograph courtesy of Hughes Photography, John Rall, president.)

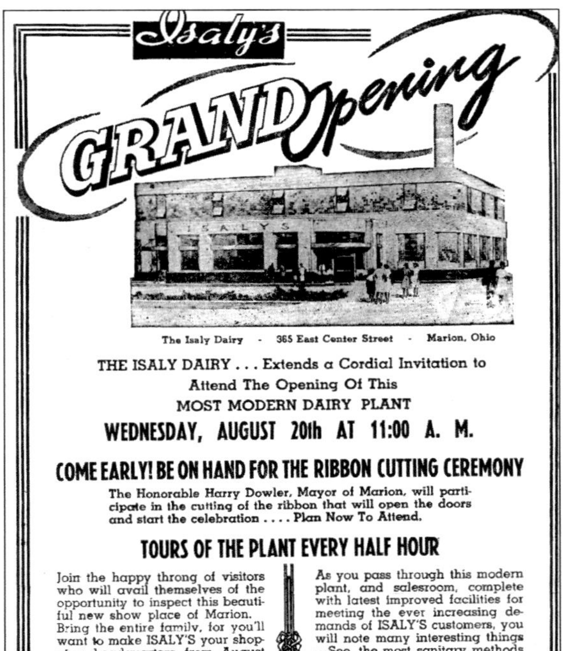

1947 GRAND OPENING OF THE ISALY DAIRY, EAST CENTER STREET. On August 20, 1947, seven years after construction began, the Isaly Diary and retail store held its Grand Opening. The skeleton of the building was steel-reinforced concrete, the outer walls cream colored brick. A ribbon of glass block windows wrapped around the first and second floors, punctuated by windows that could be opened when needed. The front of the building featured a retail store that provided counter service for ice cream and skyscraper cones, as well as sandwiches and coffee. Tissue thin slices of Isaly's brand Chip Chop Ham became a mainstay for hot and cold sandwiches in the post-war era. (Photograph courtesy of Patti Isaly Fulakis.)

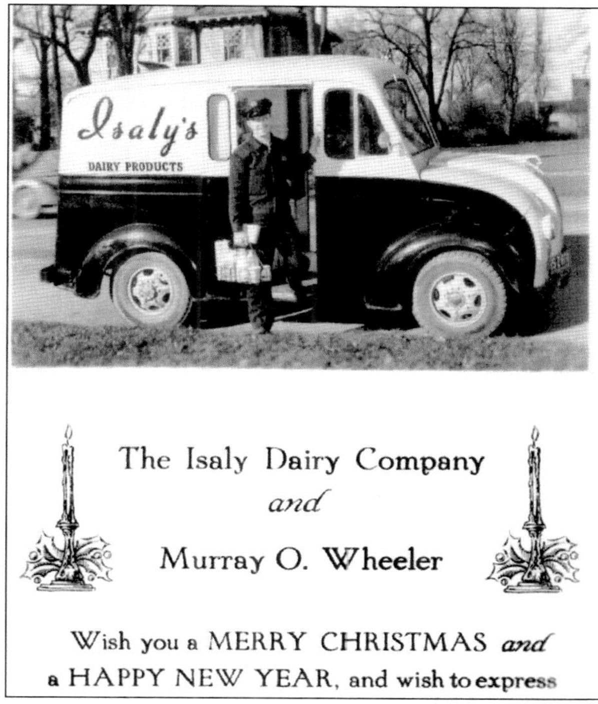

SEASON'S GREETING FROM ISALY'S. Standing in front of his DIVCO milk truck, Murray O. Wheeler posed on Center Street in front of the Isaly diary for this seasonal Christmas card. Each driver received his own personalized thank you that was provided to patrons on their respective routes. (Photograph courtesy of the Marion County Historical Society.)

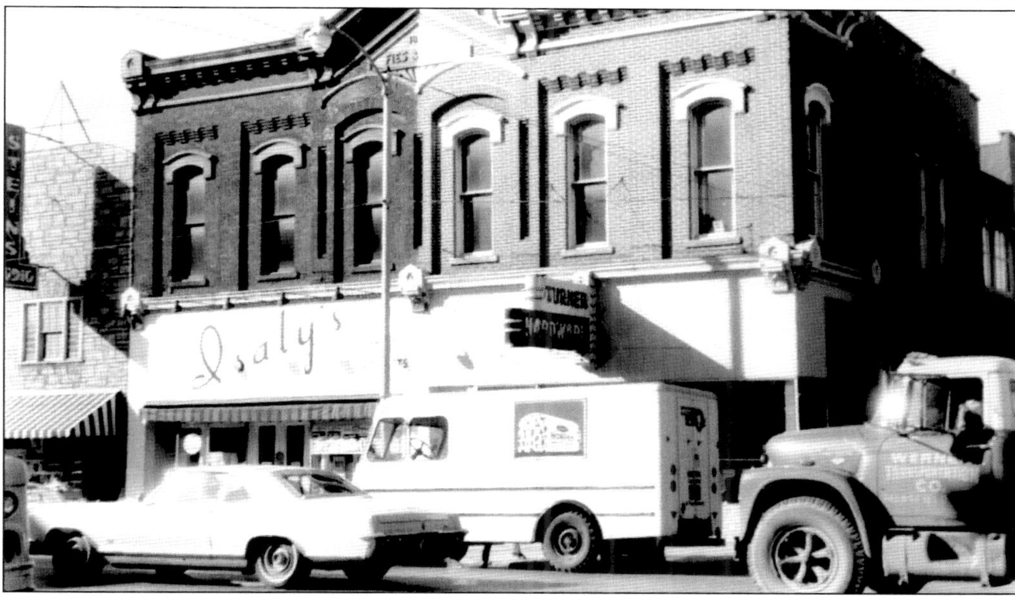

ISALY'S, SOUTH MAIN STREET. In addition to the North Prospect and East Center Street operations, Isaly's also operated a retail store on South Main Street in the Fies and Kling block immediately south of Turner's Hardware. The location, complete with a white Carrara glass store front, was advertised as "Isaly's Cafeteria." The Fies and Kling block was also interesting because until the 1980s, the building sported an "aged" look on the south side of the building, and a restored façade featuring bright white trim and cleaned brick. (Photograph courtesy of the Marion County Historical Society.)

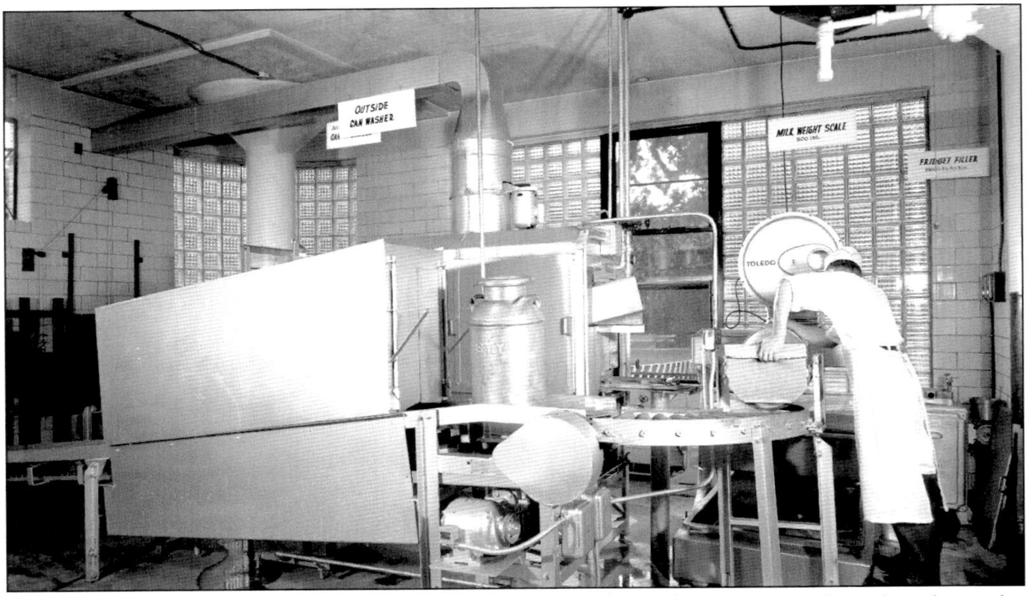

WEIGHING MILK, ISALY DAIRY. Once milk from supplying farmers arrived at the plant, the milk was introduced into the production line my measuring its weight. Milk at the plant was pasteurized in huge glass-lined vats. Milk cans were washed by automated washers and returned to await their reuse. (Photograph courtesy of Patti Isaly Fulakis.)

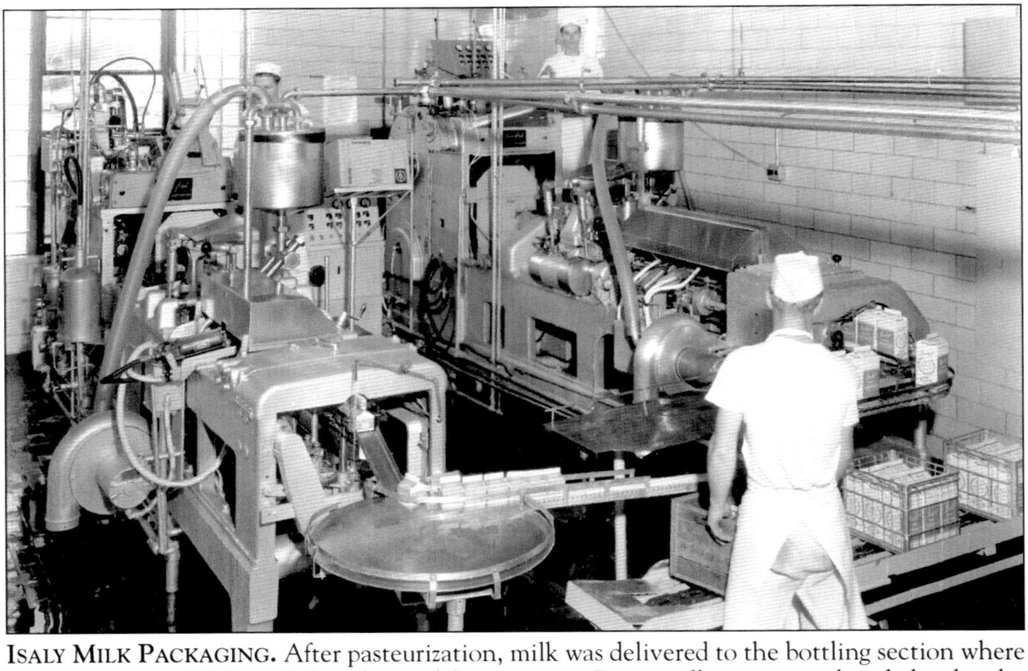

ISALY MILK PACKAGING. After pasteurization, milk was delivered to the bottling section where containers were filled, sealed, and crated for transport. Paper milk cartons replaced glass bottles in 1956. Most Isaly patrons slipped the half-gallon cartons into plastic handled caddies stamped "Isaly's," which made pouring the milk easier during home use. (Photograph courtesy of Hughes Photography, John Rall, president.)

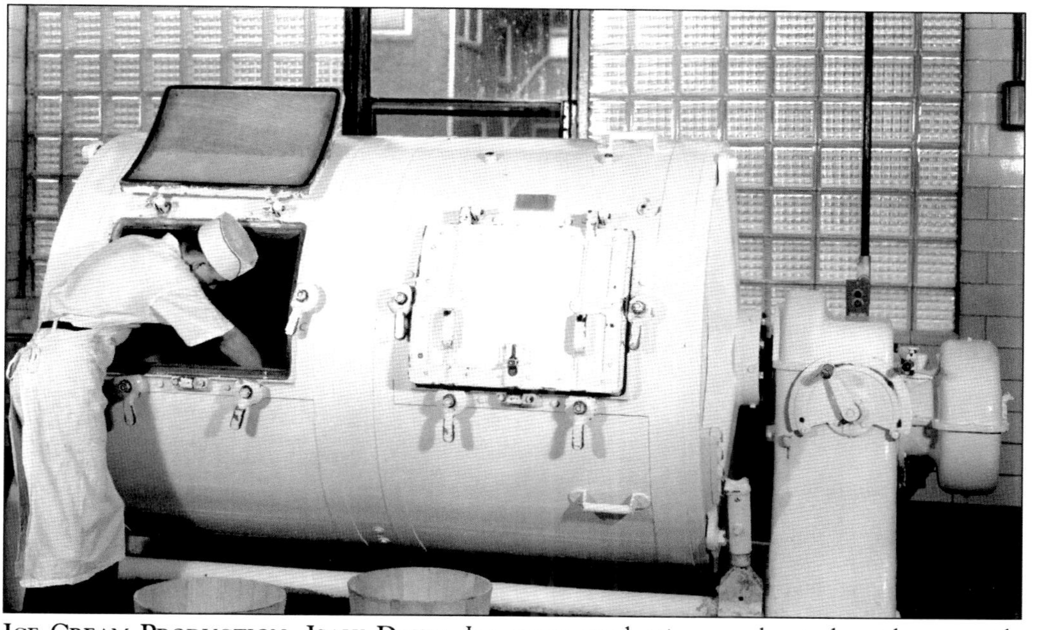

ICE CREAM PRODUCTION, ISALY DAIRY. Ice cream production was located on the east side of the building. During the ice cream-making process, milk, flavorings, color, and other ingredients are mixed; as they mix, air is infused into the product, giving the ice cream a light feel. Ice cream without air would have the same dense consistency as an ice cube. (Photograph courtesy of Hughes Photography, John Rall, president.)

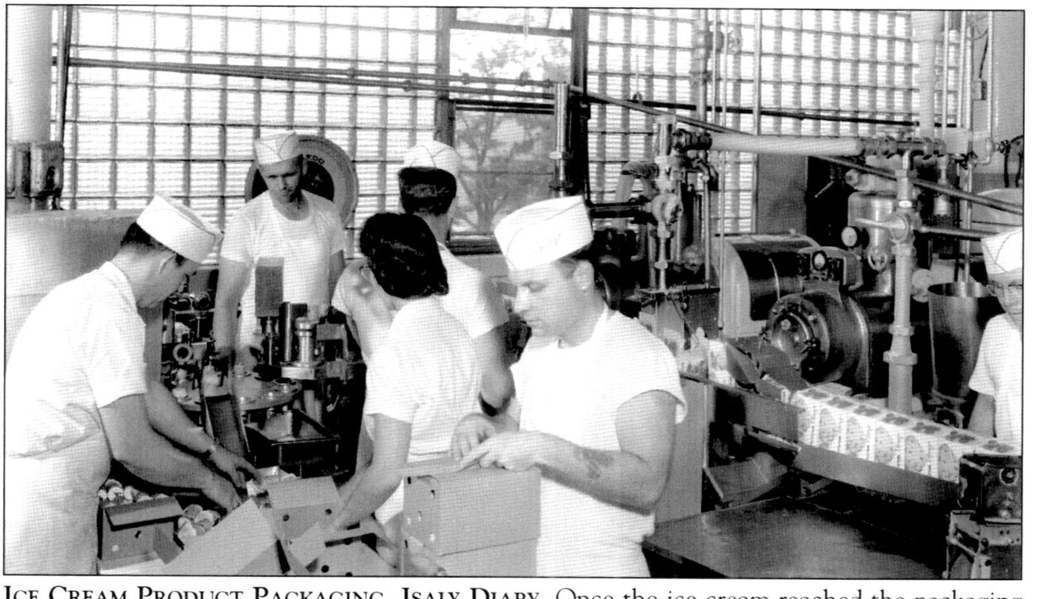

ICE CREAM PRODUCT PACKAGING, ISALY DIARY. Once the ice cream reached the packaging stage, local employees supervised the mechanical filling and sealing of the familiar white Isaly half-gallon containers. From the production line, the containers were sent into a super cold freezer known as the Hardening Room. (Photograph courtesy of Hughes Photography, John Rall, president.)

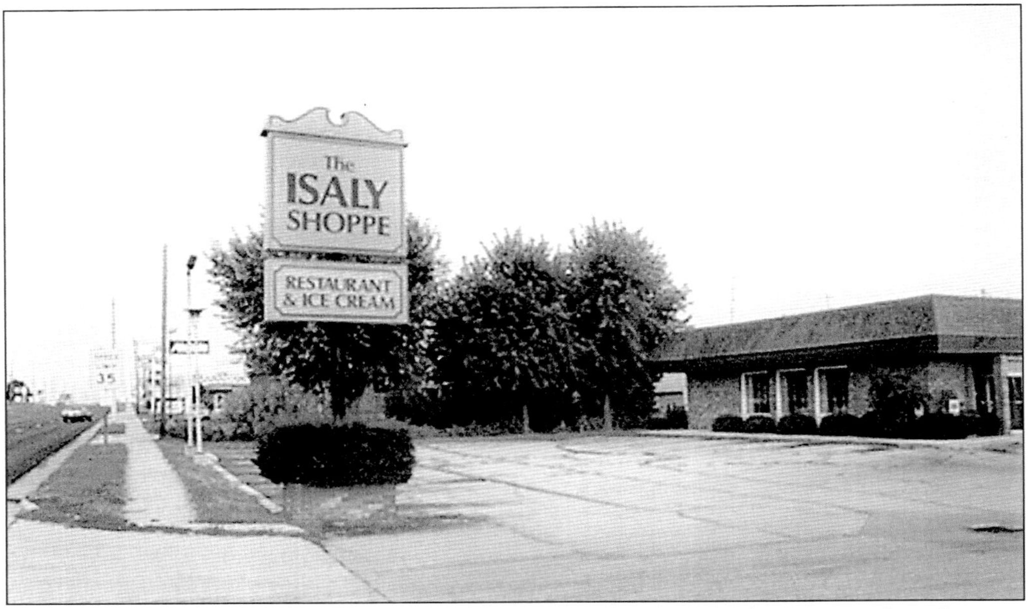

THE ISALY SHOPPE, MT. VERNON AVENUE. In the late 1960s, Isaly's was winding down as a dairy, the victim of the economy and changing consumer preferences. In 1969, The Isaly Shoppe restaurant opened on Mt. Vernon Avenue and was managed by John Isaly. The Isaly Shoppe offered a wide variety of menu items at affordable prices—and ice cream, of course. Immediately popular, and fondly remembered, the Isaly Shoppe continued to be a success until it closed in the 1990s. (Photograph courtesy of Brian Butko, author of *Klondikes, Chipped Ham, & Skyscraper Cones.*)

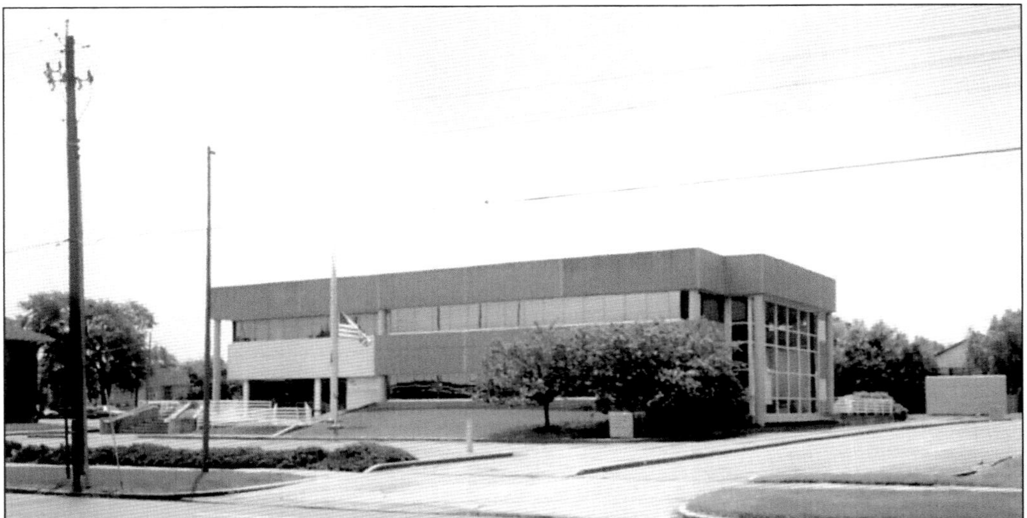

OHIO AMERICAN WATER COMPANY, EAST CENTER STREET. Closed in 1970, the Isaly Dairy plant sat empty for well over a decade before the Ohio American Water Company purchased the site. The art moderne façade was removed from the building, revealing a sound inner structure of steel reinforced concrete, which was then incorporated into a new design by Burris and Behne Architects. (Photograph courtesy of the author.)

Seven

Crystal Lake

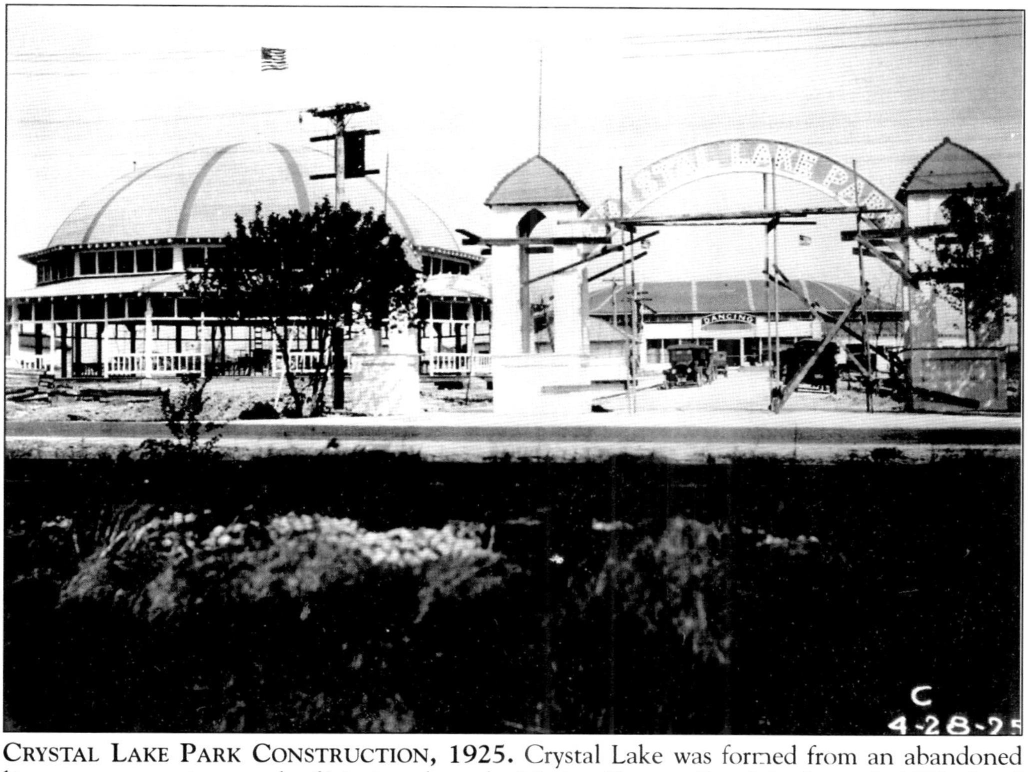

Crystal Lake Park Construction, 1925. Crystal Lake was formed from an abandoned limestone quarry just north of Marion along the Marion-Bucyrus Road. In the early 1920s, local businessmen seized upon the idea of building an amusement park next to the popular swimming spot. Construction of the amusement park began late in 1924 when local businessmen broke ground for what would be Marion County's first (and only) amusement park. (Photograph courtesy of Hughes Photography, John Rall, president.)

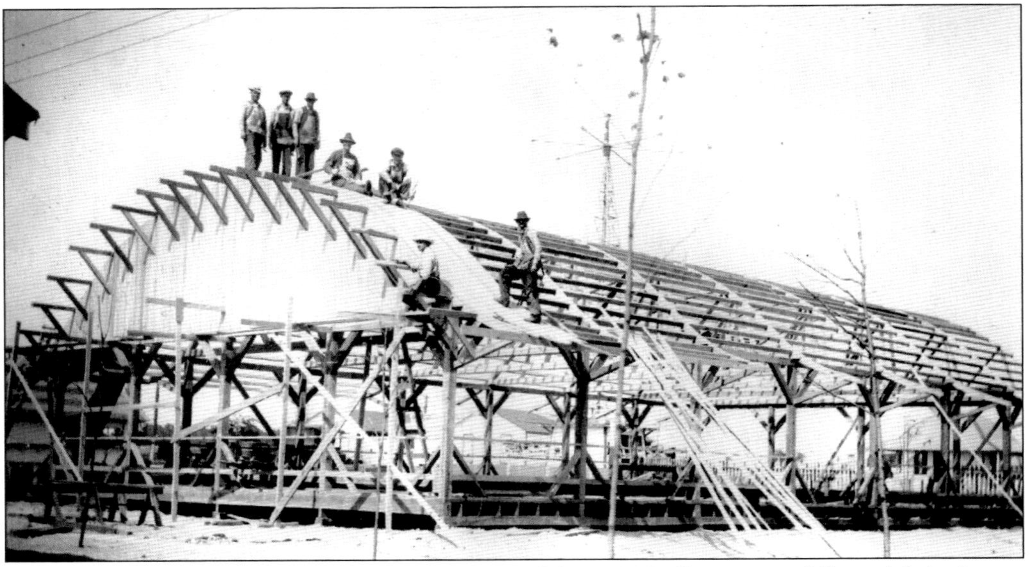

CONSTRUCTION OF "THE SKOOTER" PAVILION, MAY 1925. Operators of Crystal Lake began construction of the park attractions and shelters in 1924 and completed the first phase in 1925. Phase I included "The Skooter" and "Dutch Mill Ride." Later, Crystal Pavilion and Amusement Company of Marion was officially incorporated on January 23, 1926, with Charles King, Asa Queen, A.E. Probst, Fred Scherff, and John T. Canfield as the majority stock holders. (Photograph courtesy of Hughes Photography, John Rall, president.)

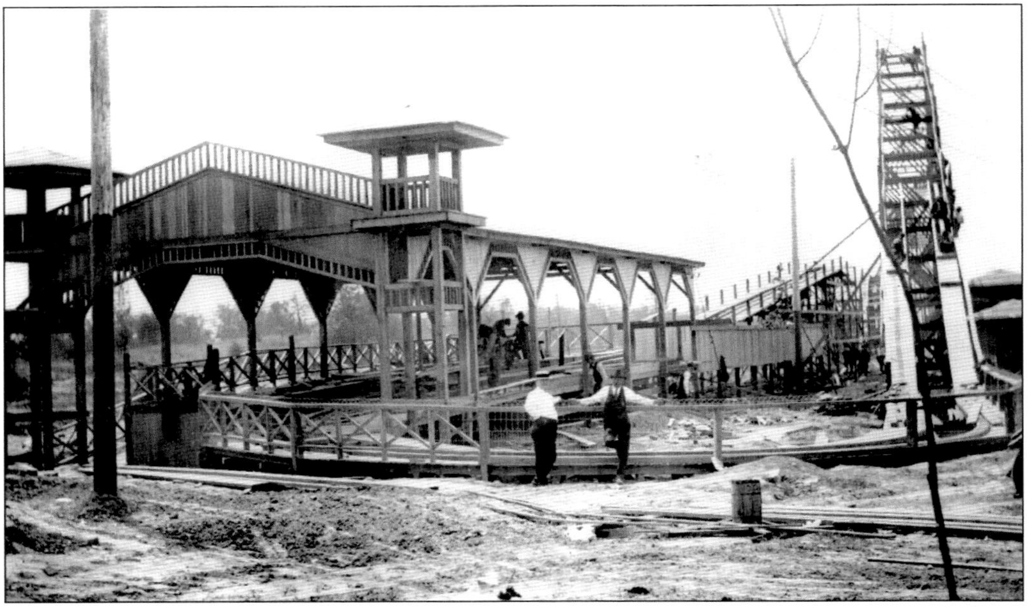

CONSTRUCTION OF "THE ZIP" AND CAR BARN, 1925. Unlike other amusement parks in small town Ohio that were built by interurban companies, Crystal Lake was built by private owners who formed their own company. Construction of high profile rides such as The Zip were intended to be trump cards to draw crowds to the park. (Photograph courtesy of Hughes Photography, John Rall, president.)

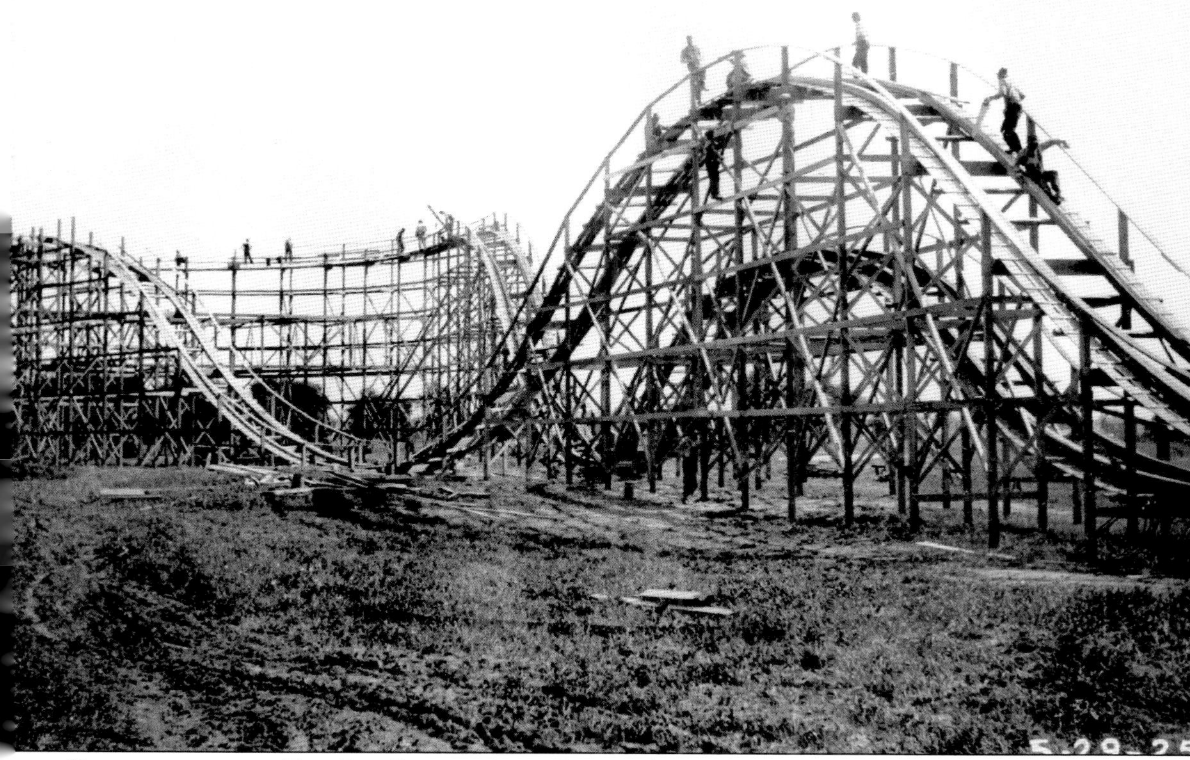

CONSTRUCTION OF THE ZIP, CRYSTAL LAKE PARK. The single most costly ride built at Crystal Lake Park was its rollercoaster, The Zip, which cost park operators $60,000. The Zip featured a 65-foot drop and a track length of 2,500 feet. Construction of the whip was overseen by Joseph Drambour of New York, who also designed the "Thunderbolt," originally built for the 1939 New York's Worlds Fair. The Thunderbolt, a descendent of The Zip, was later reassembled and is now operating at Six Flags New England. (Photograph courtesy of Hughes Photography, John Rall, president.)

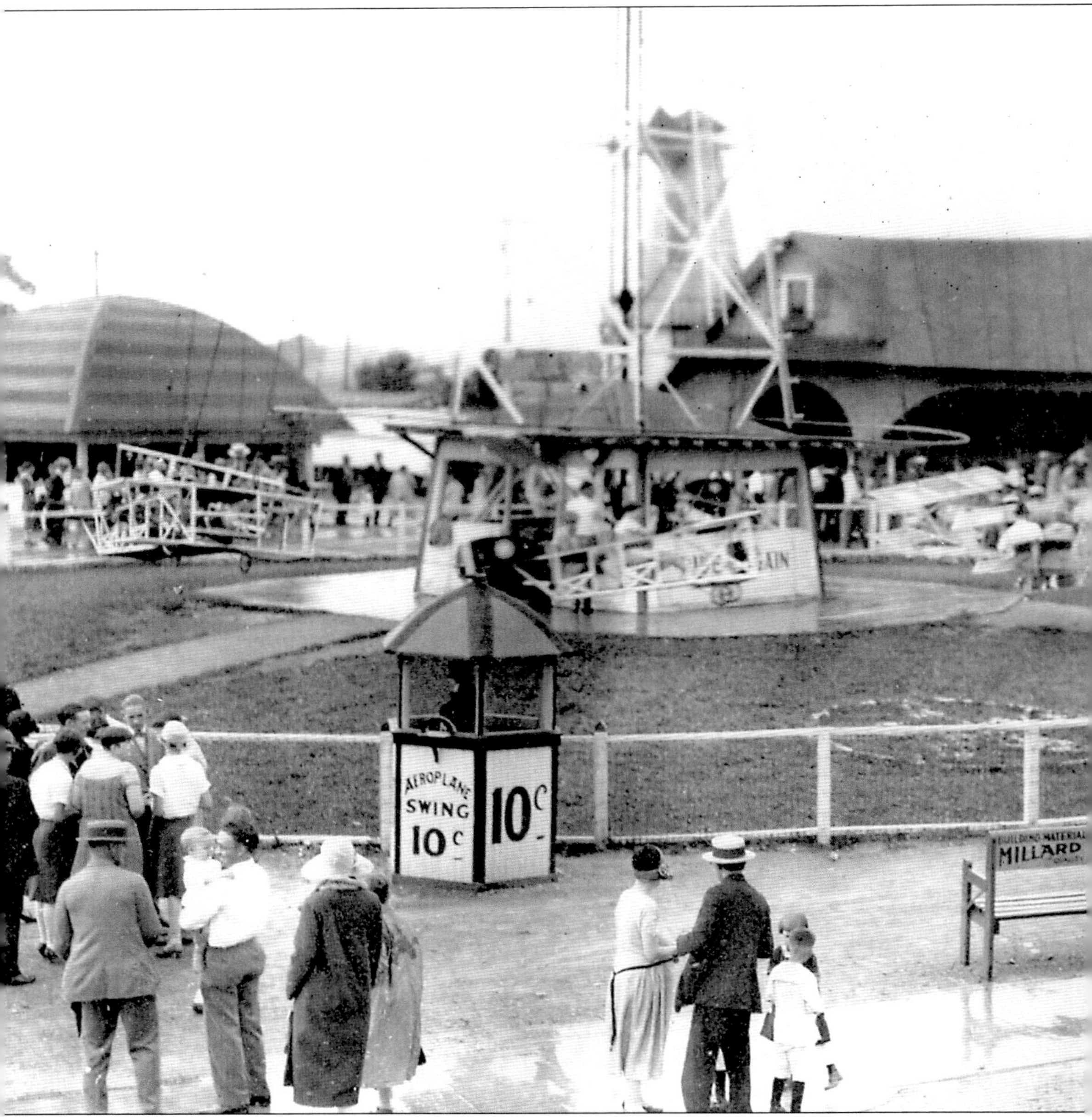

AEROPLANE SWING, CRYSTAL LAKE PARK, 1926. Crystal Lake Park's tallest structure was the metal tower constructed for the adult "Aeroplane Swing" ride on the park. For a then lofty sum of 10¢, riders "flew" in a 120-foot circle around the 70-foot tower while seated in one of six bi-plane styled gondolas. (Photograph courtesy of Hughes Photography, John Rall, president.)

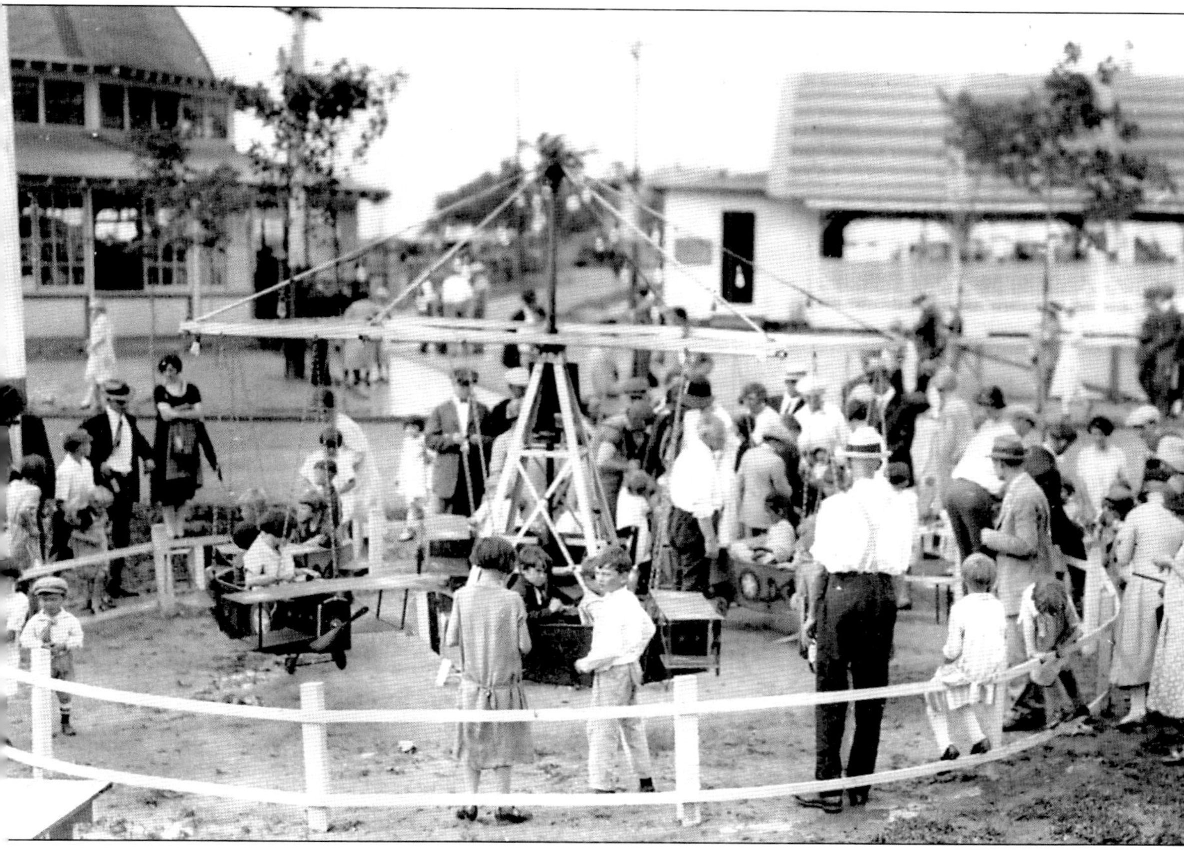

Children's Aeroplane Ride, Crystal Lake Park, 1925. Kiddies attending the park had a chance to ride their own pint-sized aeroplanes at Crystal Lake when this children's ride opened up. (Photograph courtesy of Hughes Photography, John Rall, president.)

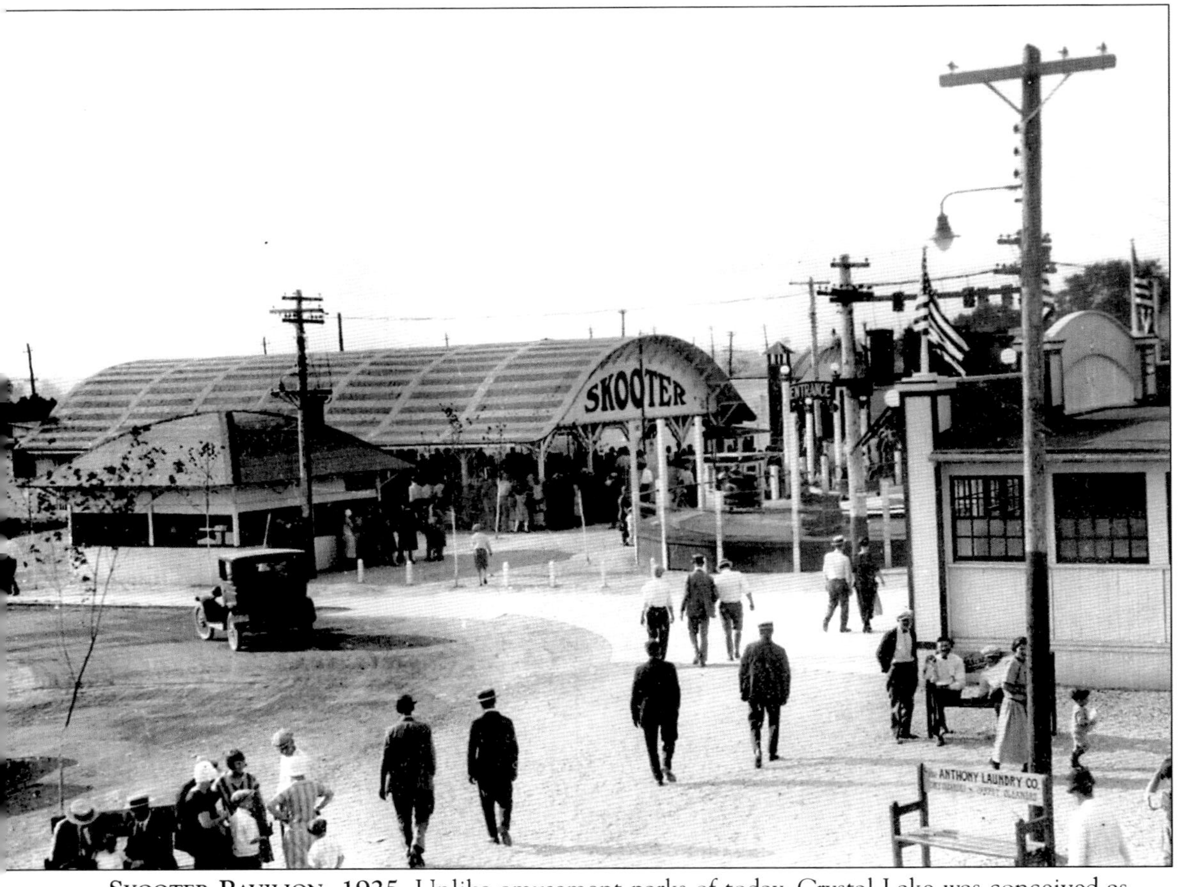

SKOOTER PAVILION, 1925. Unlike amusement parks of today, Crystal Lake was conceived as an open air park, with tickets sold only for rides that patrons wanted. The park also boasted one of the largest Merry-Go-Rounds in the State of Ohio. (Photograph courtesy of Hughes Photography, John Rall, president.)

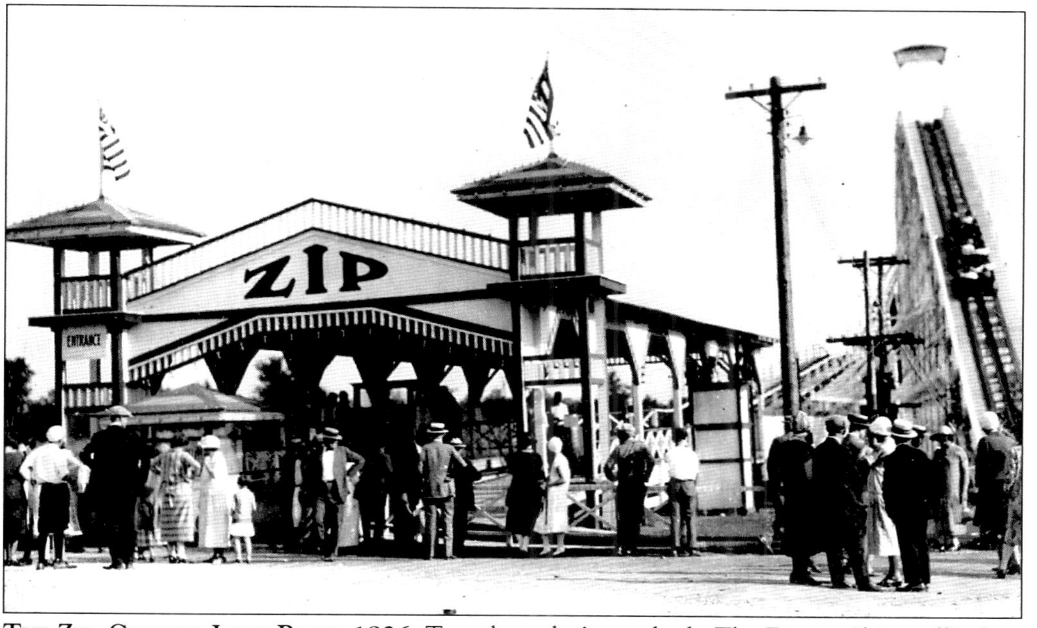

THE ZIP, CRYSTAL LAKE PARK, 1926. Tame by today's standards, The Zip was "big stuff" when it opened in May 1925. Opening day attendance was 4,000 people. Lines for the ride were long, even at the high price of 10¢ a trip. With the collapse of the Crystal Lake Corporation following the stock market crash of 1929, The Zip and the other rides were dismantled and sold to other park operators. (Photograph courtesy of Hughes Photography, John Rall, president.)

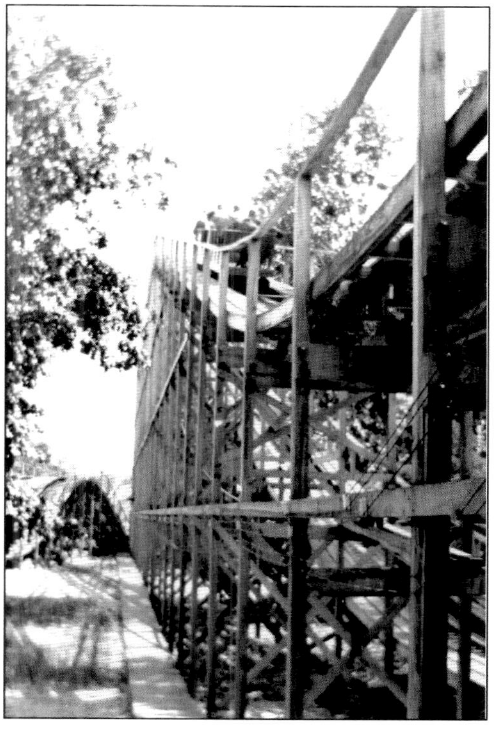

CRYSTAL LAKE'S ZIP COASTER. This image shows one of The Zip's coaster cars en route from the bottom of the first hill. Rides at this time didn't have the stringent security systems in place today. Unfortunately, The Zip recorded its first fatality within a month of its opening when a rider from Mansfield was thrown from her seat and suffered massive head trauma. (Photograph courtesy of Hughes Photography, John Rall, president.)

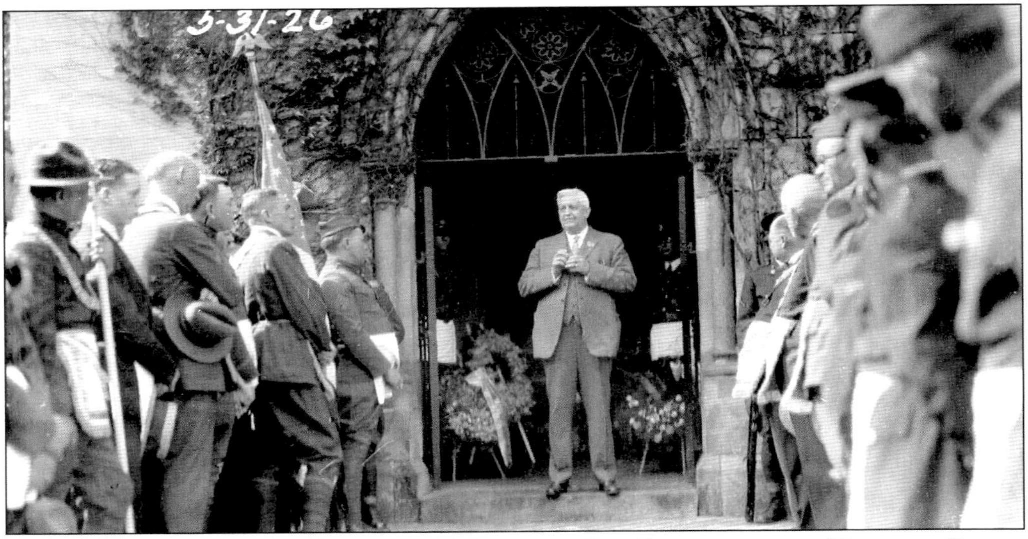

The Reverend Jesse Swank Leads a Memorial Day Service at the Harding Crypt. Serving Marion's Methodist community from 1915 to 1926, the Reverend Jesse Swank was also involved in numerous community wide organizations. Dr. Swank led a majority coalition of churches in Marion that attempted to ban dancing, rides, and swimming at Crystal Lake on Sundays during the mid 1920s. The ministers were dealt a blow when the courts ruled in favor of the fun seekers; however, young women were banned from wearing their bathing suits on Marion's street car lines. (Photograph courtesy of the author.)

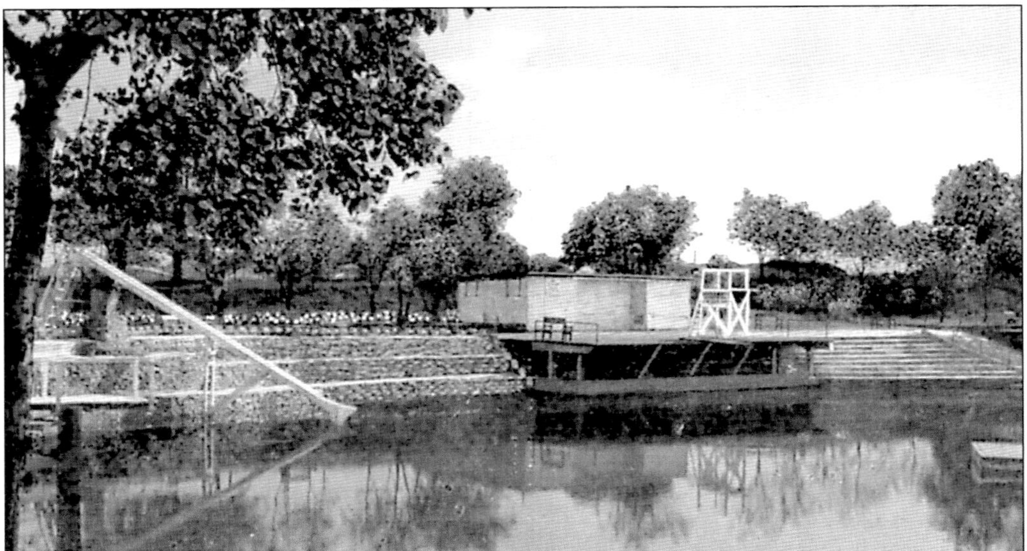

Crystal Lake Swimming Pool. Following the liquidation of Crystal Lake's amusement business, the park continued to operate the swimming pool and the massive Crystal Lake Pavilion, which operated as a dance hall, a roller skating rink, and finally housed Bargain City Department Store from 1958 to 1968. Eventually, swimming at Crystal Lake was suspended when water levels dropped to unsafe levels. The final link to Crystal Lake, the abandoned Pavilion, originally designed to accommodate 1,000 dancers, burned to the ground in June 1975. (Photograph courtesy of Robert Turner.)

Eight

BUILDING ETOWAH, PLACE OF THE SUMAC

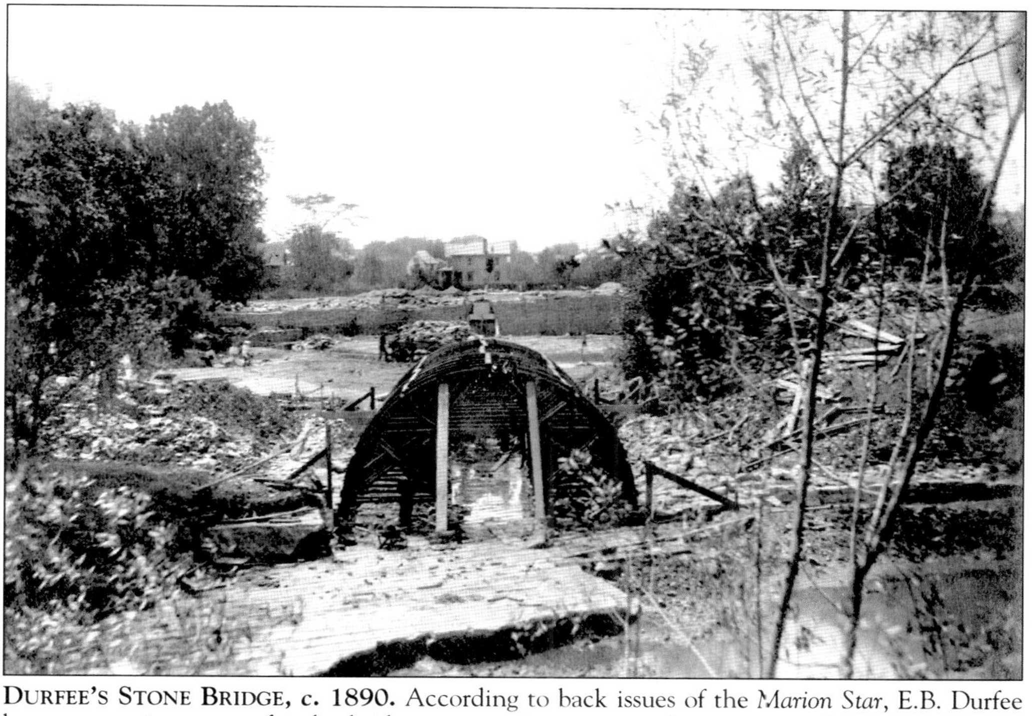

DURFEE'S STONE BRIDGE, c. 1890. According to back issues of the *Marion Star*, E.B. Durfee began quarrying stones for the bridge construction seen in this image on South Greenwood Street. Durfee's limestone quarry was east of this bridge; to the bridge's west was LaFayette Lake. This view is looking west from Durfee's property toward the first few new homes opened in the tony Lafayette subdivision. (Photograph courtesy of the Marion County Historical Society.)

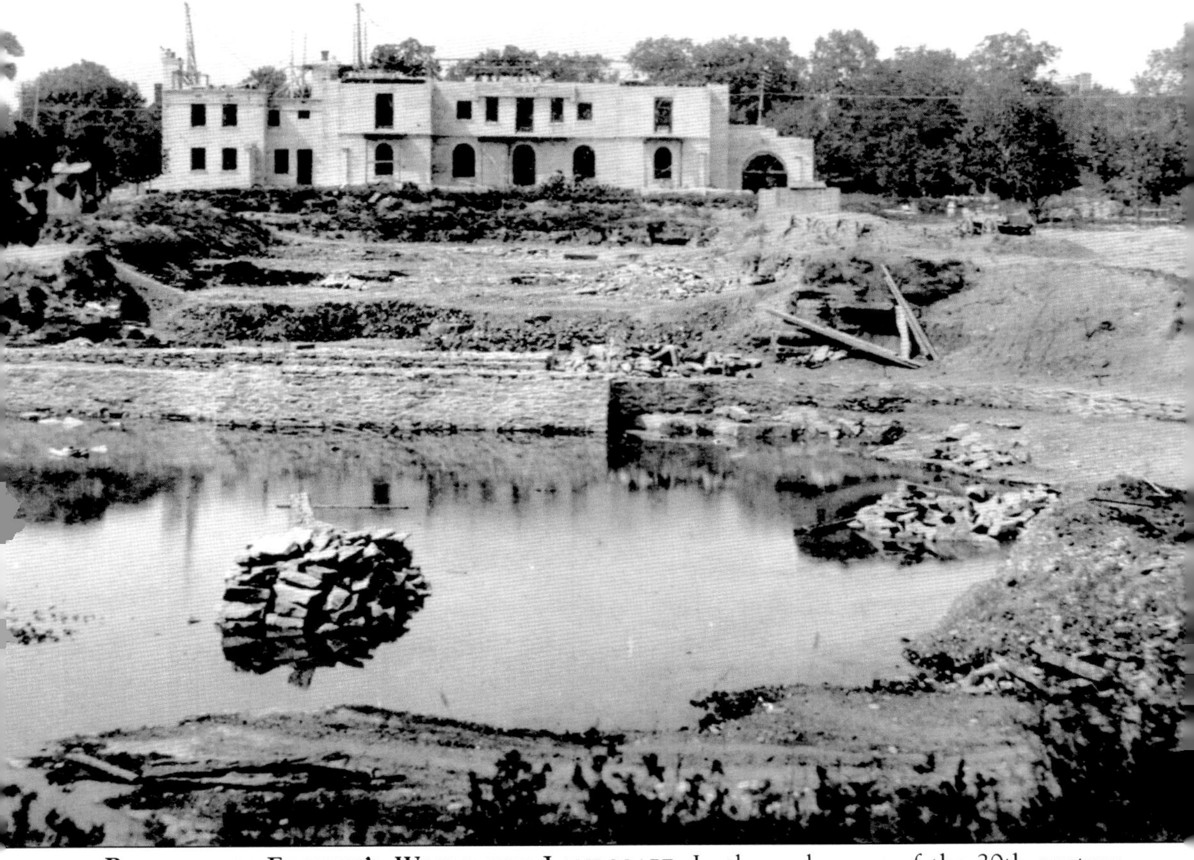

BUILDING OF ETOWAH'S WALLS AND LANDSCAPE. In the early years of the 20th century, Mr. and Mrs. George W. King decided to build a new home overlooking what was locally known as LaFayette Lake. Retaining the services of a Philadelphia based architect, the King's sought to build a house that would be at once their home and also an elegant symbol of what could be realized through hard work and innovation. The result was named Etowah, or "Place of the Sumac."

An early construction photograph from the building and landscaping of Etowah shows the building of the residence's external walls. Also visible are the cranes used to lift the cut limestone blocks and other materials to the second-floor construction areas. The landscape down to the lake is also beginning to take shape as terraces were graded down to the water's edge. (Photograph courtesy of the Marion County Historical Society.)

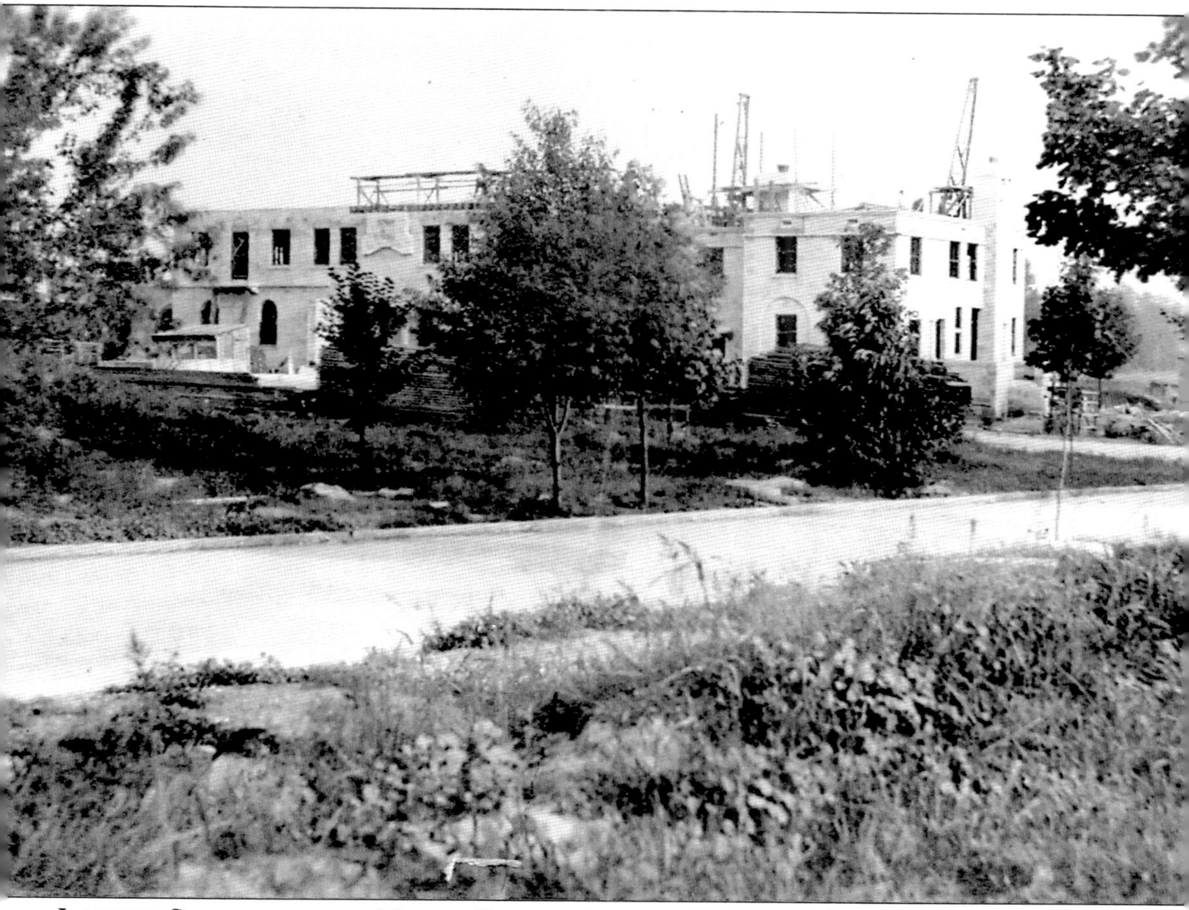

LOOKING SOUTHEAST FROM MOUNT VERNON AVENUE. This image shows the scaffolding in place for work on the home's street (north) façade. The architect hired by the Kings achieved a design that, through its simplicity, kept the house from overwhelming visitors. Avoiding a heavy hand, subtle design features were wisely placed throughout the design, instead of "gilding the lily," as they said back then. (Photograph courtesy of the Marion County Historical Society.)

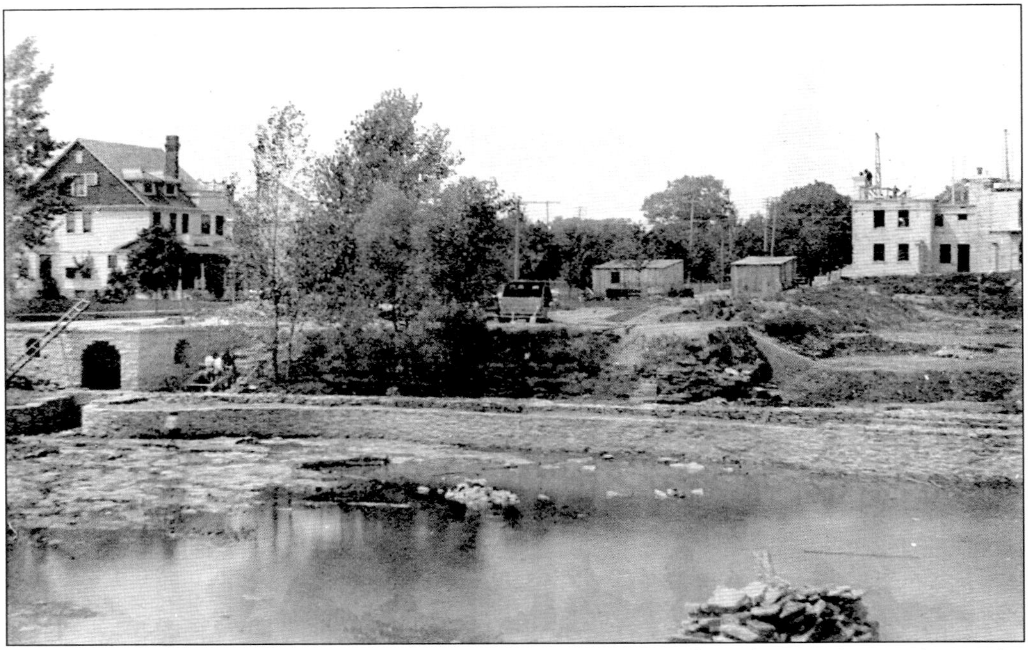

CONSTRUCTION AND LANDSCAPE WORK. This view towards Lafayette Street shows the construction shacks as well as the elaborate stone work that went into the landscape along the western edge of the property. By opening the vista across the lake, the Kings graciously shared what could otherwise have been hidden behind stone walls. (Photograph courtesy of the Marion County Historical Society.)

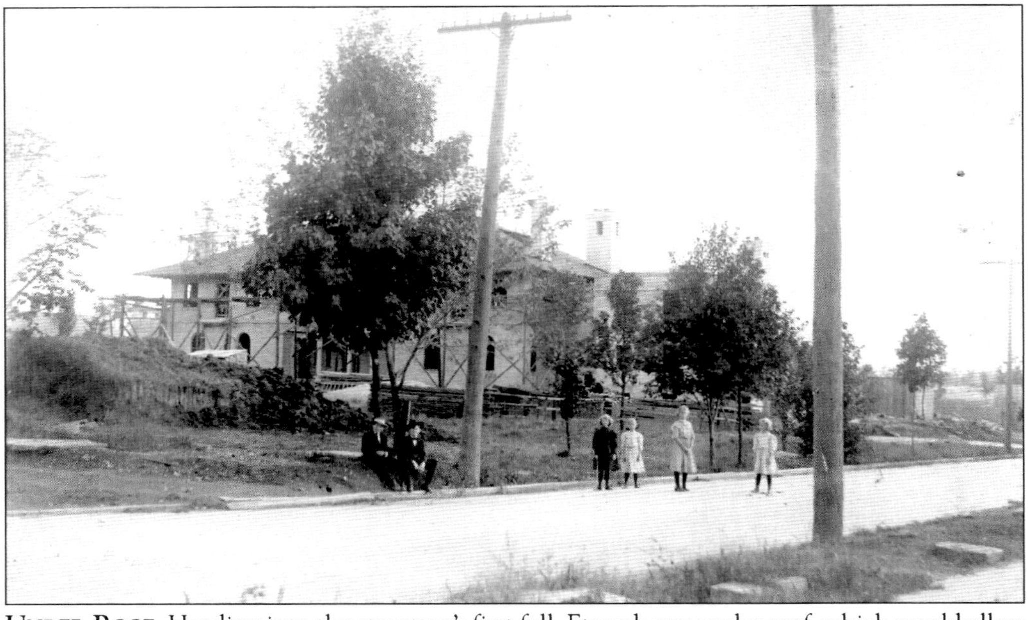

UNDER ROOF. Heading into the structure's first fall, Etowah was under roof, which would allow work to continue throughout the approaching winter. (Photograph courtesy of the Marion County Historical Society.)

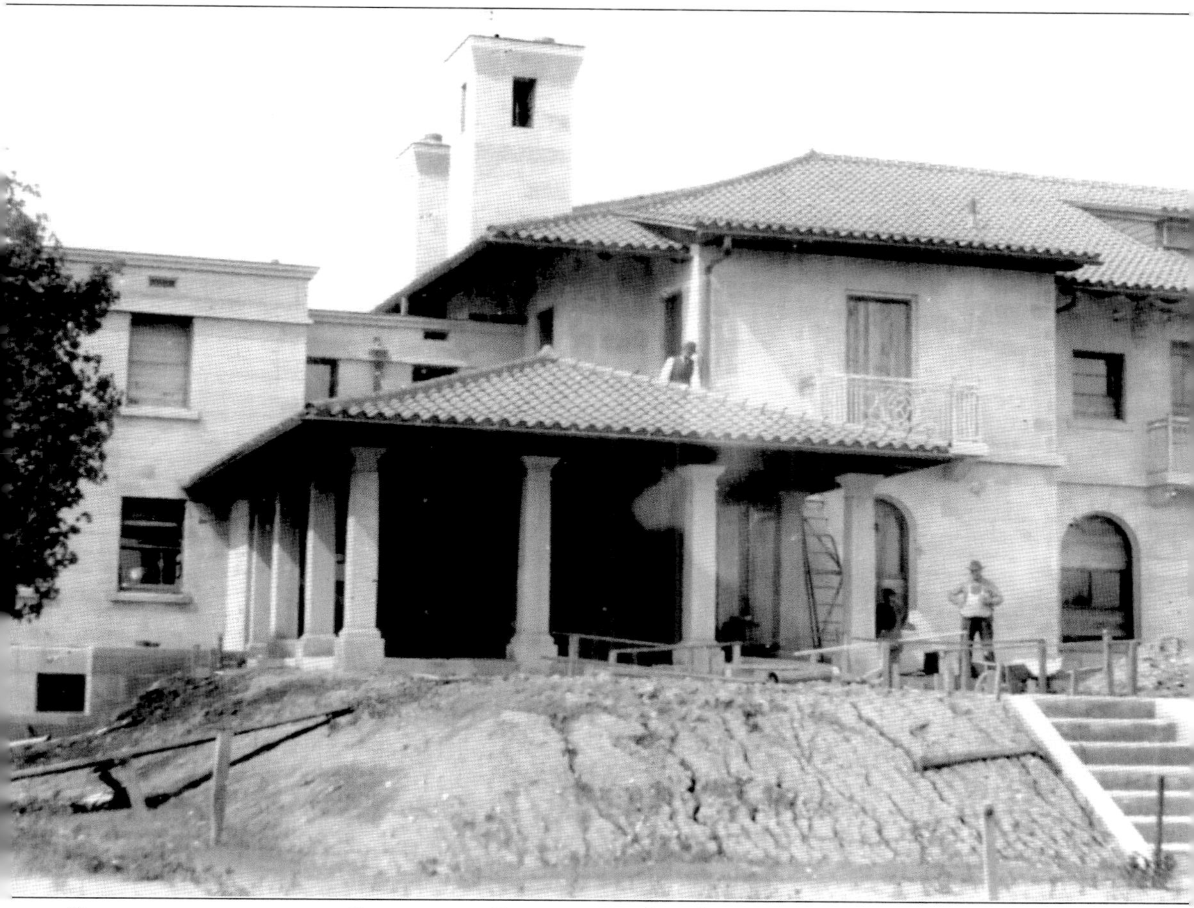

CONSTRUCTION OF THE SOUTHWEST LOGGIA. Work is being completed on the southwest loggia, overlooking the lake, and the outer walls were nearing completion when this picture was taken. However, windows for the house had yet to be installed. Decorative ironwork railings for the second-story windows featured a prominent "K" in the center of the design. This image also provides a glimpse of the "garland of plenty" carved in the stone façade, just under the eaves. (Photograph courtesy of the Marion County Historical Society.)

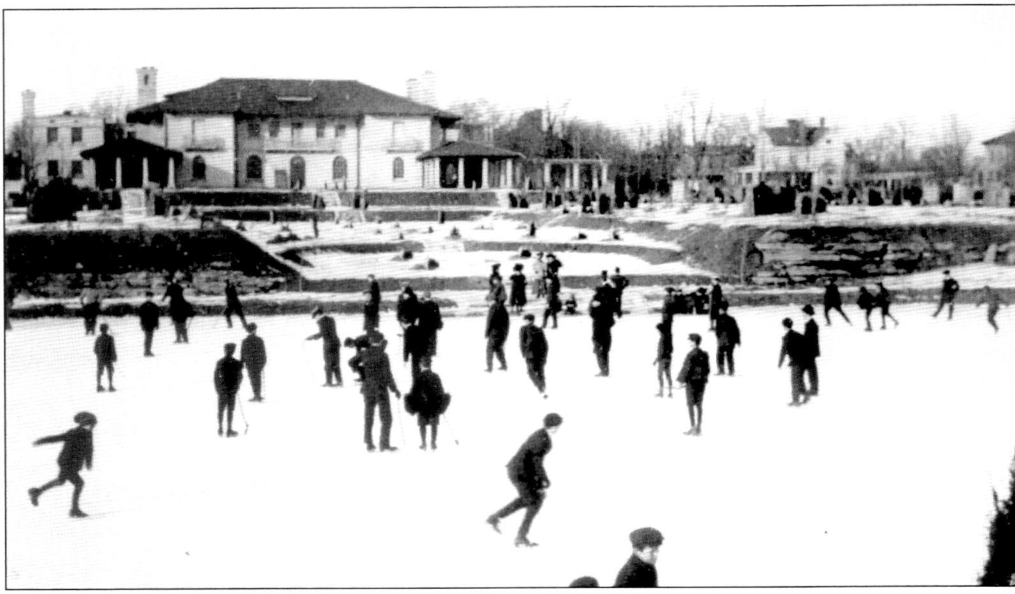

SKATING ON ETOWAH'S LAKE. Winter skating in Marion brought city residents to one of two sites, McKinley Park or to Etowah's Lake. The depth of Etowah's Lakes helped the lake freeze early and freeze hard. Skating on Etowah's Lake continued until 1924, when damage to bedrock under the lake and Durfee's Quarry resulted in the draining of both bodies of water. The white house in the background was the home of the Oswald Wollenweber family. (Photograph courtesy of the author.)

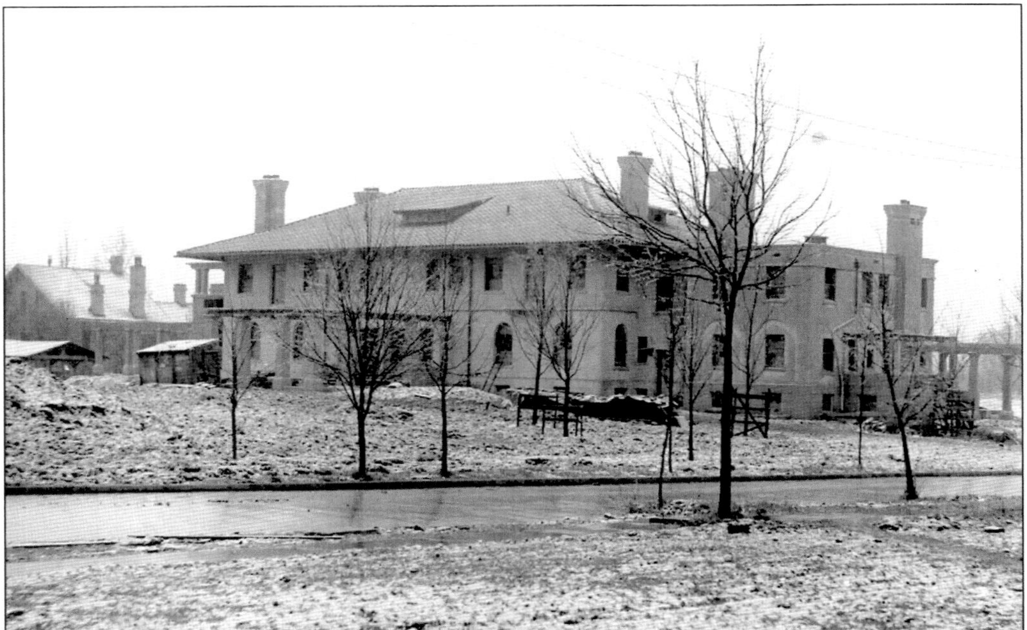

ETOWAH'S NORTH FAÇADE AND BLUESTONE MANOR. This photograph shows Bluestone Manor, located east of Etowah. (Photograph courtesy of the Marion County Historical Society.)

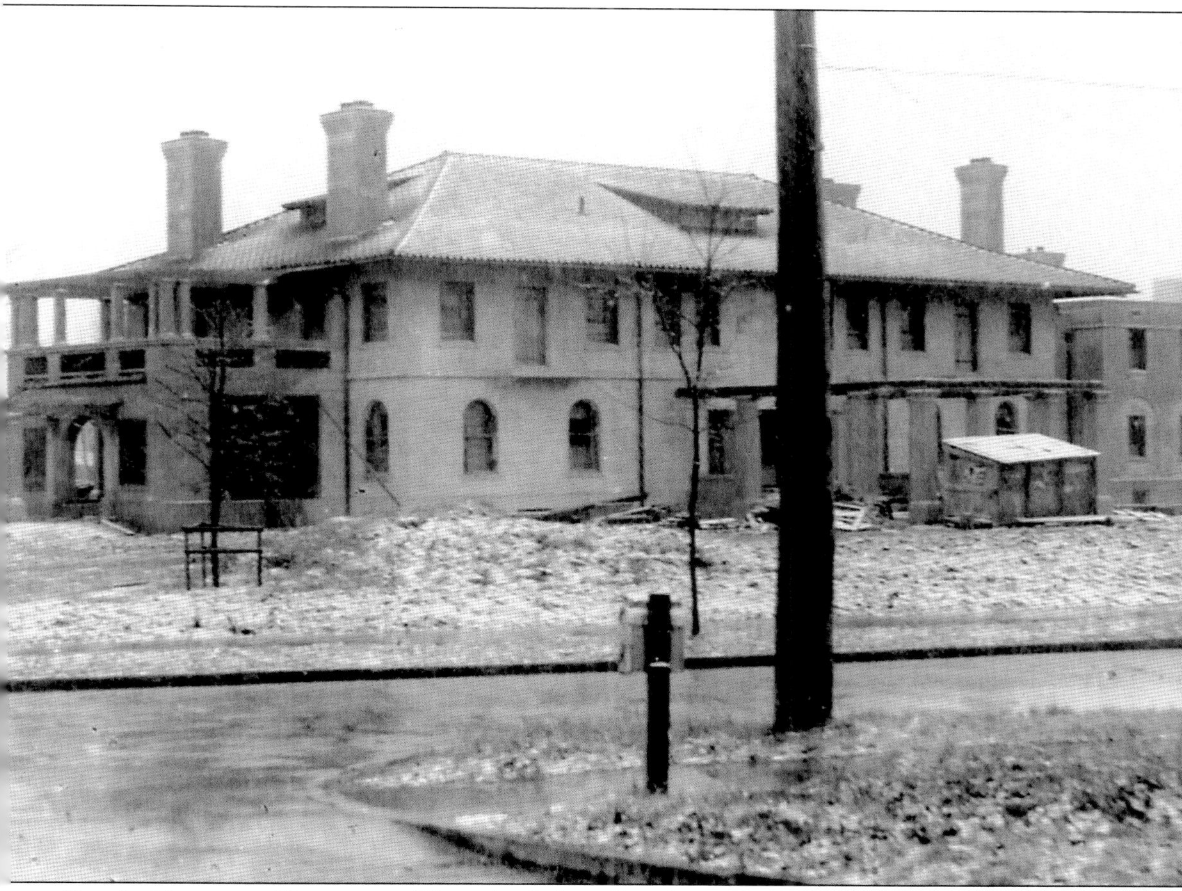

KING'S MANSION. This view of Etowah while still under construction shows the residence's original asymmetrical design. Following the death of Mrs. King, the house was divided, allowing both of the King's children and their families to live at Etowah. Ray King and his family occupied the west half of Etowah, while his sister Ava King Brown and her family occupied the east half, following additional construction to the east façade. (Photograph courtesy of the Marion County Historical Society.)

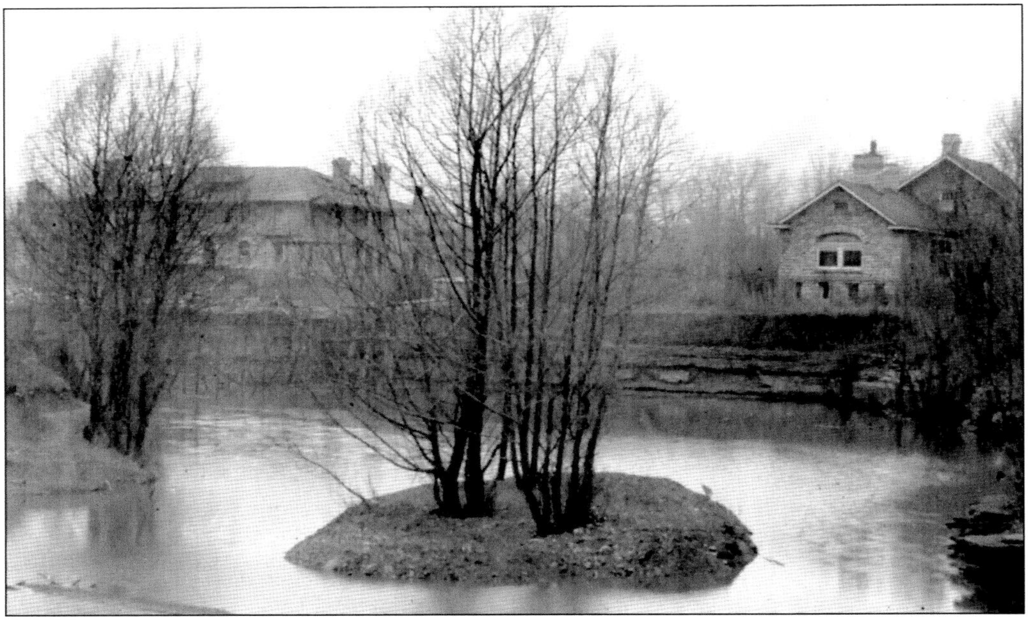

Brightwood Lake and Blue Stone Manor. Located east of Etowah, Blue Stone Manor is located on the southeast corner of Mt. Vernon Avenue and South Greenwood Street. The house derives its name from the blue-hued limestone first quarried on the property by Nathan Peters. Under the ownership of Mr. Brightman Durfee, the quarry was developed as Brightwood Lake, which fed into Etowah's Lake under the stone bridge on Greenwood Street. (Photograph courtesy of Carroll Neidhart.)

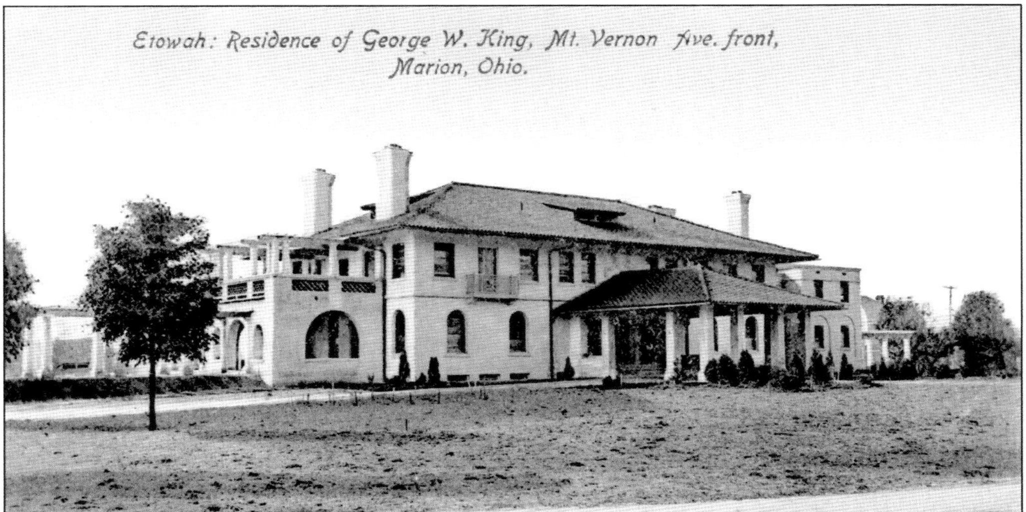

Picture Perfect, but Still Without Windows. In the early 1900s, picture postcards were all the rage. G.C. Wiant Bookseller and Stationers anxiously added the still yet unfinished King mansion to its line of Marion postcards. This postcard shows one of the more popular views of the era, showing the house far from finished with wooden boards covering the window openings, which still lacked installed windows. (Postcard courtesy of the author.)

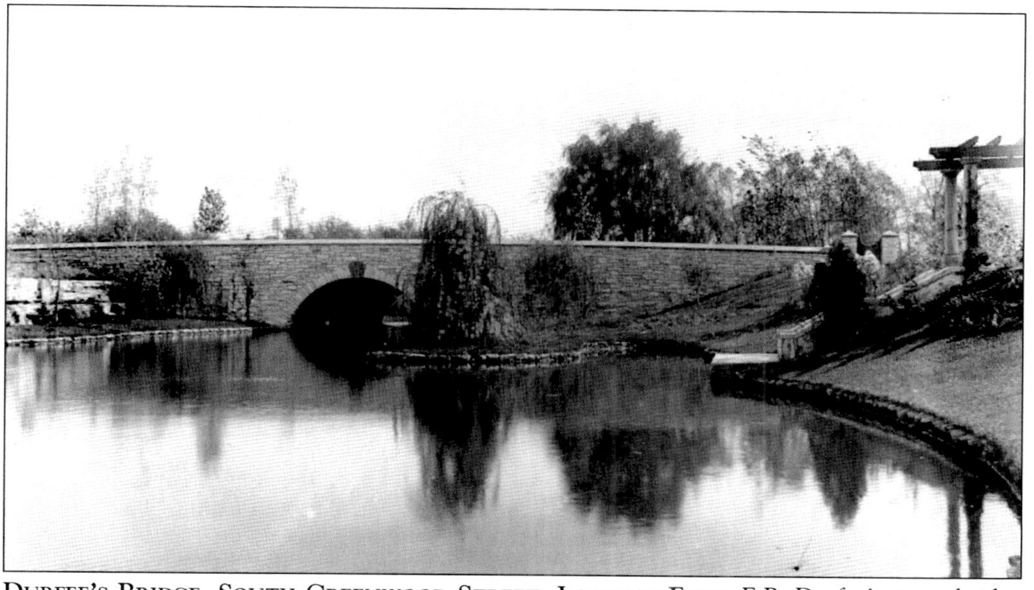

Durfee's Bridge, South Greenwood Street, Looking East. E.B. Durfee's stone bridge easily became a part of Etowah's landscape as the building project neared its end. It was possible to pass under the bridge, to move from one body of water to another, provided the boaters could duck low enough to clear the bridge's arch. To the right is the south pergola of Etowah's garden. (Postcard courtesy of the Marion County Historical Society.)

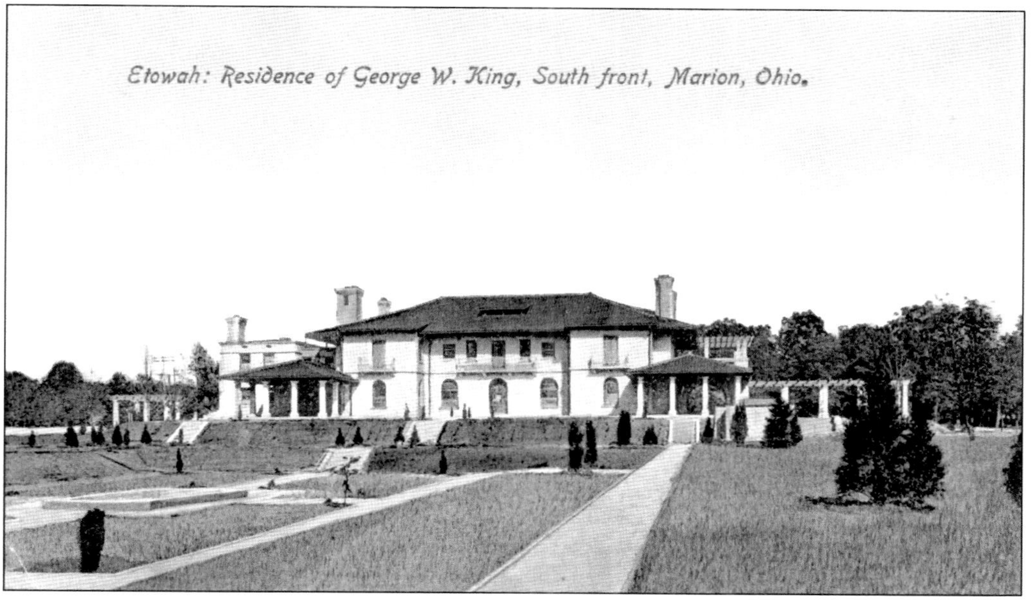

Etowah's South Lawn. Another of G.C. Wiant's postcards illustrated the dramatic terracing of Etowah's lawns near the lake. Postcard sellers like Wiant utilized printers in Germany to obtain vivid color, which was often applied by hand. Wiant would ship the photograph to Germany with instructions as to what color was placed in different areas, the instructions were translated, and the finished postcards would be shipped back to Wiant. (Image courtesy of the Marion County Historical Society.)

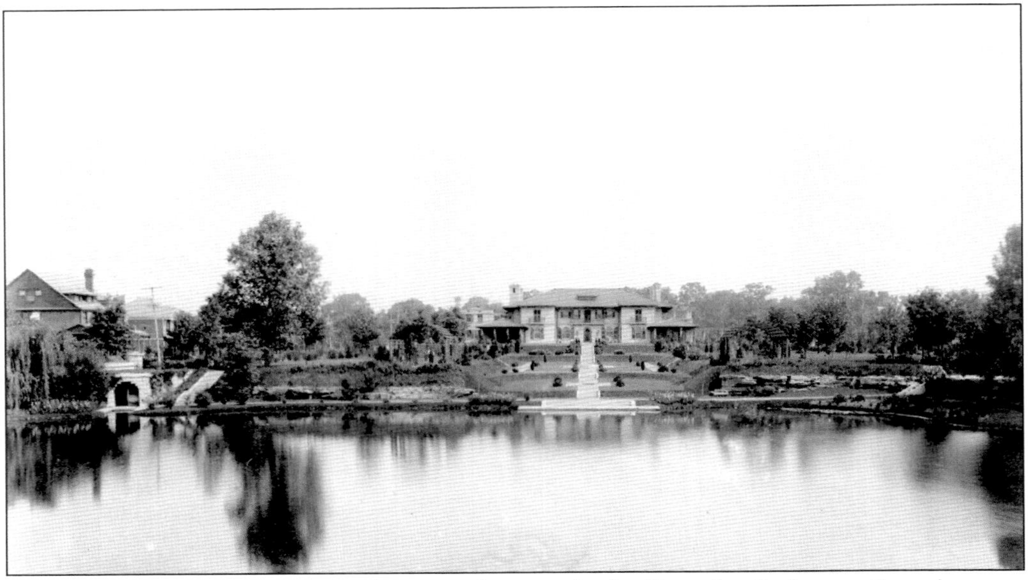

ETOWAH'S SOUTH FAÇADE. Looking north towards the King family home, Etowah was a majestic sight. According to Carroll Niedhart, when the house was finished, an evening party was thrown to celebrate; guests arrived at the south Pergola, the furthest point from the house, boarded gondolas and were ferried to the north water gate where they were welcomed by their hosts. (Photograph courtesy of the Marion Historical Society.)

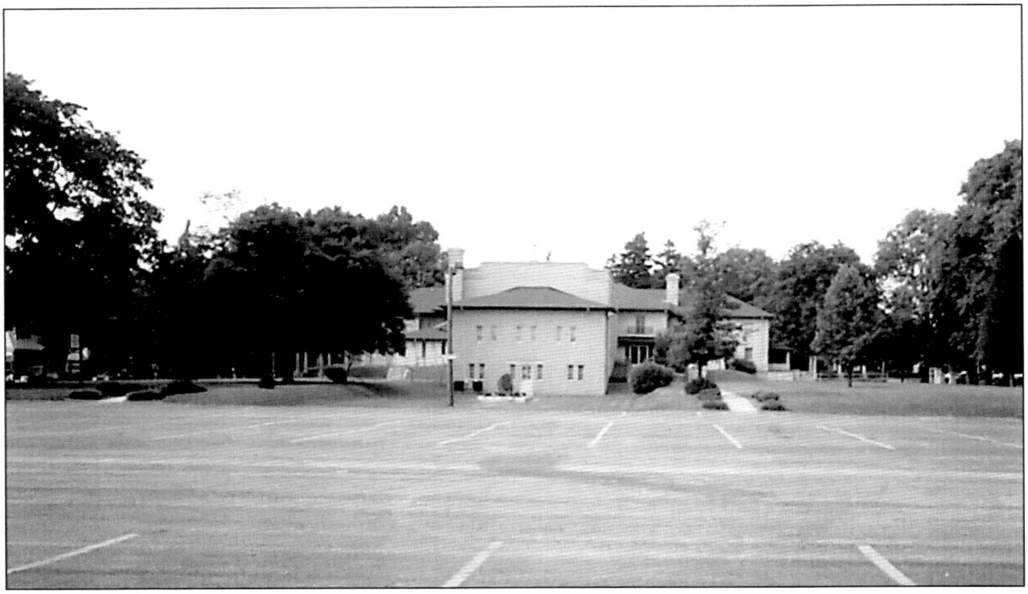

FORMER LAKE FAÇADE IN 2004. In 1947, Etowah was sold and became Central Christian Church; the families of Ray King and Ava King Brown were grateful that the estate found a new purpose and future. Etowah provided Central Christian's congregation with room to grow as its needs arose. When a larger sanctuary was needed, one was built at the rear of the property. Etowah's Lake, having long been dry, serves as the site for the church's parking lot. (Photograph courtesy of the author.)

Nine

This and That

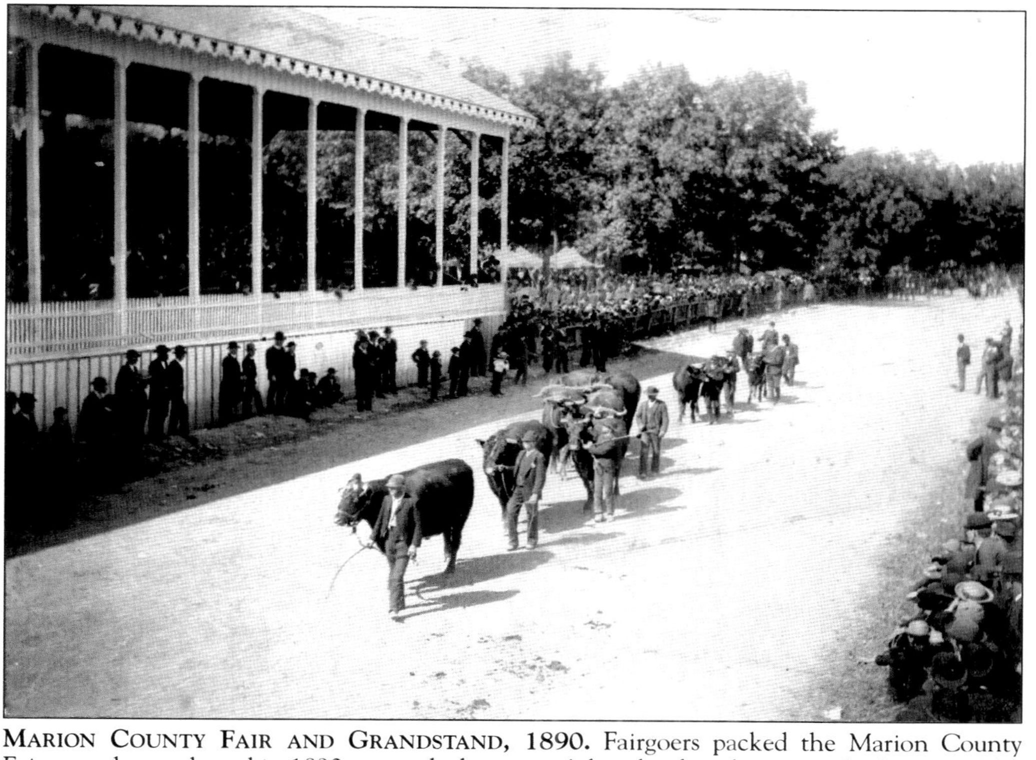

Marion County Fair and Grandstand, 1890. Fairgoers packed the Marion County Fairgrounds grandstand in 1890 to watch the county's best beef cattle on parade that year. The annual event, started in 1851, serves as a source of entertainment, as well as an exhibition of the newest ideas in farming and food production. The grandstand pictured above was replaced in 1917. (Photograph courtesy of the Marion County Historical Society.)

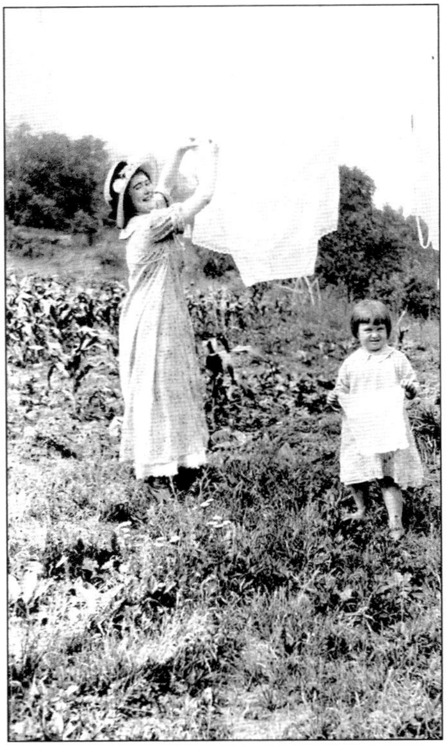

WASH DAY BLUES. Miss Agnes Davids (later, Mrs. Cecil Pugh), of Scott Township, cheerfully hangs clothes to dry in this image from 1913. In those days, water was drawn by pump and heated on the woodstove. Homemade soap made of animal fats and lye was added, and the clothes were washed by hand, or a metal plunger was used to manually agitate the clothes (if one could afford such a luxury). Once dry, the clothes were ironed using sad irons heated on the woodstove; if any stove blacking stuck to the bottom of the iron, the clothes had to be rewashed. Miss Davids had to go through this whole process, all the while keeping an eye on the children. Thus, her smile is a miracle, and it was a miracle she could smile! (Photograph courtesy of the author.)

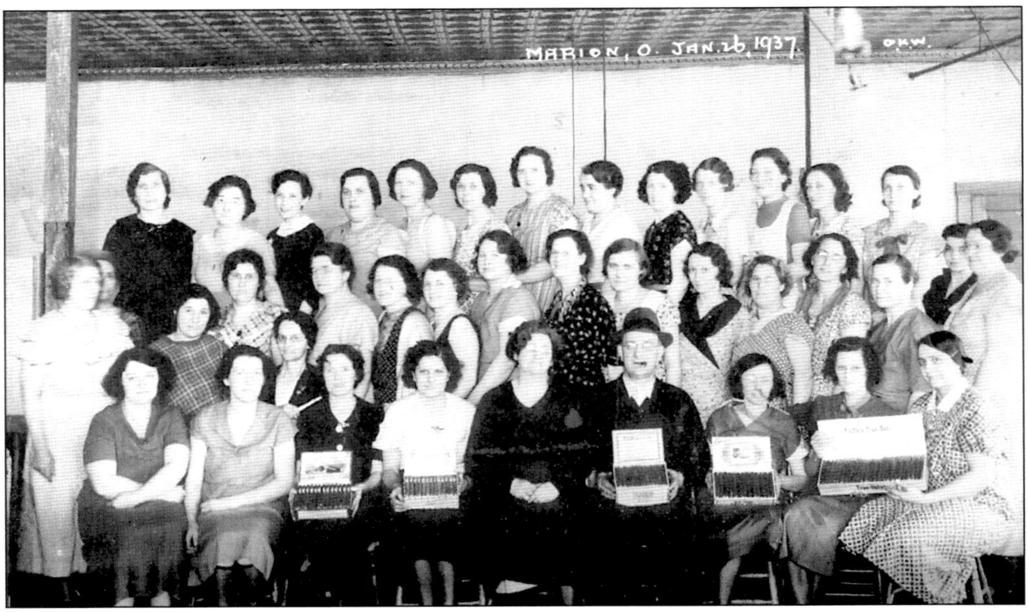

THE MARION CIGAR COMPANY, 1937. Started in 1927 on Blaine Avenue, the Marion Cigar Company moved its plant to North Main and George Street in 1932 in order to keep pace with sales. The company manufactured a variety of cigars including the San Berita, the Canon Baf, and the Josiah Peet labels. At its peek, the company employed over 65 employees. (Photograph courtesy of Hughes Photography, John Rall, president.)

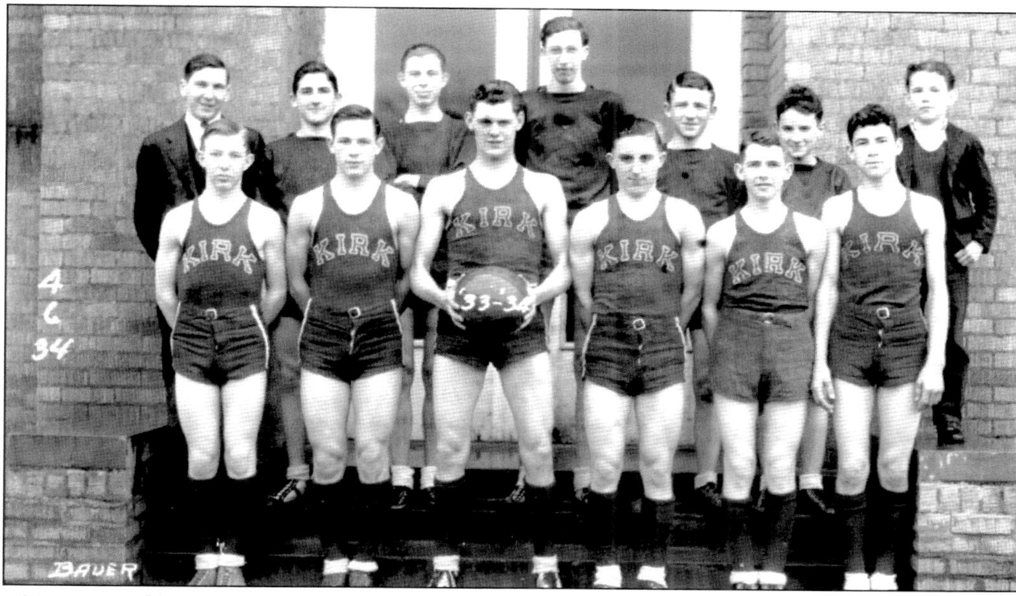

1933–1934 KIRKPATRICK MEN'S BASKETBALL TEAM, SCOTT TOWNSHIP. Consolidation of Marion County's one-room school houses began just prior to World War I. As a result, modern team sports were introduced into the new schools, pitting township against township in weekly games. Kirkpatrick fielded this team during the 1933–34 season: (front row, left to right) Cleo Grossman, Paul Monnette, Vernon Rowe, Harold Hart, Eldon Beers, and Ralph Hord; and (second row, left to right) Clyde Forry, Lloyd Hart, Harry Allen, Dallas Mason, Robert Hord, Don Baker, and Dean Baker. (Photograph courtesy of Marion County Historical Society.)

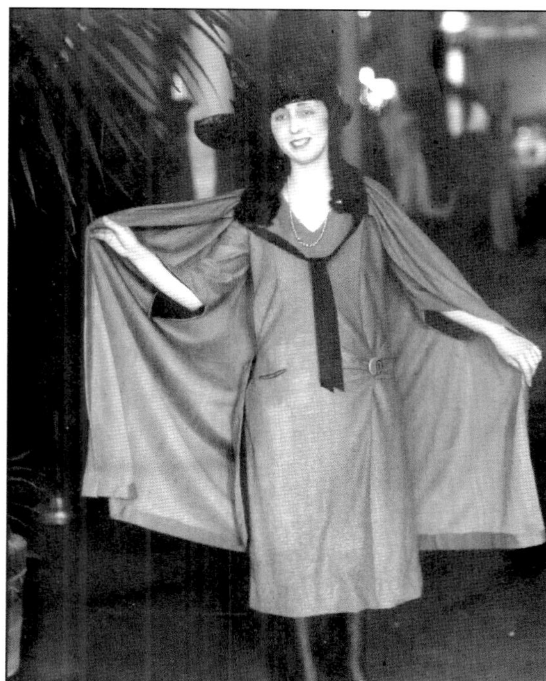

LATEST FASHIONS AT WARNER EDWARDS COMPANY. Located in the business block on West Church Street, the Warner Edwards Company competed with the Uhler Phillips and Frank Brothers' Department Stores until the 1930s. This image of Marionite Mildred Brenner Dayton was taken during one of the store's women's fashion shows in the early 1920s. The Warner Edwards block is best known to baby boomers as the longtime home of the Henney & Cooper Drug Store. (Photograph courtesy of the Marion County Historical Society.)

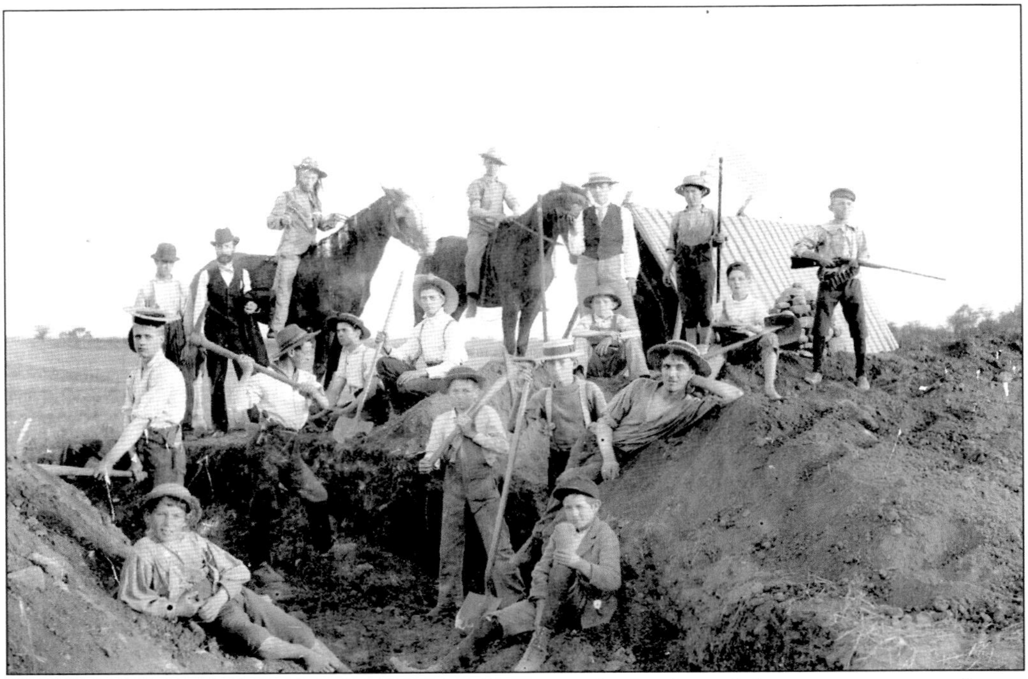

INDIAN MOUND DIG, SOUTHERN MARION COUNTY. Archeological digs were a source of great excitement throughout Ohio in the later part of the 19th century; and Marion County with its Indian Mounds, was no exception, as this image taken near Prospect in southern Marion County shows. Native American artifacts, such as arrow- and axe-heads continue to surface during plowing season. (Photograph courtesy of Marion County Historical Society.)

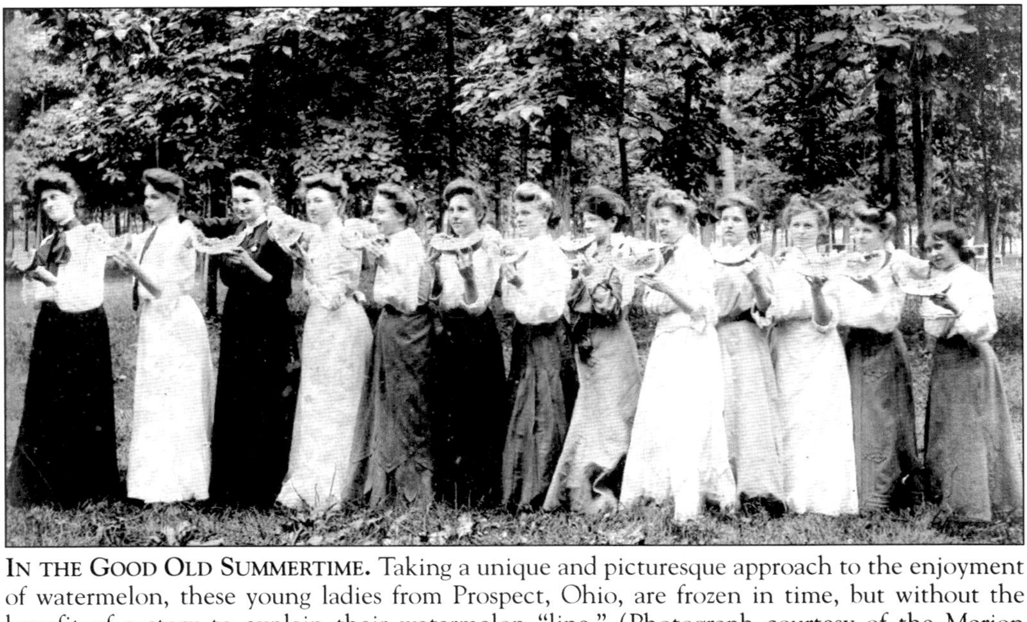

IN THE GOOD OLD SUMMERTIME. Taking a unique and picturesque approach to the enjoyment of watermelon, these young ladies from Prospect, Ohio, are frozen in time, but without the benefit of a story to explain their watermelon "line." (Photograph courtesy of the Marion County Historical Society.)

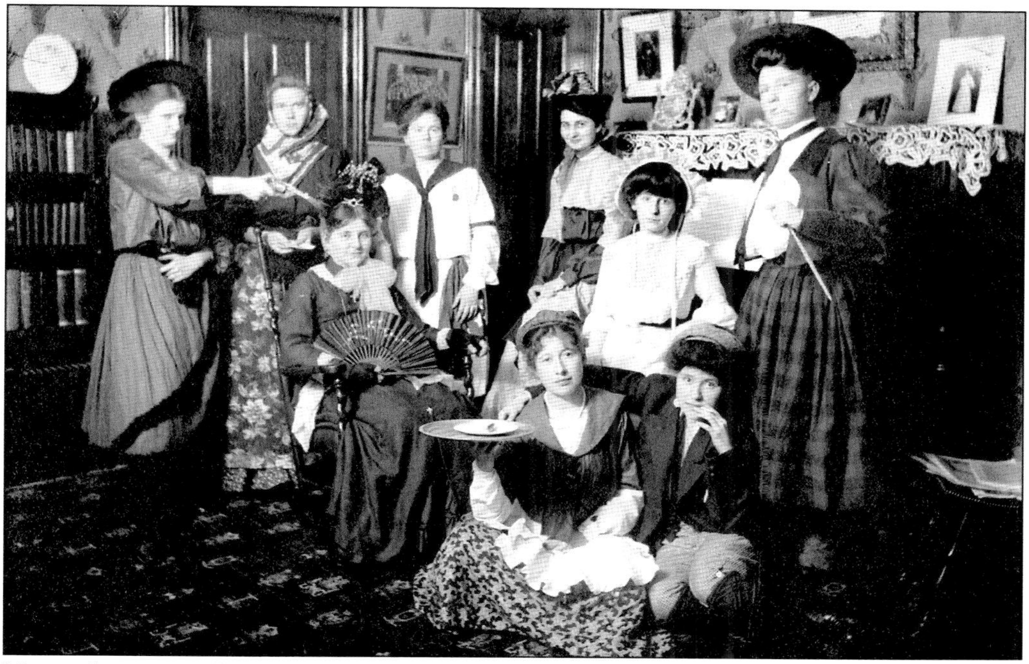

MERRY LADIES OF WINDSOR STREET, 1903. Miss Fahey T. Jones, sitting on the lower right, poses with her friends in this costumed tableau. The precise occasion is unknown, but there is foul play afoot! The young lady standing on the left seems to have been caught red-handed. It's too late to save the dowager. . . but Miss Jones beware—your victim has a friend standing behind you with an ice pick at the ready! (Photograph courtesy of Babette Dusang Jones.)

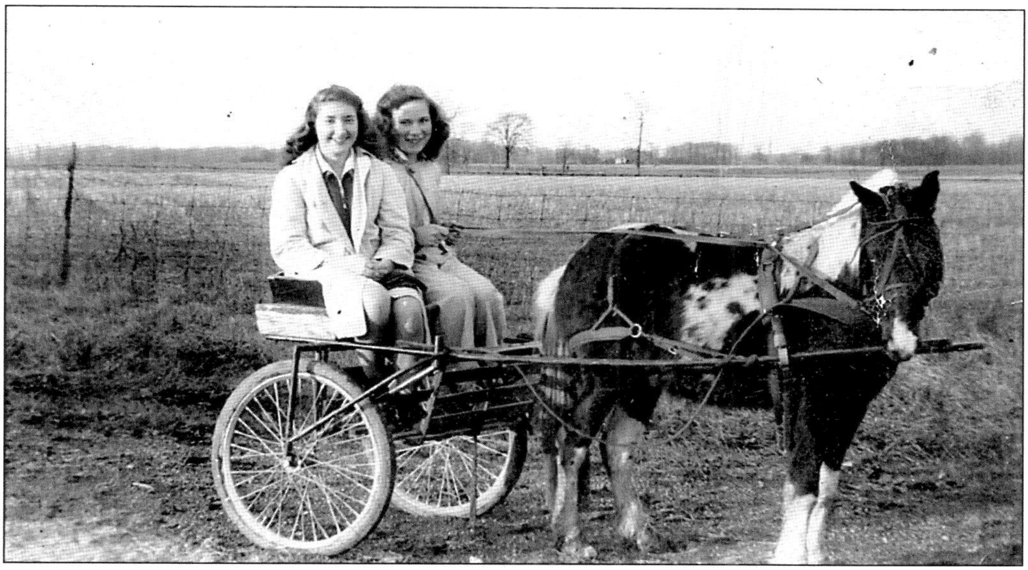

BERTHA JANE LEASE, LOUISE SPEECE, AND EDDY. Fuel rationing during World War II regulated automobile travel to necessary trips only. In 1945, when visiting friends and neighbors, Bertha Jane Lease and Louise Speece tooled around Scott Township in northern Marion County in their pony cart, pulled by Eddy. (Courtesy of the author.)

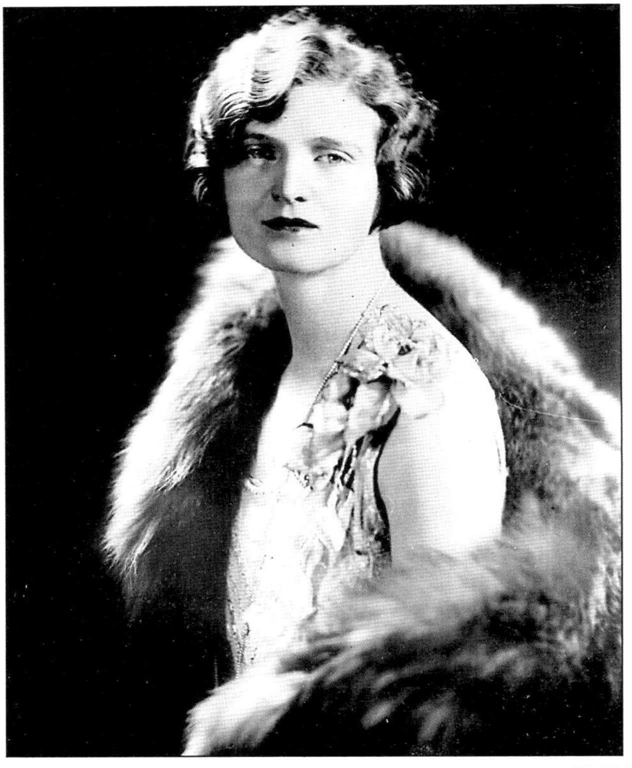

NAN BRITTON. As a young girl in Marion, Nanny Britton developed a crush on her father's friend, *Marion Star* publisher, Warren G. Harding. As she matured, her feelings for Harding intensified and ripened. Following the president's death, she was denied support for the daughter she claimed was conceived with the then Senator Harding. Britton published one of the first kiss-and-tell books of the modern era, titled, *The President's Daughter,* a best seller in its day. Though her claims were never verified in court, Nan Britton remained resolute until her final breath that Harding was the father of their daughter, Elizabeth Ann. (Photograph courtesy of Gary Barnhart.)

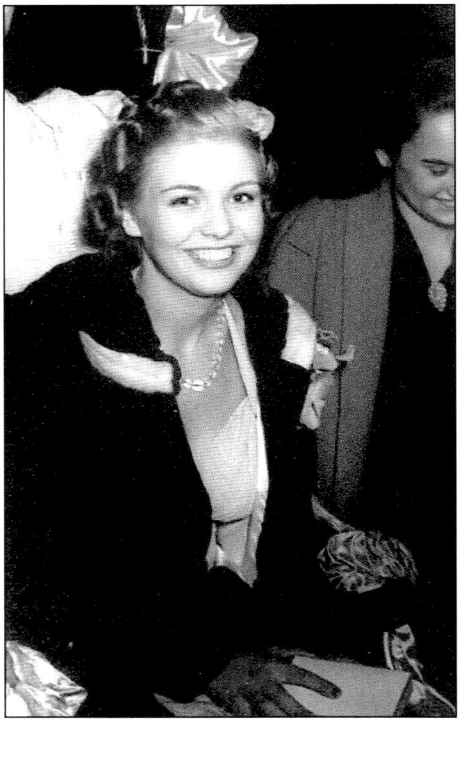

MARILYN MESEKE, MISS AMERICA 1938. Raised in Marion by her grandmother, Marilyn Meseke taught tap dance at her family's home on South Prospect Street. In 1938, Meseke won the Miss Ohio Contest, qualifying her to represent Ohio in the Miss America Pageant. Her timing and her talent fit the moment perfectly—1938 was the first year that talent became a scoring event in the competition. While Maronites listened to the pageant on the radio, Meseke won the crown on September 10, 1938. The event also marked the first time that movie audiences could see a Miss America being crowned through news reel footage shown the week following the event. Meseke's return to Marion on September 29, 1938, included a night time parade attended by 30,000 well-wishers from Marion and surrounding communities. (Photograph courtesy of Gary Barnhart.)

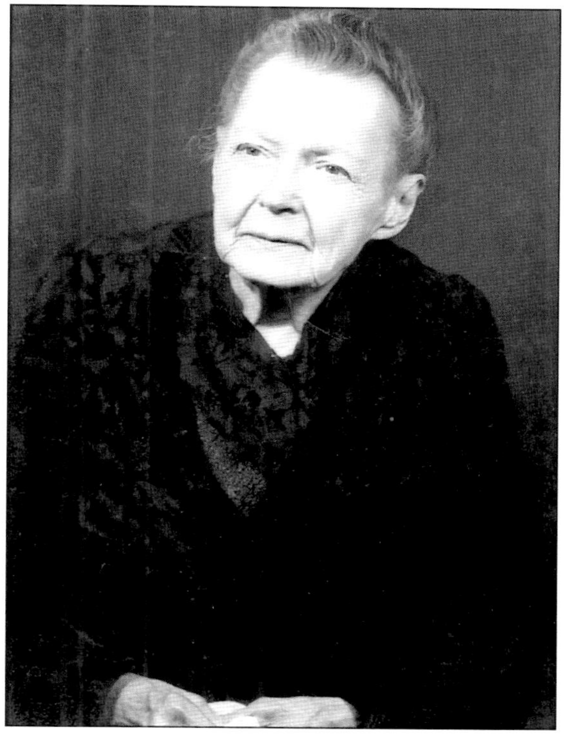

Dr. Elizabeth Maud Louise Bull, M.D. Dr. Maud Bull's medical career in Marion spanned over 60 years and included the delivery of over 9,000 babies. A graduate of the American Medical Missionary College in Chicago in 1901, and a graduate of Ohio State University Medical School in 1907, Maud Bull's service to her community reached beyond her medical practice. As one of the founders of Marion's Seventh Day Adventist Church, Dr. Bull served that body in numerous ways, including as Deaconess and as a missionary worker. Dr. Bull died in December 1961 at the age of 89; she is buried in Marion Cemetery. (Photograph courtesy of Marion County Historical Society.)

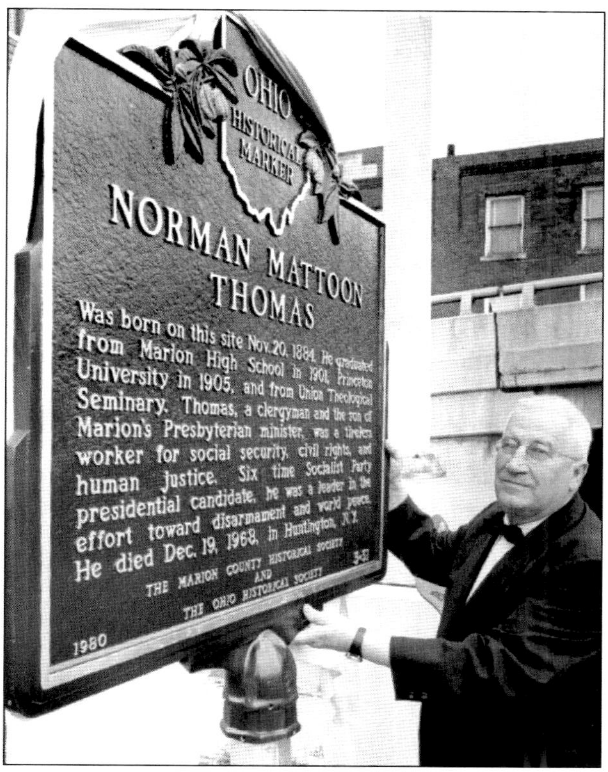

Judge Charlton Myers Unveils the Norman Thomas Historical Marker, North Prospect Street. Considered the Dean of Marion County History during his lifetime, Charlton Myers (1910–1998) was a charter member and the first president of the Marion County Historical Society. An ardent promoter and recorder of the county's history, Judge Myers began his campaign to elevate the discussion of protecting Marion County's history in the early 1960s through classes he taught to local, continuing education students. (Photograph courtesy of the Marion County Historical Society.)

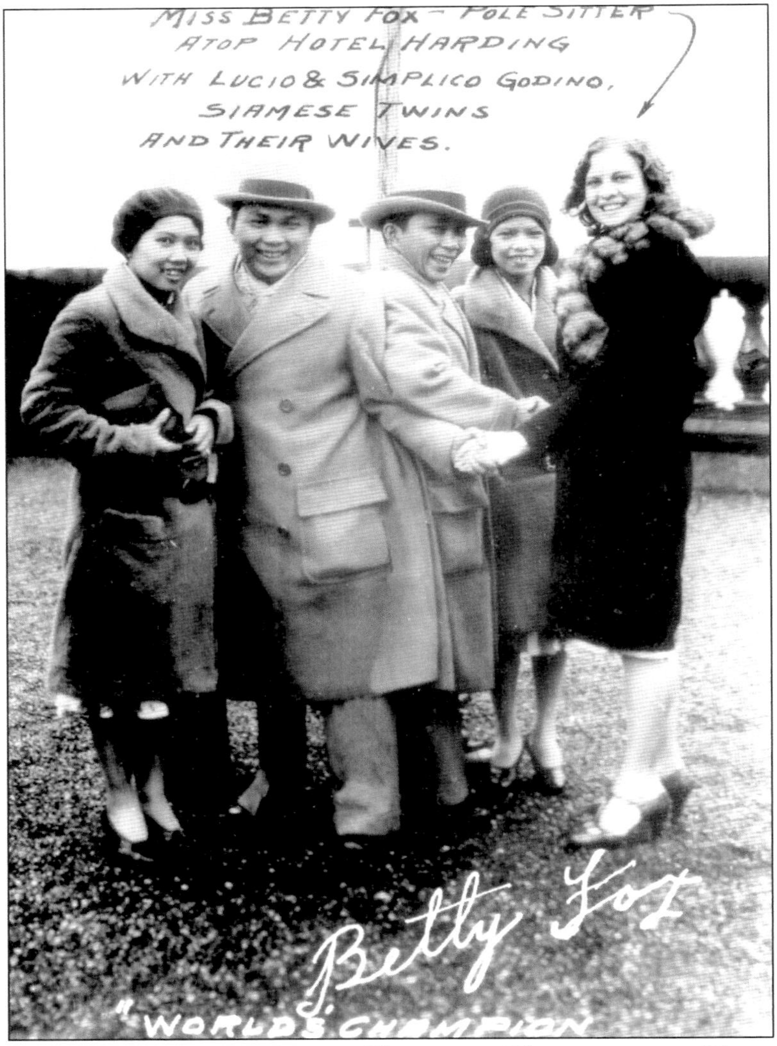

AERIALIST BETTY FOX MEETS THE GODINO TWINS AND WIVES ATOP THE HOTEL HARDING. In the late 1920s and early 1930s, an era of fantastic stunts and fads, Betty Fox's title, "World Champion Flagpole Sitter," was one for the books. Arriving in Marion on April 23, 1935, she had the good fortune to meet up with Filipino Siamese twins Lucio and Simplico Godino and their wives (twins, themselves), who were performing at the Marion Theatre that week.

Fox was in Marion to perform for the Elk's Club Circus; her career as an aerialist was impressive. When performing alone, Fox worked above the crowds on a two-foot square platform. When partnered with Benny Fox, the two would perform all of the popular dances of the day atop the same two-foot square platform! Fox continued to perform well into the late 1950s without mishap.

The Godino's stage act included singing, saxophone duets, dancing, and roller skating. The twins toured America, appearing on vaudeville stages from coast to coast. According to a Philadelphia paper from the era, the twins were avid motorists owning two cars, which allowed equal time for both behind the wheel. Their "enthusiastic" methods of driving in their native Philippines resulted in the revocation of their licenses as Philippine police were unable to arrest "the offender" without falsely incarcerating the innocent, attached twin. The twins died in December 1936. (Photograph courtesy of Gary Barnhart.)

Ten

RESIDENCES, HOMES, AND A HOUSE, OF SORTS

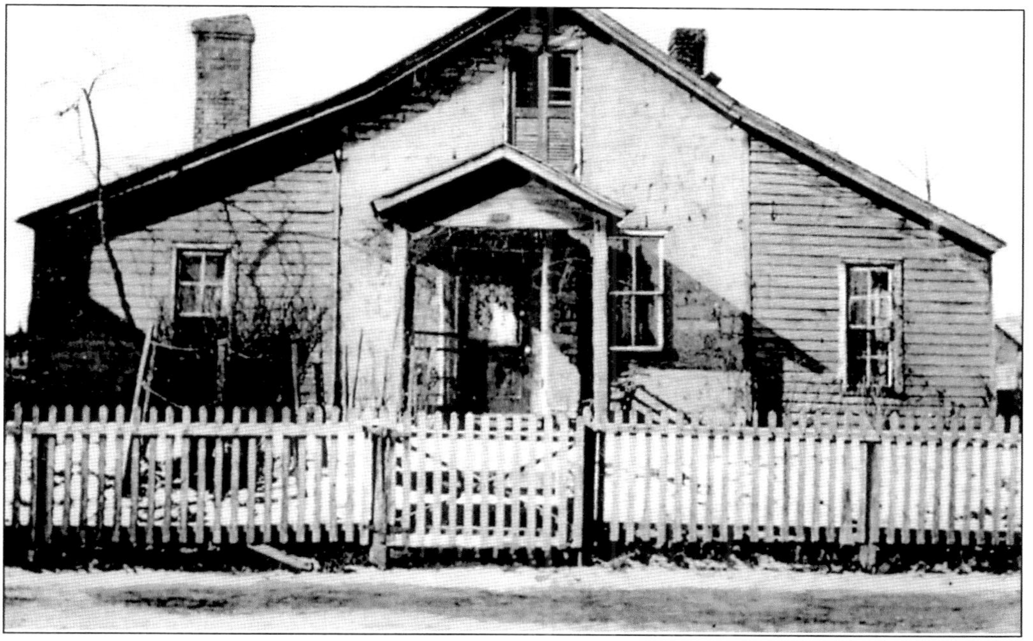

THE ALVIN AND BETSEY PRIEST HOUSE, NORTH MAIN STREET. Alvin and Betsey Priest arrived in Marion when the settlement was in its infancy. Betsey was a daughter of Marion founder Eber Baker, and his first wife, Lydia Smith. The Priest residence, built about 1830, was a simple one-and-a-half-story hewed-log house that also served as a bark house and a tannery. Betsey Priest died in Marion in 1843 and was buried in the old Marion Cemetery on Quarry Street; Mr. Priest left the city in that same year, relocating to Texas where he died in 1881 at the age of 81 years old. (Photograph courtesy of the author.)

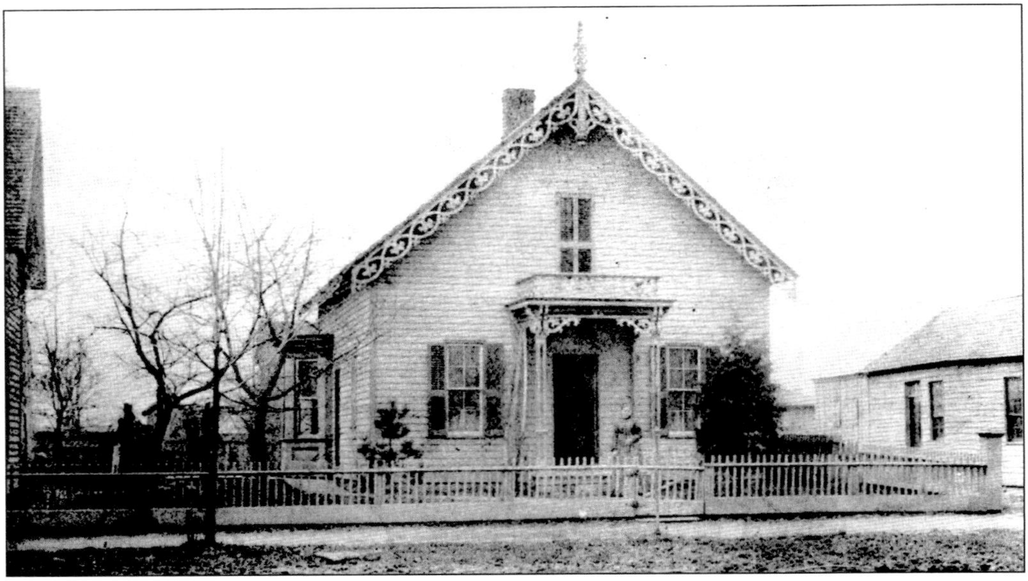

HOPKINS RESIDENCE, MARION TOWNSHIP. When built by the John Hopkins family in the 1840s, this cottage was in the country, just east of the city of Marion. By early 1900s, the growing city had surrounded the home on East Center Street, just east of South Vine Street. (Photograph courtesy of the Marion County Historical Society.)

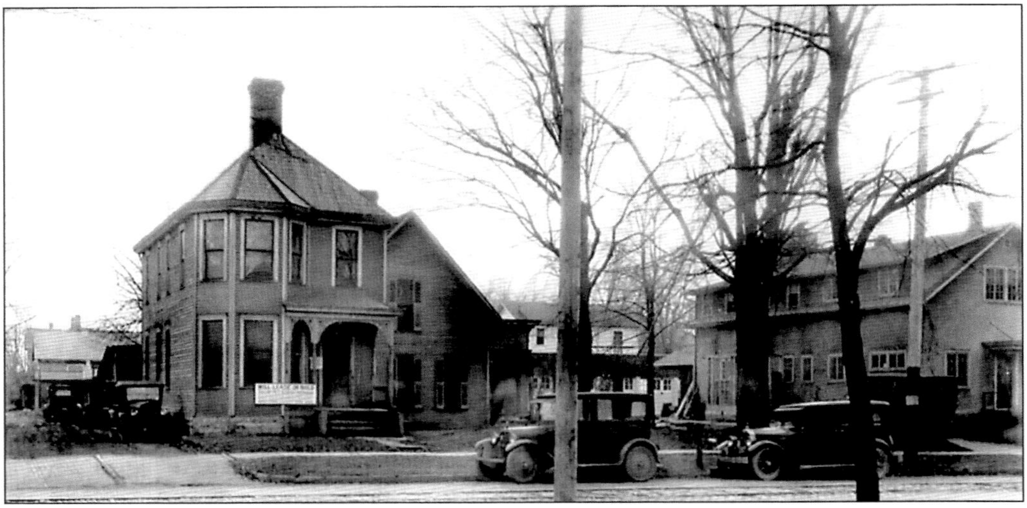

RESIDENCE AND OFFICE OF DR. HORATIO AND MILDRED CHISHOLM. When Mildred Hopkins married Dr. Horatio Chisholm, the couple set up housekeeping in the bride's family home on East Center Street. Finding the Hopkins home too small to house a family and a medical practice, the Chisholm's enlarged the homestead (shown in the picture at the top of the page) by adding a second house to the east and connecting the two; the delicate fretwork along the gable of the older home was removed. Chisholm was founder and chairman-of-the-board for the Marion C&C Hospital; later, he opened the Central Emergency Hospital on East Center Street. The site is now occupied by a commercial garage. (Photograph courtesy of the Marion County Historical Society.)

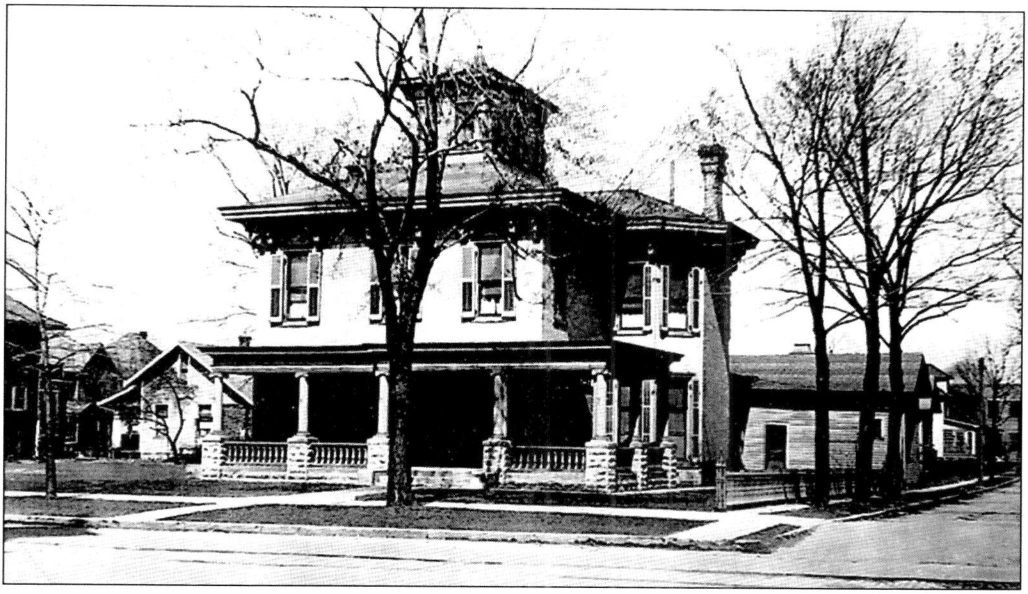

Amos and Louisa Bouton Kling Residence, 254 East Center Street. Built by one of Marion's wealthiest and most powerful citizens, the Amos Kling mansion was located on the northwest corner of North Vine and East Center Streets. Kling raised his children Florence, Clifford, and Vetallis in this home. The Italianate-style house was across from Epworth Methodist Church, until July 1951 when it was torn down for a Sun Oil Company gas station. (Photograph courtesy of Gary Barnhart.)

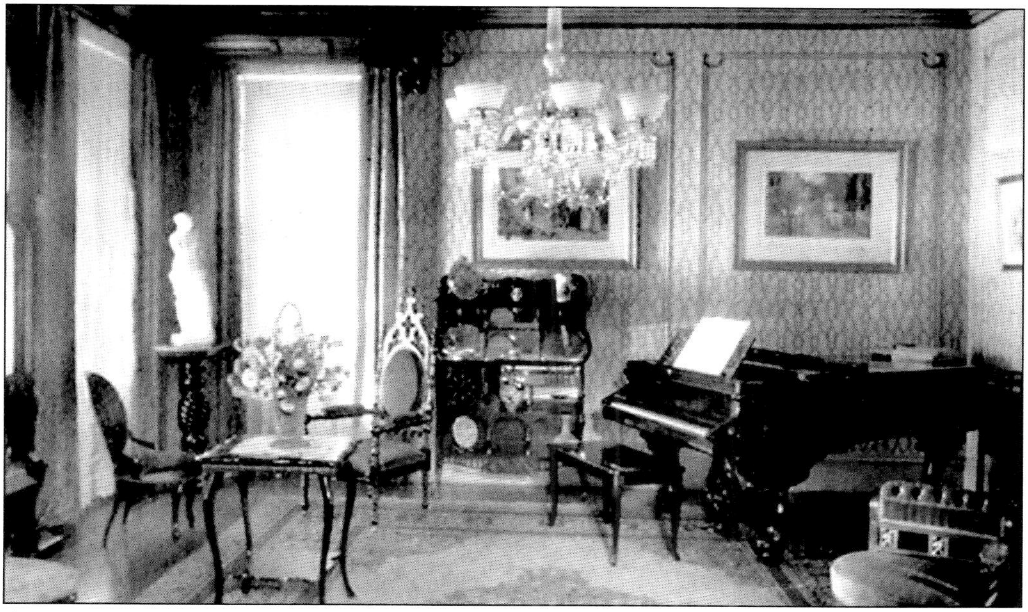

Amos and Louisa Bouton Kling Residence, Front Parlor. The front parlor in the Kling Mansion showed great restraint, given the exuberance of Victorian decorating tastes. Formal parlors were used for the receiving of guests and for more formal affairs such as weddings and funerals. (Photograph courtesy of Gary Barnhart.)

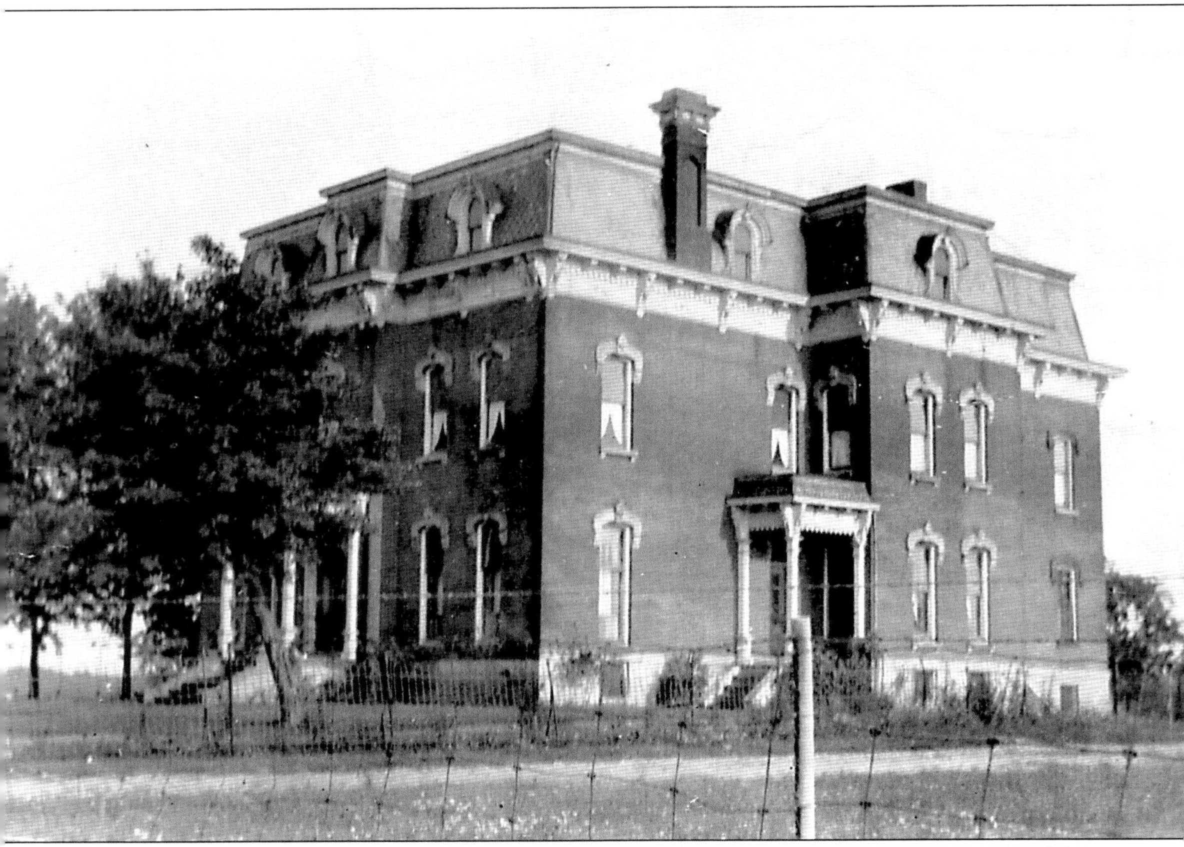

MELVIN MONNETTE'S BIG BRICK. Marion County's largest and most sumptuous "farm" house was built in 1886 by Melvin and Ella Monnette on what is now Morral-Kirkpatrick Road, west of Kirkpatrick in Scott Township. Locals referred to the 28-room mansion as "Monnette's Folly." According to the *Marion Star*, "it was elaborately finished and furnished throughout from its basement to its ballroom on the third floor. Melvin and Ella Monnette were socially inclined, and the house fully was staffed with servants; their brilliant dance and dinner parties were subjects of numerous stories. Seldom less than 100 persons attended these functions in the late (eighteen) eighties and nineties." The Monnettes left the property in the mid-1890s, and the house and its gardens fell into disrepair. After passing through several owners, the mansion was purchased by William Hobson in 1928. The house burned June 10, 1931, following a square-dance party hosted by Hobson's daughter Opal in the third-floor ballroom; a smoldering cigarette left by an attendee was identified as the source of the fire. (Photograph courtesy of the author.)

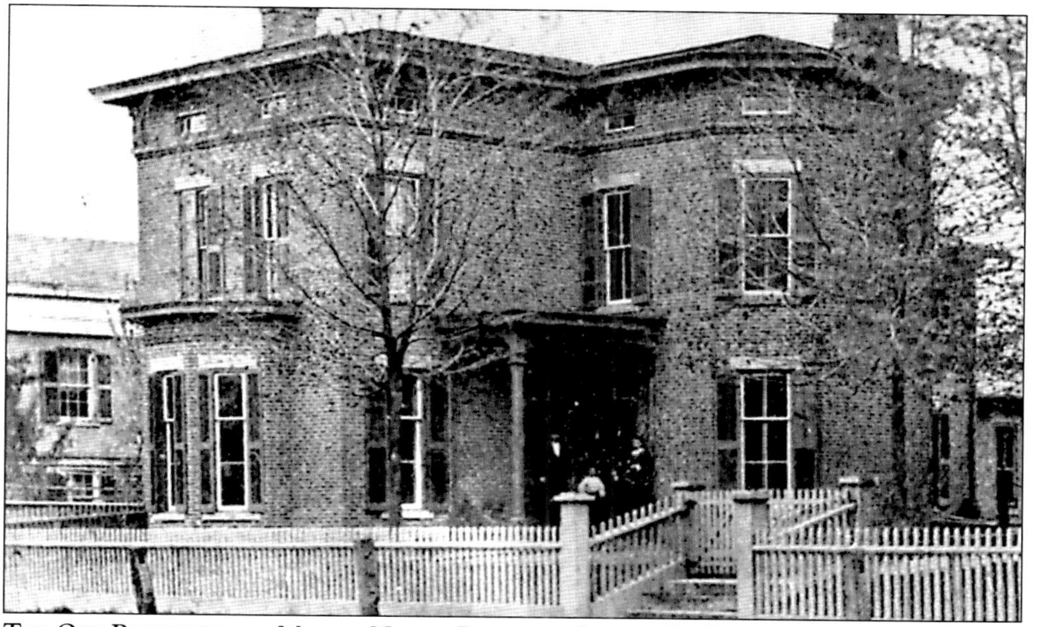

The Old Presbyterian Manse, North Prospect Street. Built next to the old Presbyterian Church on North Prospect Street, this Italianate-influenced home was the birthplace of Norman Mattoon Thomas' father, who was the minister of the Presbyterian Church in Marion from 1884 until 1901. The site of the manse is now a parking lot; an Ohio Historical Society Marker now identifies the location. (Photograph courtesy of the Marion County Historical Society.)

Norman Matoon Thomas. Less celebrated than Marion's Warren G. Harding, Norman Matoon Thomas, nevertheless, was a strong political leader who helped to shape political opinions in America through most of the 20th century. The son of the town's Presbyterian minister, Thomas was born in Marion in 1884. As a newsboy for the *Marion Star*, Thomas was one of many carriers watched over by Florence Kling Harding. An ordained minister in the Presbyterian Church, Thomas himself would run for president in the 1930s and 1940s as the Socialist Party Candidate. A pacifist and supporter of workers' rights, Thomas also helped found the American Civil Liberties Union (ACLU). Norman Thomas died in December 1968. (Photograph courtesy of the Marion County Historical Society.)

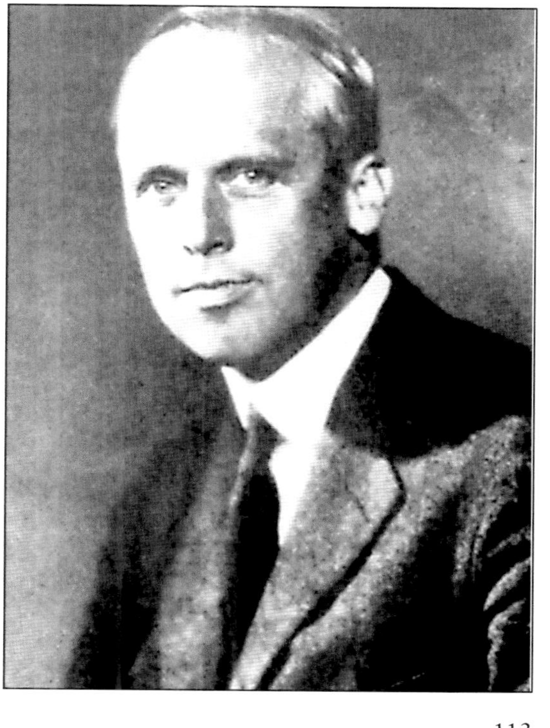

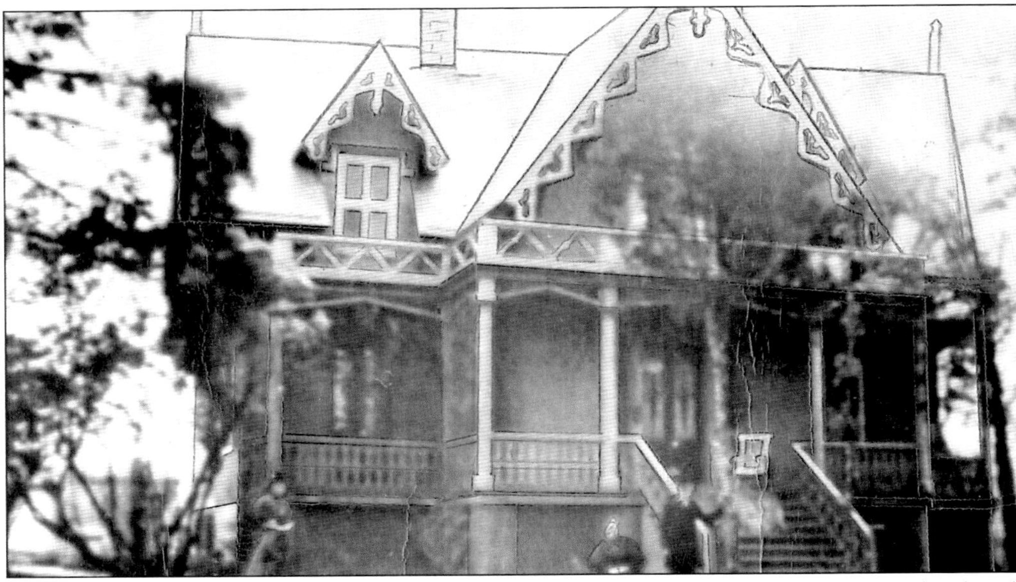

THE JAMES GODMAN HOUSE, WEST CENTER STREET. Mr. James Godman was credited with leading the campaign to bring the first rail lines into Marion in the mid-19th century. Judge Charlton Myers' passion for Mr. Godman's house is well documented; Myers took numerous photographs of the home and documented its evolution. Available photographs of the Godman's high, Gothic-style home do not clearly show the house or its detail. Unable to find a clear image of the house, Judge Myers attempted to show how the home looked by drawing in some of the washed out details on this copied image. (Photograph courtesy of the Marion County Historical Society.)

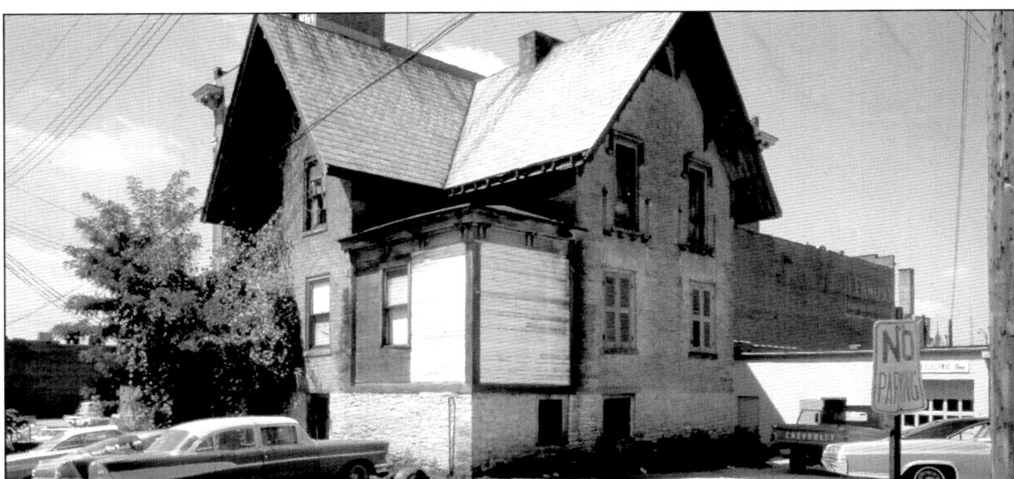

THE JAMES GODMAN HOUSE, SUMMER 1965. By the early 20th century, the Godman house, which faced West Center Street, was hidden behind a commercial building, constructed on what had been its front lawn, making a full photographic record of its main (north) façade impossible. This view of its east and south sides illustrates how a property can evolve over an extended period of time. The Godman home was torn down in 1968; the site is now home to the Marion City Hall complex. (Photograph courtesy of the Marion County Historical Society.)

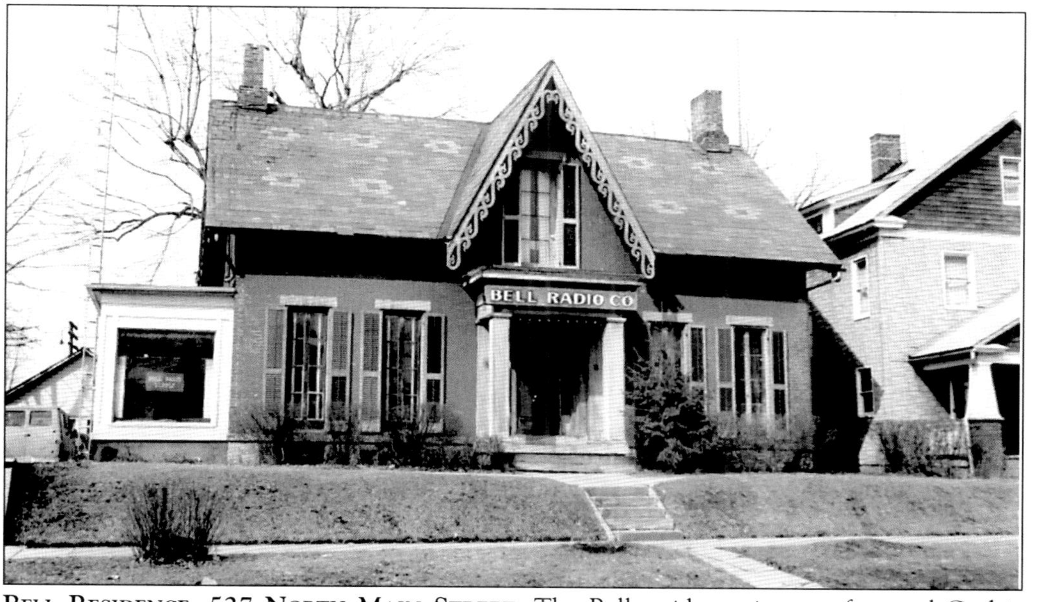

BELL RESIDENCE, 527 NORTH MAIN STREET. The Bell residence is one of several Gothic Revival "cottages" built in Marion County dating to the mid-19th century. The Henry True House on East Church Street is of a similar design. The gingerbread trim was designed to provide visual interest as decoration itself and to also provide shadow patterns made through the daylight hours. Three generations of the Bell family called this home between 1875 and 1969. (Photograph courtesy of Seton Counsul.)

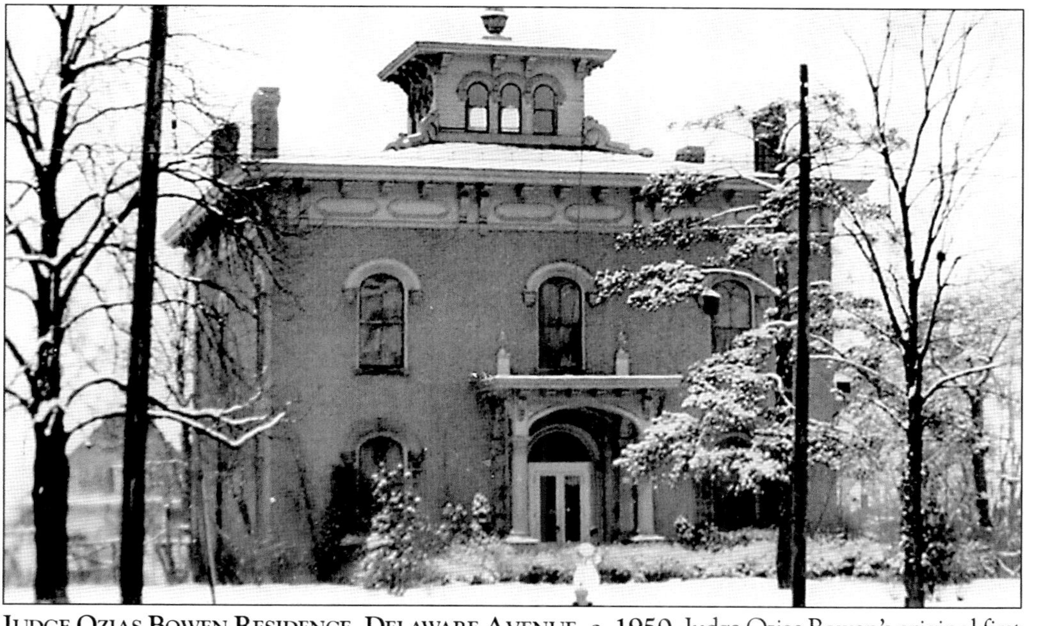

JUDGE OZIAS BOWEN RESIDENCE, DELAWARE AVENUE, c. 1950. Judge Ozias Bowen's original first brick home was a modest, yet dignified dwelling, designed in the Greek Revival style. The judge's second home, begun in 1862 on Gospel Hill, was built in the fashionable Italianate villa style. The home is now known as the Stengle-True Museum. (Photograph courtesy of the author.)

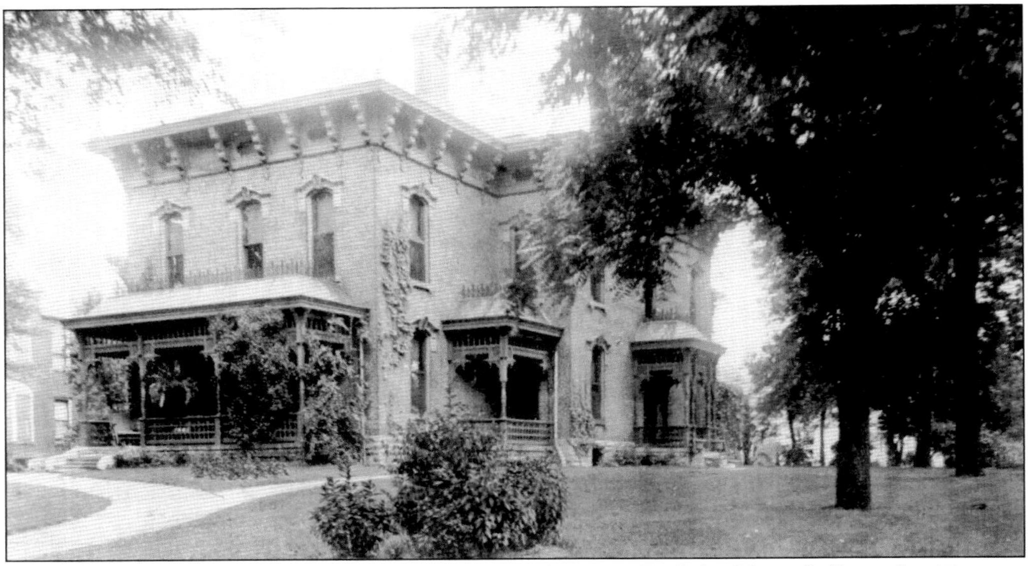

URIAS SEFFNER RESIDENCE, 365 EAST CENTER STREET. Built by Urias Seffner, the 22-room Italianate mansion featured state of the art materials, including modern poured concrete molds for building details. The home was also the residence of the Hane family for many years. In the late 1939, the mansion was acquired by the Isaly Dairy Company and was converted into apartments; a commercial store front structure was built onto the front of the residence and was used by Isaly's as a sign shop. Later, this structure housed a donut shop, and, finally, Faajar's dry cleaners. The building was razed in 1976. (Photograph courtesy of the author.)

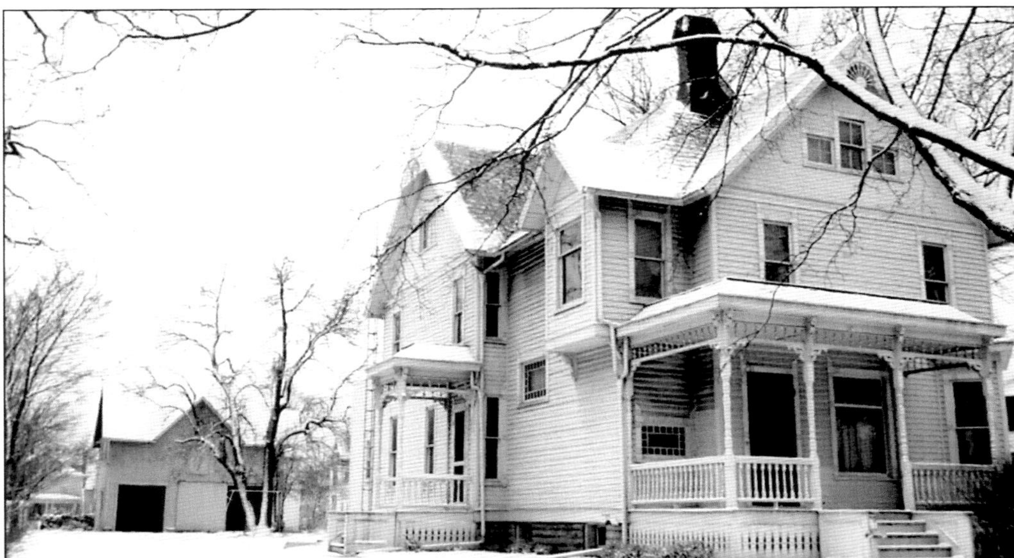

WILLIAM HENRY HARRISON THOMPSON RESIDENCE, 1965. The Thompson residence was located at 347 East Center Street, immediately west of the Urias Seffner mansion. The highly ornamented Queen Anne-style house remained in the Thompson family until it was raised in the late 1970s. Scantland Communications' corporate headquarters was later built on the site. (Photograph courtesy of the Marion County Historical Society.)

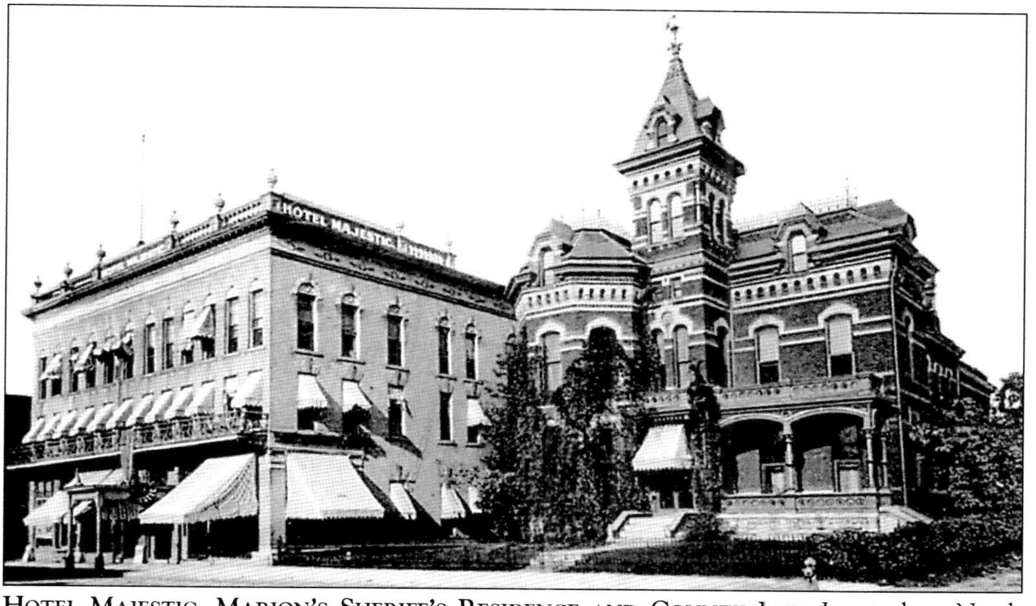

HOTEL MAJESTIC, MARION'S SHERIFF'S RESIDENCE AND COUNTY JAIL. Located on North State Street, the county jail and the Hotel Majestic made ironic neighbors; The Majestic was a place that was difficult to get into, while the jail was most difficult to get out of. (Photograph courtesy of Robert Turner)

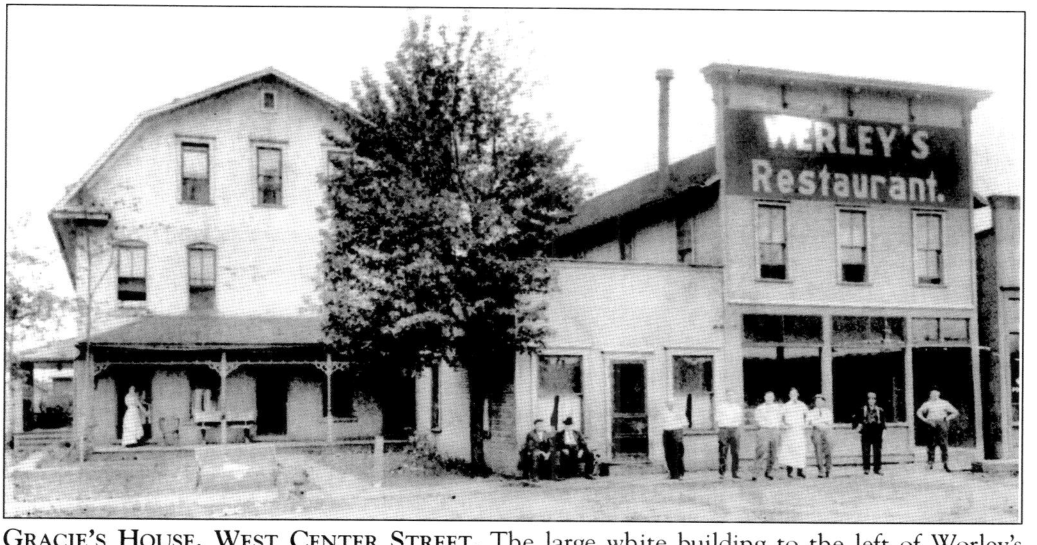

GRACIE'S HOUSE, WEST CENTER STREET. The large white building to the left of Worley's Restaurant was once known as the Railroad Hotel. In the 1930s, the hotel came under the proprietorship of one Grace Pollack, or "Gracie," as she liked the men in town to call her. Gracie operated a "house" of sorts, which she filled with "her girls." Periodically, she and her girls would get hauled into court, where Gracie would be charged with operating a"house of ill repute," but someone always posted bail. After Gracie moved the operation to the country near the Scioto Ordnance Facility in the 1940s, business was so good that one annoyed neighbor posted a sign in her front yard that read "We Give Green Stamps." (Photograph courtesy of Gary Barnhart.)

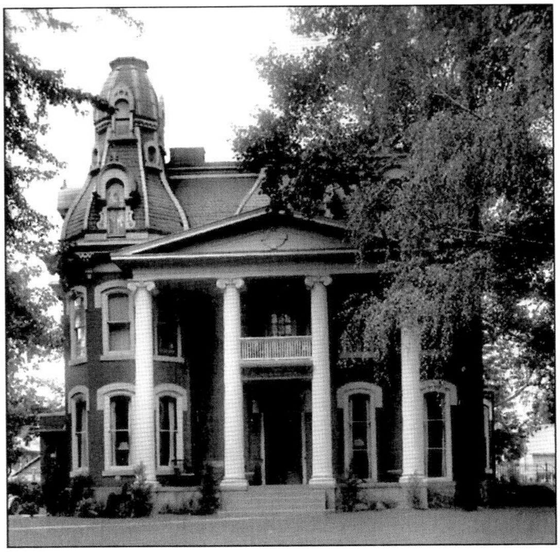

SCHAFFNER QUEEN FUNERAL HOME. Acquired by the Schaffner Queen Mortuary in 1928, the former Cummins-Barnhart residence is located on the north side of East Center Street. Advertisements for the new funeral home described services offered, including overnight accommodations for out-of-town family members. Following the death of Mr. Queen, the funeral home was renamed the Schaffner Denzer Funeral Home. Today, the building houses the Denzer-Farison-Hottinger Funeral Home, Inc. (Photograph courtesy of Carol and Gary Robinson.)

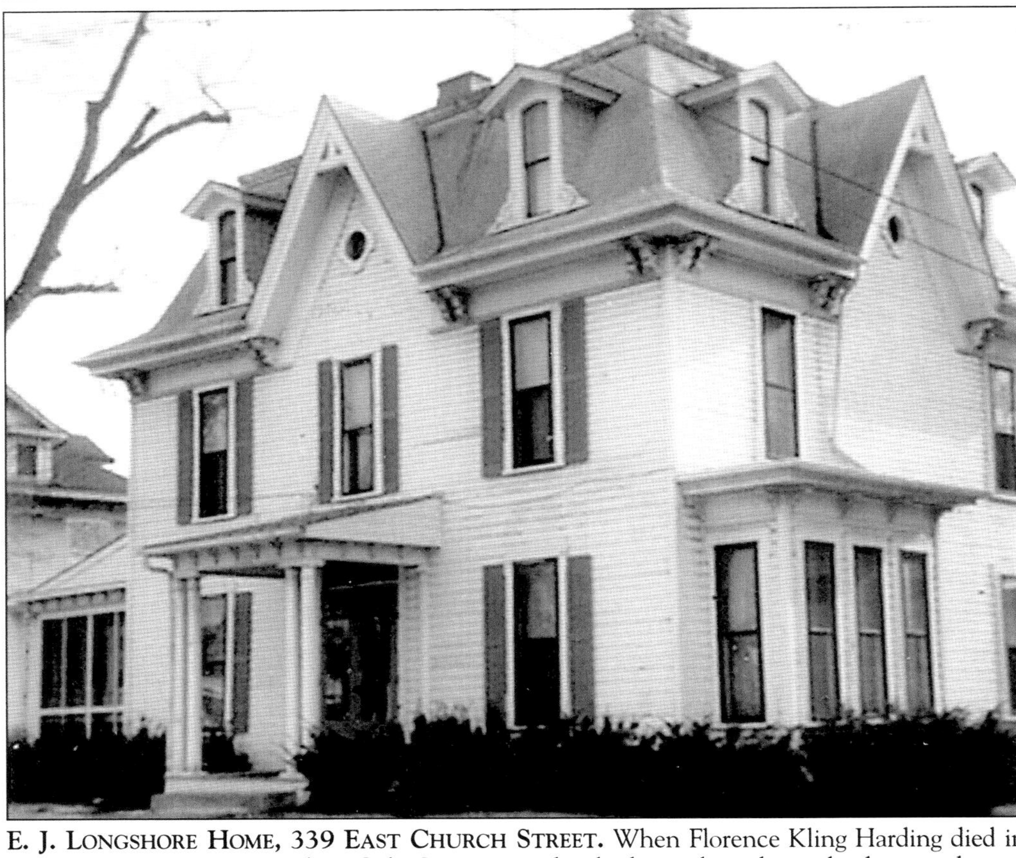

E. J. LONGSHORE HOME, 339 EAST CHURCH STREET. When Florence Kling Harding died in Rose Cottage at Sawyer's White Oaks Sanatorium, her body was brought to this home, where it laid in state until her funeral. An estimated 12,000 waited in line to pass by her bier prior to her burial. One of Marion's most eclectic Victorian houses, the Longshore residence was demolished in the 1970's. (Photograph courtesy of Gary Barnhart.)

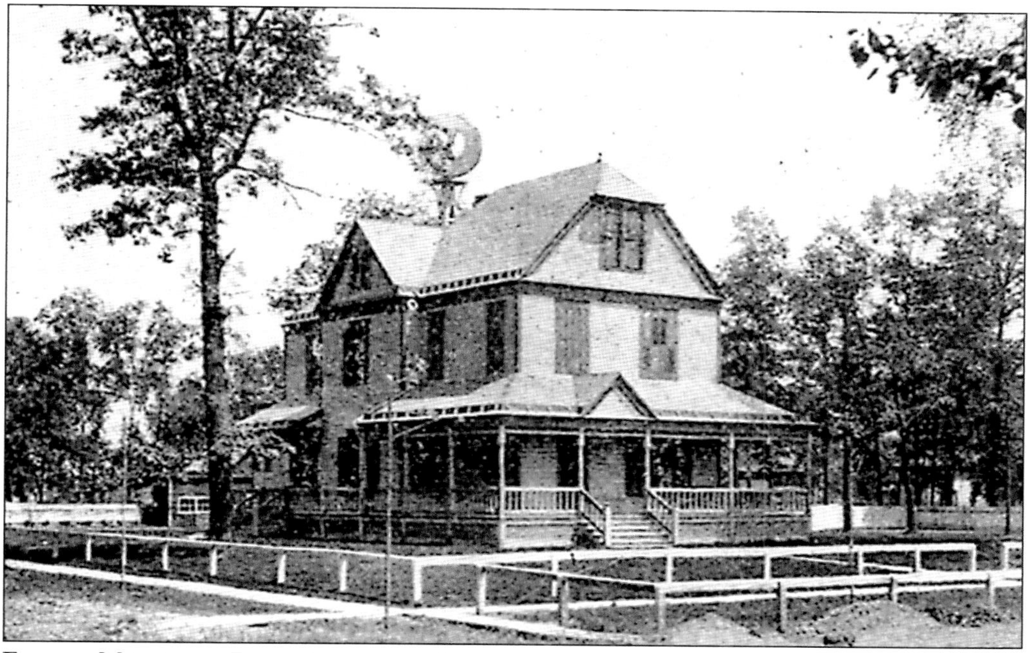

ELI AND MARGARET BUSH RESIDENCE, 1044 EAST CENTER STREET. Located on the northeast corner of East Center Street and True Avenue, the Eli and Margaret Bush residence was once a working fruit farm. By trade, Bush was a real estate developer, however, he could be found working in his orchards during the growing season. The house is still standing and used for commercial and rental purposes (Photograph courtesy of the Marion Public Library.)

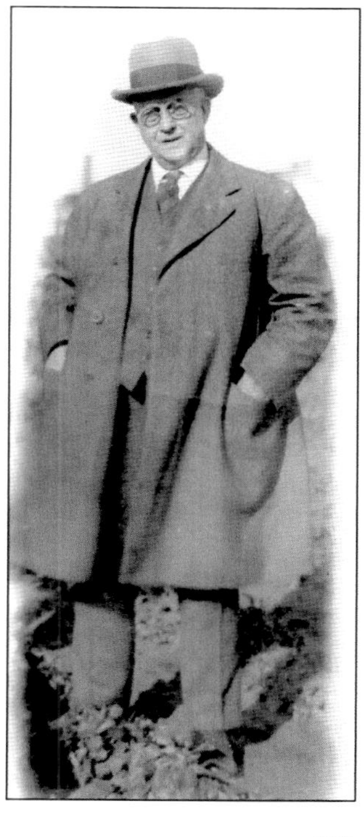

ELI E. BUSH SR. A native of Wyandot County, Ohio, Eli E. Bush Sr. helped to develop Marion's east side residential sections during the housing boom in the early 1900s. In 1882, Bush married Margaret L. Jones of Marion; the couple settled into their home located on the northeast corner of East Center Street and True Avenue, where they raised their five children. The Bushs' son, Edson, served as chairman of the Marion County Bank. Their grandson Harry (Sonny) Copeland was a well-known motorcycle racer. Following the death of his wife in 1911, Bush married his late wife's sister, Ethel M. Jones, with whom he had one son. (Photograph courtesy of Jane Clevenger Vierow.)

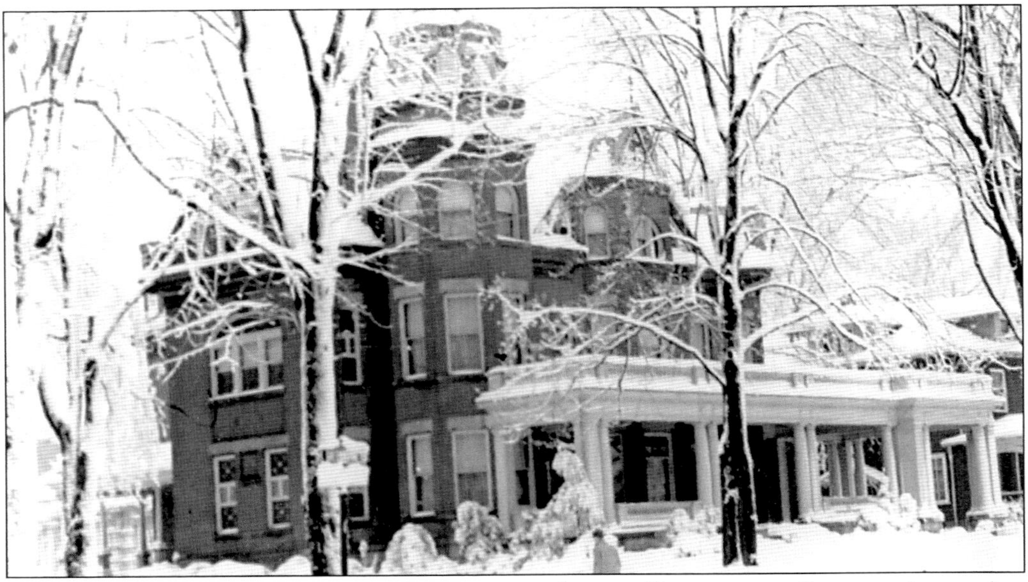

Edward Huber Mansion, East Center and South Greenwood Streets. Located at 417 East Center Street, the Edward Huber residence's design falls into the Queen Anne style of Victorian architecture. The grand residence, built in 1883 when Center Street was the preferred address of Marion's leading citizens, was a single family home until 1958, when it was sold and converted into a motel and later into apartments. The Huber residence was razed in the late 1960s for a small commercial building. (Photograph courtesy of Hughes Photography, John Rall, president.)

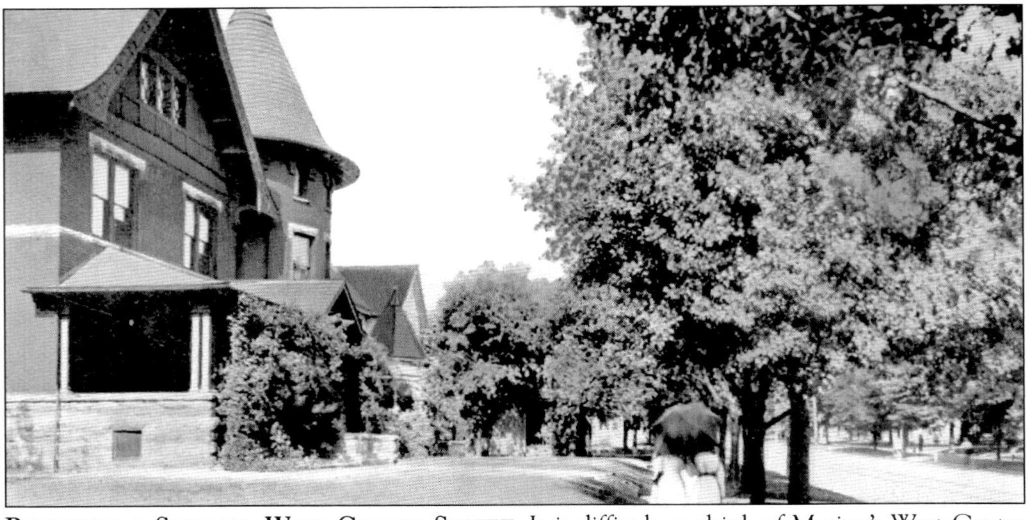

Residential Section, West Center Street. It is difficult to think of Marion's West Center Street as a fashionable street lined with large finely furnished homes, but it was once a desirable neighborhood. Looking east towards downtown along the north side of the street, the photograph shows the John Evans home and its massive tower. Evans made his fortune in limestone and built the house shortly before his death. Lavishly furnished, the home was the site of numerous social events until Mrs. Evans' death in 1931. The Evans' house was torn down in 1968 after serving as the local office of the Standard Oil Company. (Photograph courtesy of the author.)

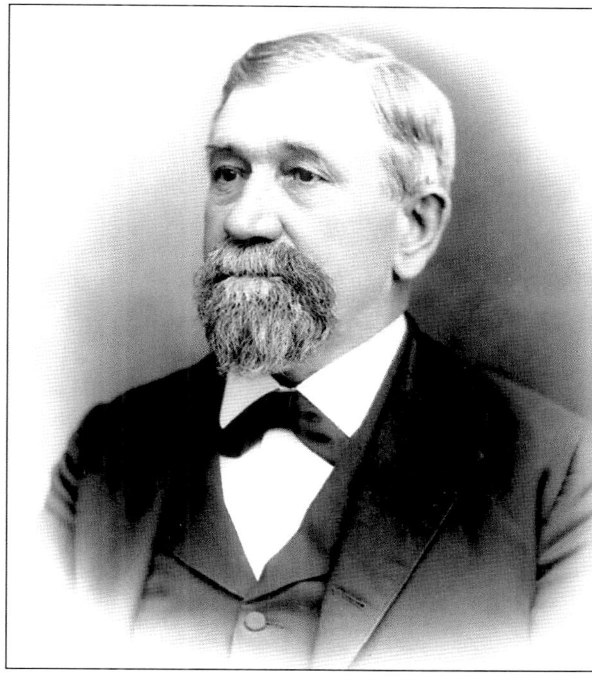

Edward Huber (1837–1904). Marion owes a great amount of its success to Edward Huber, who came to the community in 1865 to build his revolving hay rake. Huber's other ideas lead his Huber Manufacturing Company to develop the first gasoline-powered tractor in 1898. Huber also made possible the start of the Marion Steam Shovel Company, helped to bring affordable electricity to the community, established the first library in Marion, and also provided a credit program to allow his employees to purchase homes. (Photograph courtesy of the Marion County Historical Society.)

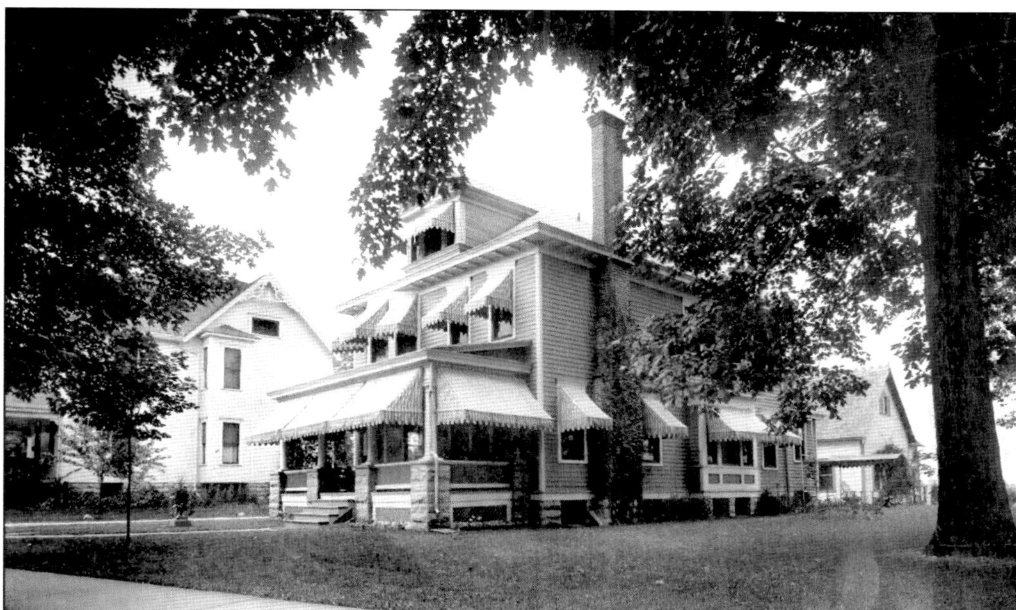

Hughs Residence. The Frank and Mary Hughs residence was located at 564 Delaware Avenue, just north of Walnut Street. Mr. Hughs owned and operated Hughs' Men's Clothiers at 147 West Center Street from 1904 to 1925. He was later associated with Jim Dugan's Men's Wear. After the death of President Harding, the Millard Hunt family, who had been renting the Harding's home, moved into this home while the Harding's home was converted to a museum. The house has since been torn down for a filling station. (Photograph courtesy of the Marion County Historical Society.)

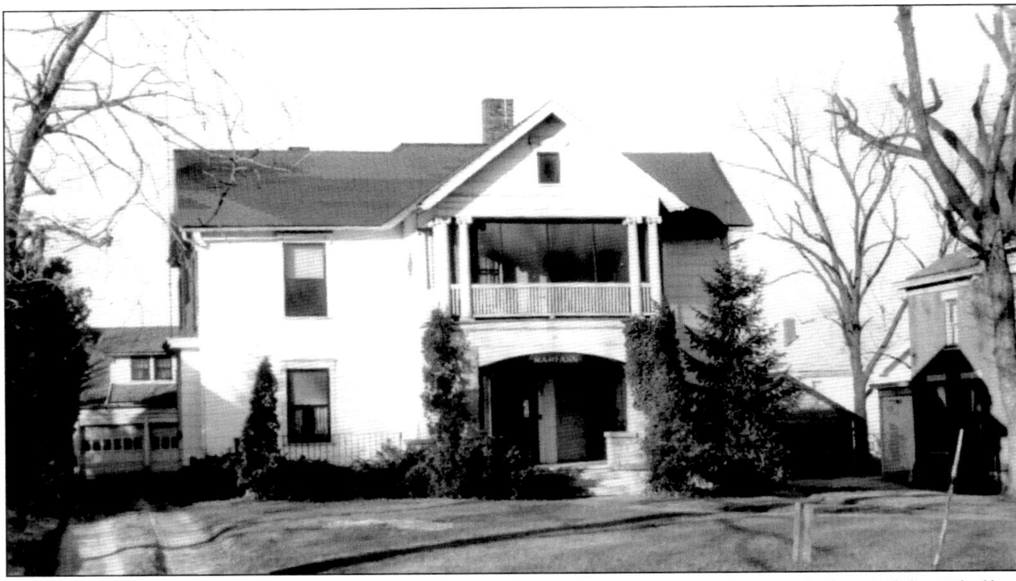

THE PHILLIPS RESIDENCE, "MARIANN." James Phillips, president of the Uhler-Phillips Company and the American Building & Loan Company, bought this home at 419 South Main Street for his bride, Carrie Fulton Phillips. They lived here until 1927 when they moved to 885 Mt. Vernon Avenue. James Phillips died in 1939. (Photograph courtesy of the Marion County Historical Society.)

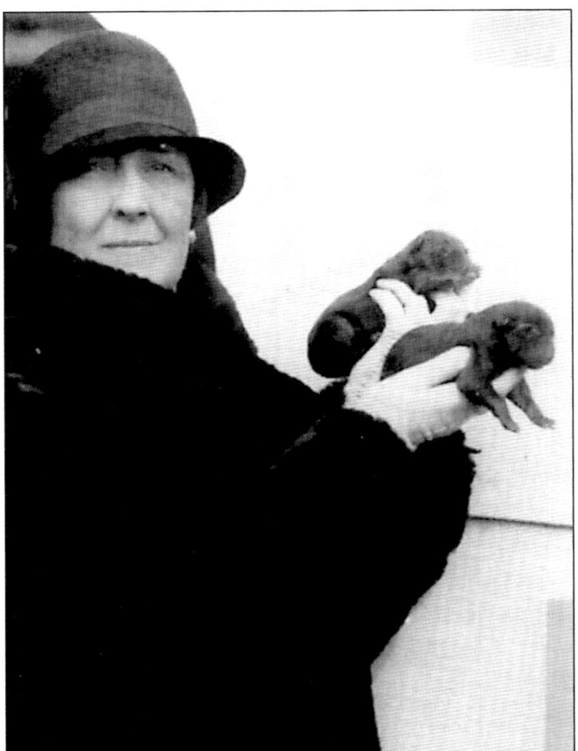

CARRIE FULTON PHILLIPS, c. 1920S. In her youth, Carrie Fulton Phillips was considered to be the most beautiful young woman in all of Ohio. Prior to the presidential election of 1920, she became one of the most infamous figures in presidential history. Following Mrs. Phillips' well-documented personal relationship with Harding, she became the only person known to have successfully blackmailed a national political party. After returning to Marion, Mrs. Phillips' political beliefs (she was a backer of Germany during both World Wars) and eccentricities (she was very fond of German Shepherds, which overran her home) caused people to "raise their brows" whenever she appeared. Carrie Phillips died in 1960 and is buried in Marion Cemetery. (Photograph courtesy of Gary Barnhart.)

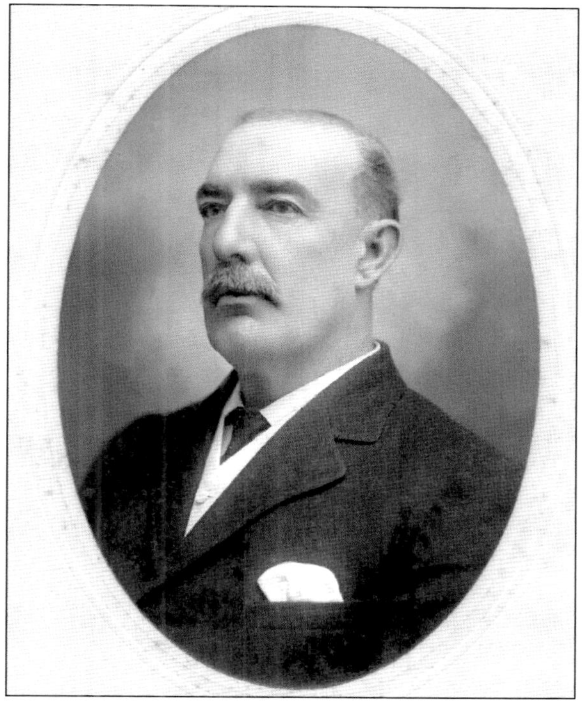

"Lord" Edward P. Houghton. A native of Liverpool, Edward P. Houghton could have risen to great heights in British society. However, his love for Jeanette Drew, a housekeeper in the employment of the Houghton household, made that impossible—Houghton chose Miss Drew over the social status of his birthright. The couple sailed for America, settling first in Union County, Ohio, and then in Marion. Highly respected for their civic leadership, the Houghton's enjoyed a lofty place in Marion Society. Edward P. Houghton died in 1917 at his home at 221 Gurley Avenue and is buried in Marion Cemetery. (Photograph courtesy of The Marion County Historical Society.)

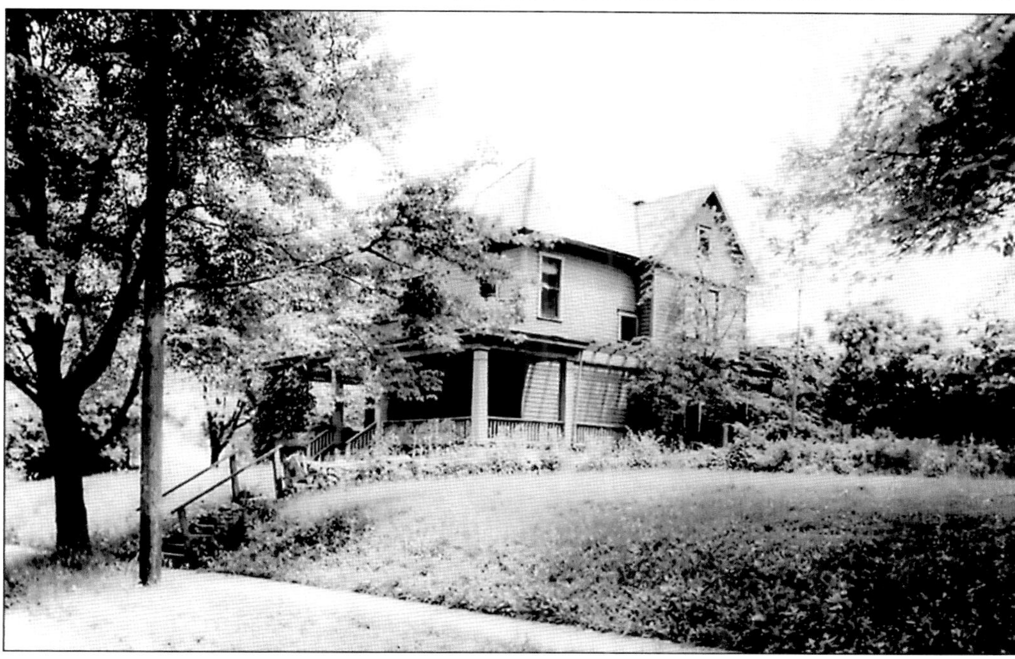

The Edward and Jeanette Houghton Residence. The former home of Edward and Jeanette Houghton is located overlooking Marion on the brow of Gospel Hill on Gurley Avenue. Maintained as a single-family residence for many years, the house has since been converted into a multiple family dwelling. (Photograph courtesy of the Marion County Historical Society.)

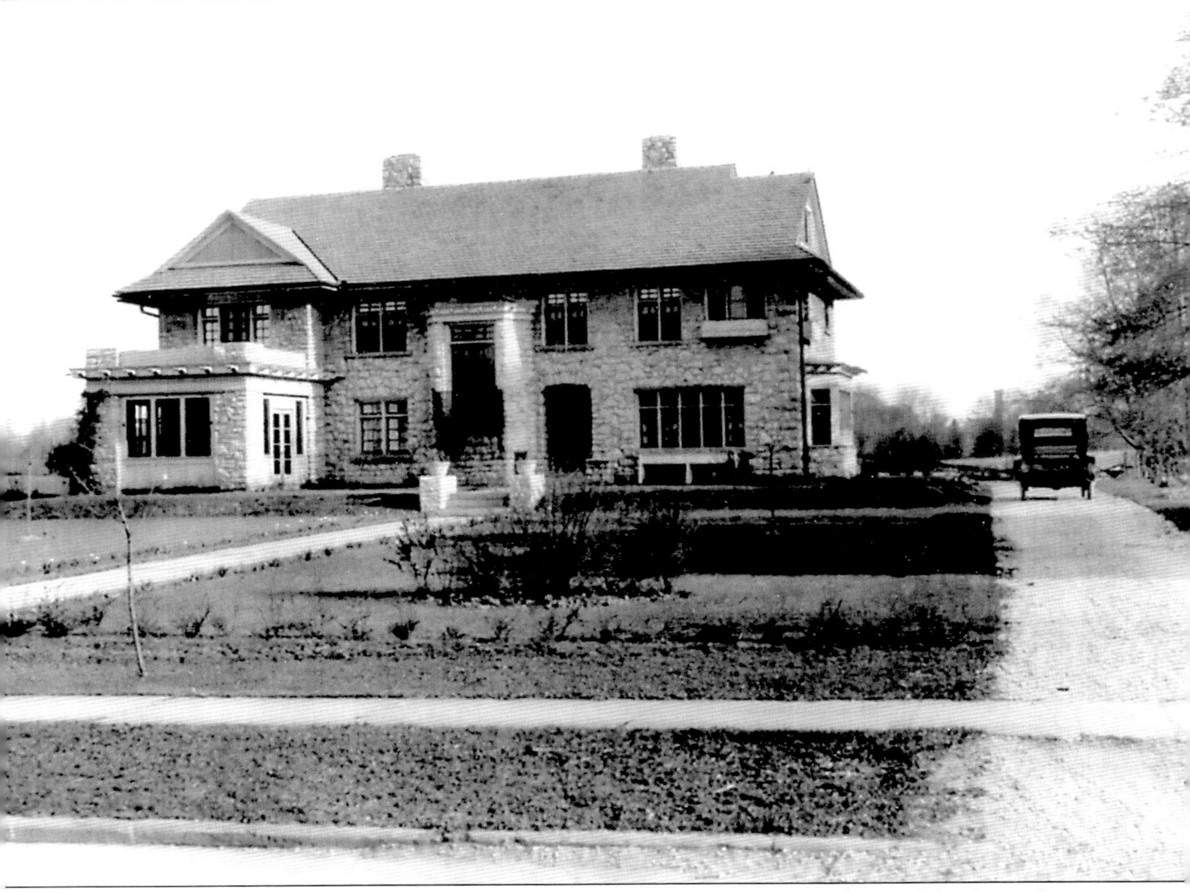

LIMESTONE PLACE. The home of Daniel and Mary J. Evans was located at 245 St. James Street at the corner of Vine Street. Stone for the prairie-style residence was quarried at the Evans Quarry northwest of Marion off of West Fairground Road. The house is presently owned by Steve and Marsha Adams, who offer its elegance as a bed and breakfast facility called Old Towne Manor. To the right of the house, peeking through the trees, is the bell tower of the Civil War Memorial Chapel at the Marion Cemetery. (Photograph courtesy of Mike and Linda Perry.)

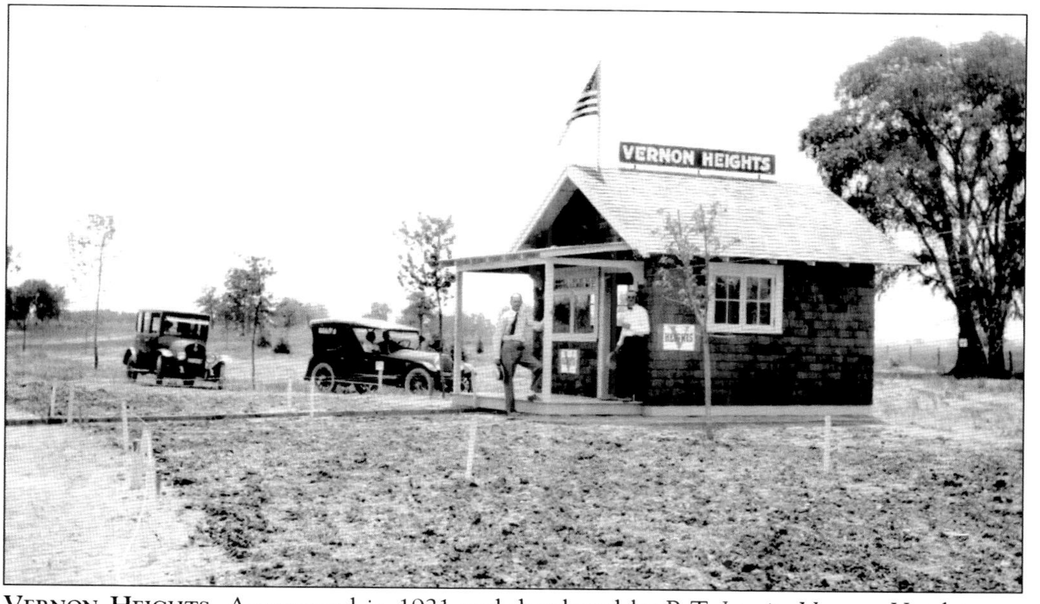

VERNON HEIGHTS. Announced in 1921 and developed by R.T. Lewis, Vernon Heights was designed to become Marion's most desirable neighborhood, on par with Upper Arlington and Shaker Heights. Dominating the planned development was a grand boulevard that would connect Mt. Vernon Avenue on Marion's east side with Delaware Avenue on the south. (Photograph courtesy of the Marion Historical Society.)

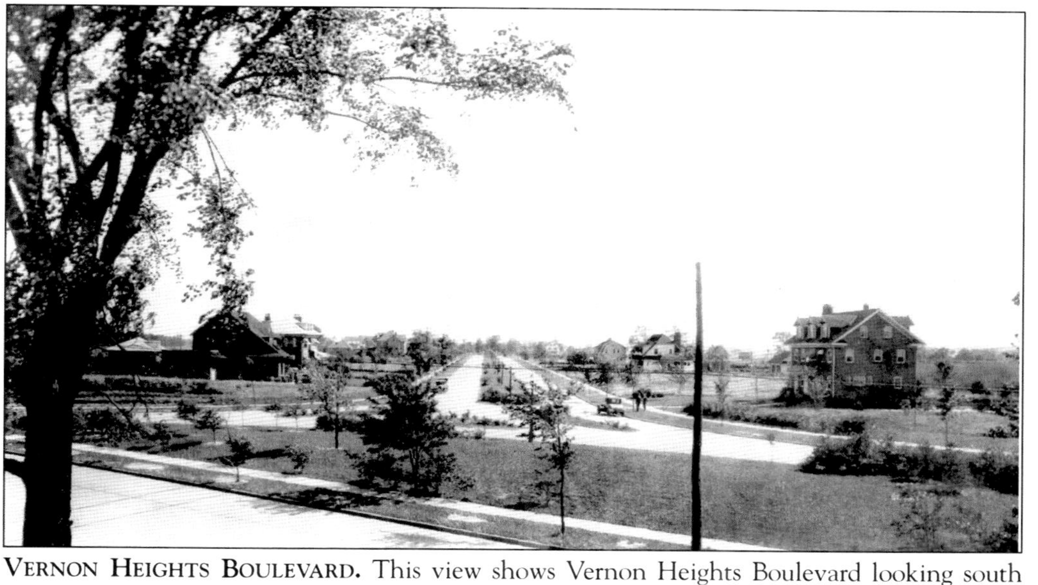

VERNON HEIGHTS BOULEVARD. This view shows Vernon Heights Boulevard looking south from Mt. Vernon Avenue. In the infancy of the project, owners were restricted to minimum square footage, set back and specific to allowable designs. Developer R.T. Lewis argued that if the community was to be as desirable in 50 years as it was at the time, certain standards had to be met and maintained. Married to Daisy Harding, Lewis had also hoped to lure his brother-in-law, Warren G. Harding, to build his post-Whitehouse retirement home in the heights. (Photograph courtesy of Hughes Photography, John Rall, president.)

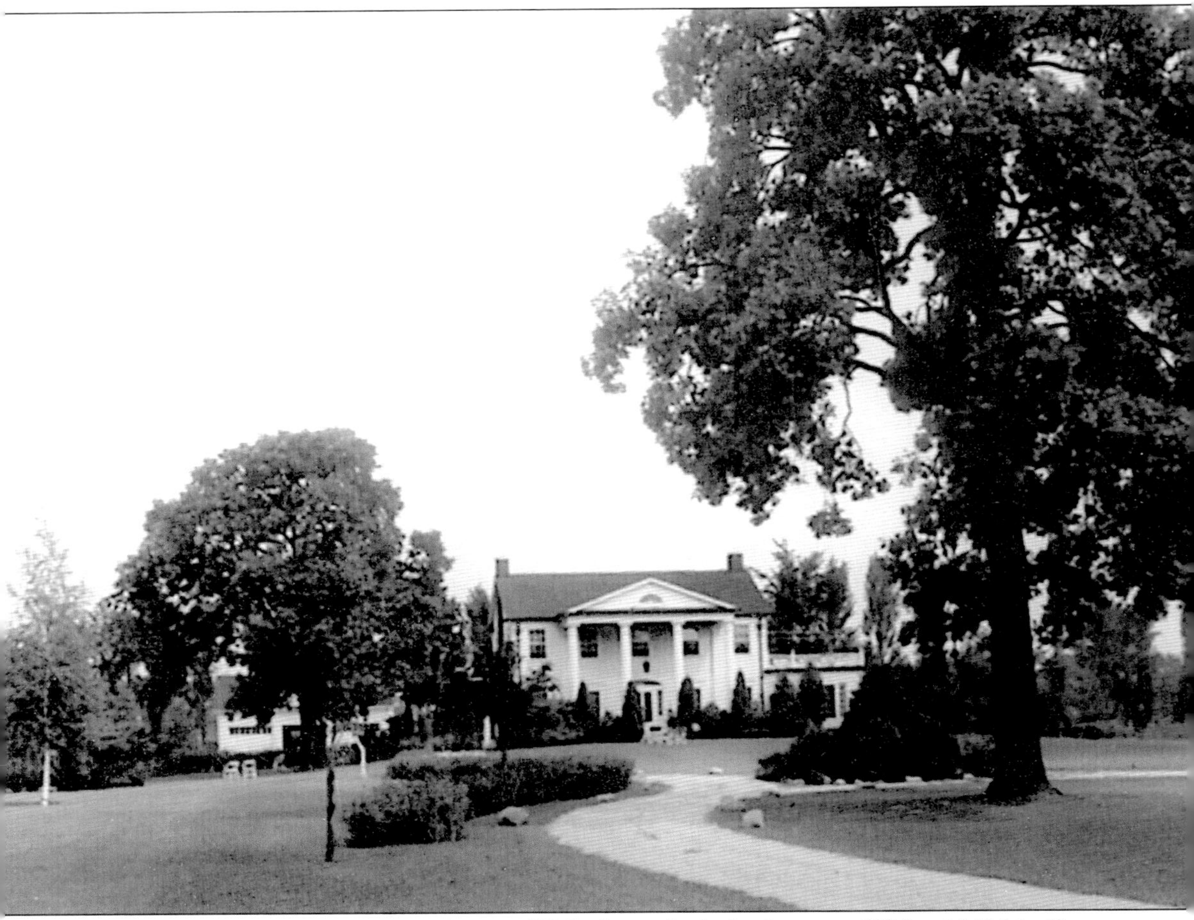

ZACHMAN-STRELITZ MANSION. Harvey W. Zachman built this house in 1928 at 1048 Mt. Vernon Avenue at the corner Merchant Avenue. It featured broad lawns and manicured gardens. Zachman fell on hard times during the Depression, and the house was sold to J. Malcolm Strelitz by 1934. And so, the house became known to a generation or so of Marionites as "the Strelitz Mansion." In 1956, Mrs. Strelitz hosted a formal tea for 250 people on the front lawn in honor of her daughter, Julia Marie Strelitz. Mrs. Strelitz and Julia Marie were aboard the *Andrea Doria* the night that the ocean liner collided with the *Stockholm* in the Atlantic Ocean. Both survived the ordeal.

The Strelitz family was as much at home in New York City as they were in Marion, and Miss Strelitz had made her debut into society that December at the annual Debutants Cotillion and Christmas Ball at the Waldorf Astoria Hotel.

Following the sale of the property by Mrs. Strelitz, the estate was rezoned, and the frontage along Mt. Vernon Avenue rezoned commercial, occupied by the L&K Royal Buffet, and a filling stations in the 1960s. The elegant house was demolished by Frank Bennett in 1973 to make way for an apartment complex, presently known as Vanover Square at 583 Merchant Avenue. (Photograph courtesy of Gary Barnhart.)

FAIRPARK. Following World War II, the demand for modern and affordable housing gave rise to Fairpark, a planned development on Marion's far north side, opened in the late 1950s. The developers of Fairpark also set aside land for an elementary school and a park with a pool. A three-bedroom house in the development could be purchased for as little as $7,000 or $61.05 a month if the buyer made at least $75 a week. (Photograph courtesy of the author.)

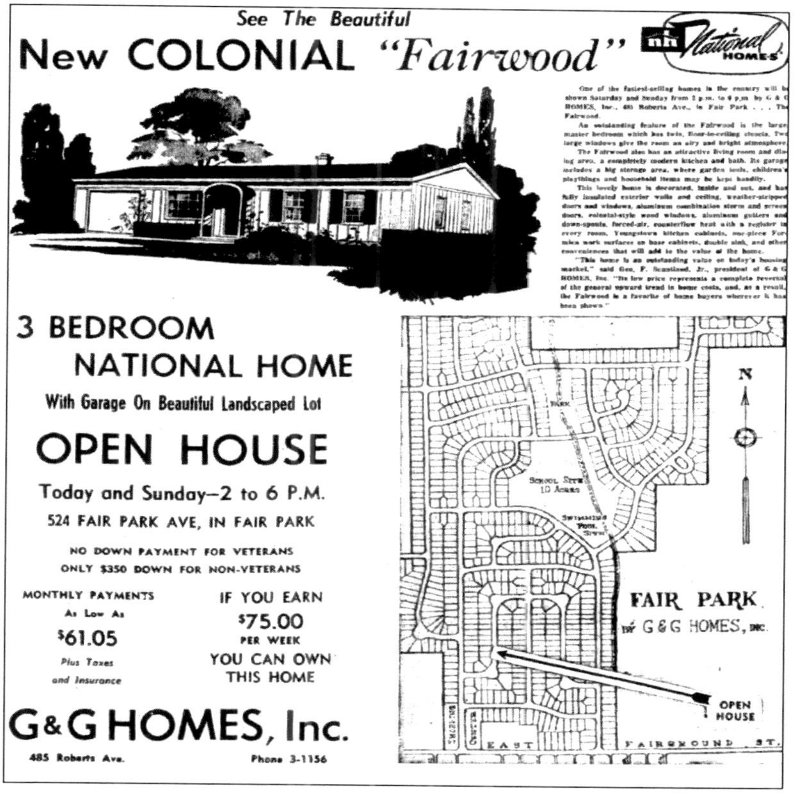

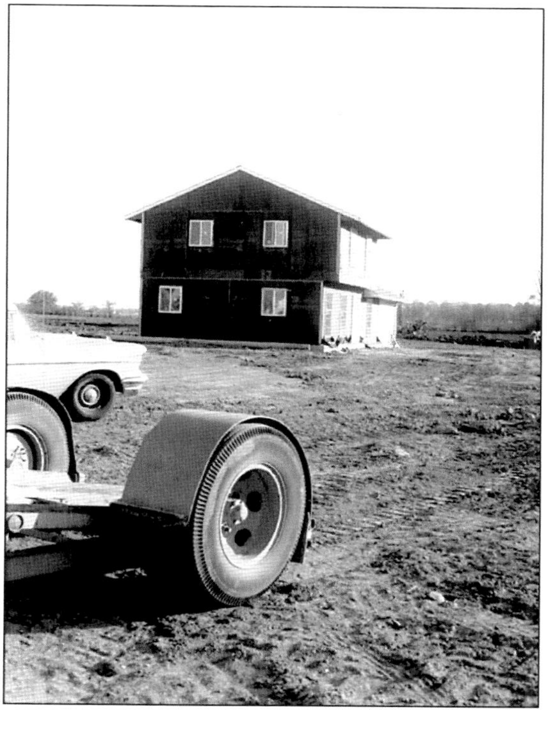

CHATEAU RIDGE OPENS, 1960. Designed to meet the needs of middle class families, Chateau Ridge was developed on Marion's east side by G&G Homes. Surveying for the development began in the late winter of 1960 with the first model home open for tours that August. The target price for the homes at that time ranged from $16,000 to $30,000, with 206 lots available at that time. Chateau Woods, east of Richland Road, was developed concurrently, with houses priced in the $40,000 range. (Photograph courtesy of Marion County Historical Society.)

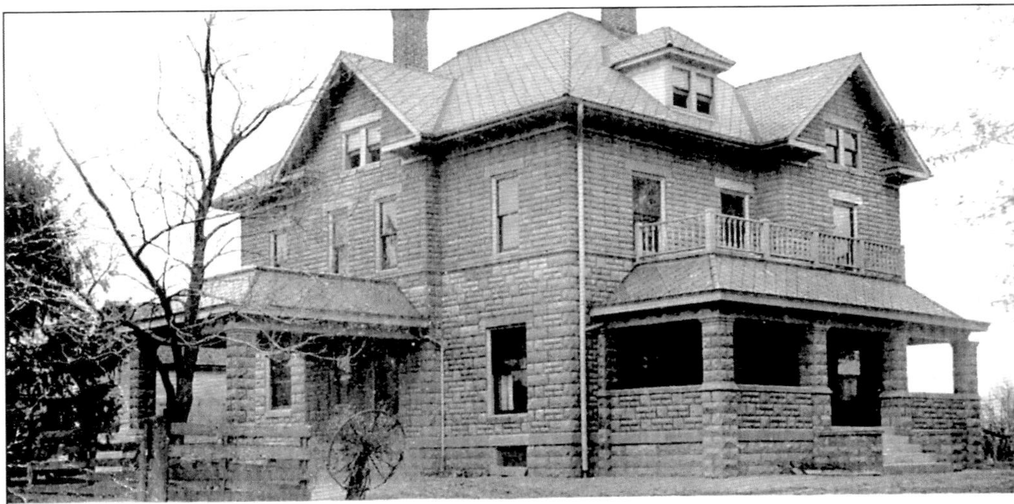

FARM RESIDENCE OF MR. JAMES HILL, MARION, OHIO.
Roofed with Asbestos "Century" Shingles.
From plans by J. J. SLOAN, Architect, Marion.

HILL RESIDENCE, SCOTT TOWNSHIP. Hoping to entice their mother to return to living in the country, James Hill and sister Maud Hill, built this home on Marseilles Galion Road, just northeast of Pole Lane Road. The Hill's spared no expense. The house was equipped with electric and pressurized indoor plumbing at a time when neither was found in the country. Their effort was for naught. Mother Hill found the house nice enough, but preferred to live in the city. Maud Hill continued to live in the home until the 1950s. (Photograph courtesy of the author.)

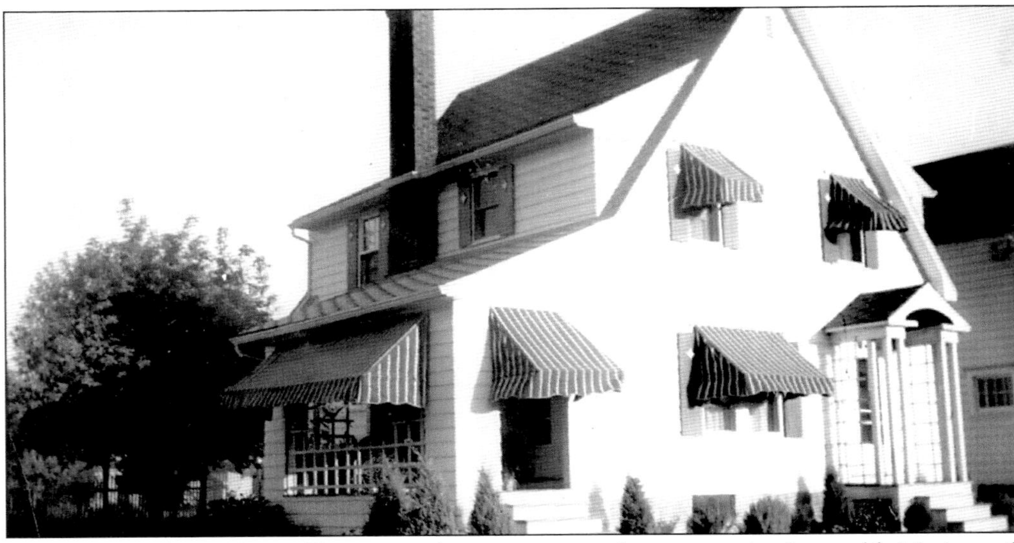

A PLACE TO CALL HOME. For many of us, no matter where we go in the world, Marion will always be our hometown. A place where our grandparents lived, cousins played on warm summers evenings, and parents watched over and provided for their families. Simple houses, like this one at 214 Forest Lawn Boulevard, have given us shelter and security that have allowed us to dream our dreams within their walls. This house was one such home for a young man who hoped to one day write a book about his hometown of Marion, Ohio—you now hold that book in your hands. (Photograph courtesy of the author.)